EXPERIMENTS
— *with* —
ECONOMIC
PRINCIPLES

Theodore C. Bergstrom
University of Michigan

John H. Miller
Carnegie Mellon University

The McGraw-Hill Companies, Inc.

New York St. Louis San Francisco Auckland Bogotá Caracas Lisbon
London Madrid Mexico City Milan Montreal New Delhi
San Juan Singapore Sydney Tokyo Toronto

McGraw-Hill

A Division of The McGraw·Hill Companies

The editors were Lucille H. Sutton and Joseph F. Murphy;
the production supervisor was Denise Puryear.
The cover was designed by Christopher Brady.

Quebecor Printing/Dubuque was printer and binder.

EXPERIMENTS *with* ECONOMIC PRINCIPLES

2 3 4 5 6 7 8 9 QPD QPD 9 0 9 8 7

ISBN 0-07-005952-7

Library of Congress Catalog Card Number: 96-76999

About the Authors

Theodore C. Bergstrom

Ted Bergstrom was an undergraduate mathematics major at Carleton College and received his Ph. D. from Stanford University. He has taught at Washington University in St. Louis, and is currently a Professor of Economics at the University of Michigan. Professor Bergstrom is a coauthor, with Hal Varian, of *Workouts in Microeconomic Theory*. His research interests include microeconomic theory, public finance, welfare economics, game theory, international trade theory, demography, economic anthropology, and evolutionary biology. His most recent research interests have been the economics of the family and the evolution of human preferences.

Address: Department of Economics, University of Michigan
Ann Arbor, MI 48109
e-mail: tedb@umich.edu

John H. Miller

John H. Miller earned his Ph. D. from the University of Michigan after receiving undergraduate degrees from the University of Colorado. He is currently an Associate Professor of Economics at Carnegie Mellon University, where he has taught since 1989, and an External Professor at the Santa Fe Institute. In 1995 he received the Elliot Dunlap Smith Award for Distinguished Teaching and Educational Service from Carnegie Mellon University. His research interests include microeconomic theory, experimental economics, computational economics, game theory, political economy, complex adaptive systems, and adaptive computation. His recent research has focussed on experimental approaches to understanding cooperation and on the computational modeling of complex social systems.

Address: Social and Decision Sciences, Carnegie Mellon University
Pittsburgh, PA 15213-3890
e-mail: miller@zia.hss.cmu.edu

On the Internet

We plan to maintain a dialog with users of our text by means of the World Wide Web. On our Website, we will include reports of experimental results from our classes and the classes of others. Users who have suggestions, comments, or questions can contact us through the Website or directly by e-mail or ordinary mail. We will try to publish comments that we think are of general interest on the Website.

The address of our Website is:

```
http://zia.hss.cmu.edu/miller/eep/eep.html
```

Preface

Taking a course in experimental economics is a little like going to dinner at a cannibal's house. Sometimes you will be a diner, sometimes a part of dinner, sometimes both.

If you take a laboratory course in the physical sciences, you get to mix smelly chemicals, or monkey with pulleys, or dissect a frog, but you are always the experimenter and never the subject of the experiment. In the experiments conducted in this class, you and your classmates will be the *participants* as well as the scientific *observers* who try to understand the results.

It is hard to imagine that a chemist can put herself in the place of a hydrogen molecule. A biologist who studies animal behavior is not likely to know what it feels like to be a duck. You are more fortunate. You will be studying the behavior and interactions of people in economic situations. And as one of these interacting economic agents, you will be able to experience first-hand the problems faced by such an agent. We suspect that you will learn nearly as much about economic principles from your experience as a participant as from your analysis as an observer.

Acknowledgements

Like everyone in the economics profession, we owe a great debt to Vernon Smith of the University of Arizona and Charles Plott of the California Institute of Technology for convincing us that economics can be a laboratory science. Their pioneering research has been followed by important advances in experimental economics by a generation of talented researchers in experimental economics and the economics of auctions. While working on this book, we have been fortunate to receive advice and encouragement from several of these people, including Ken Binmore, Dan Friedman, Mark Isaac, John Kagel, Preston McAfee, John McMillan, Peter Morgan, Jack Ochs, Al Roth, and Shyam Sunder.

John Miller thanks his colleague Steve Spear, with whom he initially developed a course in which the principles of economics were taught by means of classroom experiments, and Robert Dalton, Mark Kamlet, Steven Klepper, George Loewenstein, and Shyam Sunder, who were generous with their support and ideas for this enterprise. Many of the ideas in this book emerged from discussions with these people and were first tested in Carnegie Mellon classrooms. Ted Bergstrom is grateful to the University of Michigan for making resources available for teaching a new course in experiments with economics and to present and former Michigan colleagues, Janet Gerson, Ken Binmore, and Hal Varian, for encouragement and assistance in developing this course.

We were fortunate to be able to work with some skilled and cooperative teaching assistants, Scott Fay, Young Lee, and Elizabeth Newlon, and we had extremely valuable editorial assistance from two talented undergraduates, Karen Bergstrom and Teddy Kang. Our editor, Lucille Sutton, at McGraw Hill has been a pleasure to work with.

This book is written in LaTeX, making use of graphics routines from Timothy Van Zandt's delightful PSTricks package. We are especially grateful to TeX wizards, Oz Shy and Hal Varian, for teaching us to cast a few of the powerful and mysterious typesetting spells that lie at their command.

Finally, we thank several classes of students at Carnegie Mellon and Michigan, who enthusiastically carried out their dual roles as scientists and lab rats. We hope that they learned as much from us as we did from them.

A Note To Users

We got tired of it. Lecturing to sleepy students who want to "go over" material that they have already highlighted in their textbooks so that they can remember the "key ideas" until the midterm. We wanted to engage our students in *active learning*, to exploit their natural curiosity about economic affairs, and to get them to ponder the questions before we try to give them answers. We found that conducting economic experiments in class, with discussions before, during, and after the experiments, was an effective way of getting students involved in economics as a means to understanding their own experience. *Experiments With Economic Principles* is the result of these efforts.

This book is designed for students who have not previously taken any economics courses, but we have discovered that students who have already taken traditional economics courses also find these experiments to be instructive and interesting. Each chapter in the book contains an *experimental section* containing instructions for an experiment and a lab report, and a *discussion section*, containing a discussion of the theory related to the experiment and a homework assignment. This alternation between experiment and discussion sets the rhythm of the class. In the lab, students participate in a market or in some kind of social interaction. As they complete their lab reports, they can begin to organize their thoughts about what happened. At the next class meeting students should be ready to discuss the experimental results, to look for a theoretical explanation of what happened in the lab, and to explore applications of these ideas to the real world. Finally, at the end of each chapter, there is a homework assignment which will help students to solidify the ideas that they have explored.

Each of us has long been tempted to try a course based on participatory experiments, but wondered whether it would really work. Would students actually take an interest and participate according to the rules? Will the students actually learn in this way?

We have tried it and it works. Students have no trouble grasping the rules for the experiments and, while they do not always play as cleverly as they might, they always play competently and seriously. Better yet, they are enthusiastic about what they are doing. They love getting involved with markets and then figuring out what happened rather than simply being lectured at. They have fun. As instructors, we feel the same way. This classroom experience is a lot more rewarding than trying to interest sleepy students in abstractions with which they have no experience. Evidence from their performance on homework and examinations suggests that students are learning well.

If you try it, we think you'll be convinced.

Instructor's Manual

Instructors who adopt this book can obtain a copy of the Instructor's Manual by request from the publisher. The Instructor's Manual has detailed instructions on how to conduct each experiment. It also includes original copies of all of the information sheets and sales contracts which are to be distributed to students at the beginning of the experimental sessions. Instructors can make photocopies of these information sheets for distribution in class. The Instructors' Manual also has reports on the outcomes of several classroom experiments that we have conducted in our own classes.

The Literature of Experimental Economics

The experiments in this book are intended primarily for teaching purposes, rather than for gathering new scientific data. Many of these experiments, however, are similar to experiments that have been carried out in experimental laboratories under carefully controlled conditions. Since in the classroom we are dealing not with paid subjects, but with tuition-paying students, we made some changes in design from that used in the scientifically-motivated experiments. These changes reflect our efforts to set a brisk pace of activity in the classroom, in order to maintain students' interest and enthusiasm, and to give them a good rate of return per unit of time that they invest in learning.

In most of the market experiments in this book, we use a "trading-pit" design which is quite similar to trading procedures used in commodities markets like the Chicago Board of Trade futures market. Market participants move around the classroom until they find someone with whom they can make a deal. When a deal has been made, the transactors deliver a slip of paper to the market manager, which identifies the buyer and seller and records the sales price, Buyer Value and Seller Cost. As sales information is turned in, the market manager records prices (in the case of a large class this can be just a sampling of prices) on the blackboard for all to see. This procedure is essentially the same as that used almost 50 years ago in a series of experiments by Professor E.H. Chamberlin [2] in his classroom at Harvard. Chamberlin, who had developed a theory of imperfect competition, emphasized the *difference* between his experimental outcomes and that predicted by competitive theory.

Professor Vernon Smith [8], who as a student had participated in Chamberlin's classroom experiments, decided to try experimental markets in his classes at Purdue. Smith changed Chamberlin's procedures in two ways that he thought would be likely to lead to outcomes more in accord with competitive theory. Smith conducted transactions by means of a "double oral auction" in which bids and offers are made publicly and all transactions are cleared through a central auctioneer. In each trading session, Smith also ran multiple rounds, which repeated the same trading environment. This enabled participants to use their experience of market outcomes from previous rounds in deciding their actions in later rounds. Smith discovered that usually by the second or third round, prices and quantities were strikingly close to competitive equilibrium values. Smith's double oral auction experiments have been replicated hundreds of times throughout the world and with many variations in the shapes of demand and supply curves and in market institutions. Experimenters have almost uniformly found a close correspondence between the experimental results and the predictions of competitive equilibrium theory.

For classroom instructional purposes, we have followed Smith in running more than one round with the same trading environment, but we have deviated from Smith's procedure by using a "trading pit" rather than a double oral auction. We find that this trading-pit procedure is faster and is more easily administered in a classroom than a double oral auction. Like Smith, for most of the markets that we tried, we found that after two or three repetitions of trading with the same market conditions, most transactions occur at prices that are very close to the competitive equilibrium price. Because sales occur simultaneously in a trading-pit market, even large classes can conclude a round of trading in about 5 minutes.[1] For most of the experi-

---

[1]In a very large class, recording all of the transactions on the blackboard would slow things down but, for a large class, it is sufficient to simply record a random sample of transaction prices as they are brought to the market manager.

ments that we have run, we find that running two rounds of trading for each market environment is sufficient. This enables us to comfortably run three, or sometimes even four, different experimental sessions during a single class period, where each session tests a different market environment.

Chamberlin and Smith both emphasized that the informational conditions in the trading-pit environment are not the same as those posited in the standard competitive model. The standard (Walrasian) competitive model assumes very large numbers of market participants, all of whom have perfect information about the best price at which they can buy or sell. This information is not available in either Smith's or Chamberlin's experimental environment. Smith argues on this account that the results of his repeated double oral auction experiment are remarkable evidence that near-competitive outcomes are likely to be achieved under much more realistic informational conditions than those usually assumed. Accordingly, the theory of competitive supply and demand is likely to be a more powerful tool for approximate prediction of market outcomes in the real world than had been previously suspected.

There is interesting evidence from market simulations that the trading-pit environment is likely to lead to a close approximation of competitive outcomes, even with very unsophisticated traders. D. K. Gode and Shyam Sunder [5] ran simulations of a trading pit with random encounters between traders, who make *random* bids and offers, subject only to the constraint that no trader makes money-losing bids or offers. Trades occurred at either the buyer's or the sellers' price whenever the buyer bid at least as much as the seller's offer price. They found that prices converged quite closely to competitive equilibrium prices. We have run similar simulations with the demand and supply curves for our experimental markets and have found results similar to those of Gode and Sunder.

Suggested Reading

For those of you who want to read more about economics laboratory experiments, we recommend three recently-published books. *Experimental Methods: A Primer for Economists* by Daniel Friedman and Shyam Sunder [4] is an engaging discussion of the methods and philosophy of experimental economics. *Experimental Economics* by Douglas Davis and Charles Holt [3] is a textbook on experimental economics, suitable for advanced undergraduate or graduate courses. *The Handbook of Experimental Economics*, edited by John Kagel and Alvin Roth [6] contains authoritative and well-written surveys of several areas of experimental economics.

If, after completing these experiments, you want to find out more about topics such as demand and supply analysis, taxation, price floors and ceilings, monopoly, the theory of the firm, or comparative advantage, you will find more extended discussions in any of the standard intermediate microeconomics textbooks. Topics related to information, auctions, and bargaining are less well covered in the standard texts. For those who want to learn more about these topics, *Games, Strategies, and Managers* by John McMillan [7] is an entertaining mixture of real-world observations and theory which is readily accessible to undergraduate students and *Auctions and Auctioneering* by Ralph Cassady [1], is a fascinating account of the many different kinds of auctions used in markets around the world.

Bibliography

[1] Ralph Cassady. *Auctions and Auctioneering*. University of California Press, Berkeley, 1967.

[2] E. H. Chamberlin. An experimental imperfect market. *Journal of Political Economy*, 56(2):95–108, April 1948.

[3] Douglas Davis and Charles Holt. *Experimental Economics*. Princeton University Press, Princeton, New Jersey, 1993.

[4] Daniel Friedman and Shyam Sunder. *Experimental Methods: A Primer for Economists*. Cambridge University Press, Cambridge, 1994.

[5] D. K. Gode and Shyam Sunder. Allocative efficiency of markets with zero-intelligence traders: Market as a partial substitute for rationality. *Journal of Political Economy*, 101:119–137, 1993.

[6] John Kagel and Alvin Roth. *The Handbook of Experimental Economics*. Princeton University Press, Princeton, N.J., 1995.

[7] John McMillan. *Games, Strategies, and Managers*. Oxford University Press, New York, 1992.

[8] Vernon Smith. An experimental study of competitive market behavior. *Journal of Political Economy*, 70(2):111–137, April 1962.

Contents

Part I

Competitive Markets

Experiment 1

Supply and Demand

An Apple Market

It is a sunny Saturday morning at the Farmers' Apple Market. You and your classmates have come to the Market to buy and sell apples. Your objective is to make as much profit as possible. Profit will be measured in "laboratory dollars."[1]

Buying and Selling

In today's experiment you are going to try to make profits by buying or selling (imaginary) apples. At the beginning of class, you will be given a personal information sheet that indicates whether you are a **supplier** or a **demander** in each market session. A sample personal information sheet is found on page 6.

If you are a supplier, you may be able to make money by selling a bushel of apples to one of your classmates. You will find your **Seller Cost** for a bushel of apples listed on your personal information sheet. If you sell a bushel of apples for a price P, and your Seller Cost is C, then your **profit** is the difference, $P - C$. If you don't sell any apples, your profit is zero. Sometimes you may not find a demander who is willing to pay you as much as your Seller Cost. If this is the case, you are better off not selling your apples and taking zero profits rather than selling for a loss.

---

[1]Unless your instructor is unusually rich and generous, laboratory dollars will not be exchangeable at face value for regular currency. In some classes, however, laboratory dollar profits count toward money prizes and/or credit toward one's grade.

Example:

   A supplier has a Seller Cost of $10 and she has one bushel of apples which she can sell. If she sells her bushel of apples for a price of $16, she will make a profit of $16-$10=$6. If she sells her bushel for $30, she will make a profit of $30-$10=$20. If she sells her bushel for $7, she will make a *loss* of $3. If she does not sell, her profit is zero.

If you are a demander, you may be able to make money by buying a bushel of apples from one of your classmates. Your **Buyer Value** for a bushel of apples is found on your personal information sheet. If your Buyer Value is V, and you buy a bushel of apples for a price P, your profit will be $V - \$P$. It is as if you pay the seller P for the apples and then you sell them to the market manager for V. If you don't buy any apples, your profit is zero. If you cannot find a supplier who is willing to sell you a bushel of apples for your buyer value or less, then you are better off not buying any apples and taking zero profits.

Example:

   A demander has a Buyer Value of $40. If he buys a bushel of apples for $16, he will make a profit of $40-$16=$24. If he buys a bushel of apples for $30, he will make a profit of $40-$30=$10. If he buys a bushel of apples for $45, he will make a *loss* of $5. If he doesn't buy any apples, his profit is zero.

In any single round of trading, buyers cannot buy and sellers cannot sell more than one bushel of apples, nor can anyone buy or sell fractions of a bushel of apples.

To make a purchase or sale, first find somebody who might be willing to make a deal with you. Suppliers can only make deals with demanders and demanders can only make deals with suppliers.[2] When a supplier meets a demander, they can negotiate about the price in any way they wish. You don't have to reveal your Seller Cost or Buyer Value to your bargaining partner, but you can if you want. You might want to take a look at the prices displayed on the blackboard for transactions that have already been made.

When a supplier (seller) and demander (buyer) reach agreement on a price, they should fill out a *sales contract* and bring it to the market manager who will record the transaction. The sales contract will record the seller's and buyer's identification numbers, the price at which the sale was made, and a few other details about the sale. As sales contracts are brought to the

---

[2]We have found it helpful to give each student in the class a red card and a green card. A supplier who wants to sell holds up a *red* (apples are red) card and a demander who wants to buy holds up a *green* (money is green) card. Students keep these cards and can use them in future market sessions.

market manager, the prices are recorded on the blackboard so that those who have not yet made a deal can see them.

If you have completed your transaction and turned in your sales contract, please return to your seat.

Sessions, Rounds, and Transactions

In this experiment and in future experiments, we define transactions, rounds of trading, and market sessions as follows. A *transaction* is a deal between a single buyer and seller and is completed when a filled-in sales contract is brought to the manager by the buyer and seller. A *round* of trading begins when the market manager declares trading to be open and ends when there are no two people left who can make a deal with each other. In the course of a single round of trading, nobody can buy or sell more than one bushel of apples, so those who have bought or sold a bushel have nothing more to do, until the next round of trading starts.

A market *session* can include two or more rounds of trading. After the first round of trading is completed, we will often conduct one or more additional rounds within the same session. In a new round of a session, buyers and sellers "start over." Everyone has the same Buyer Value or Seller Cost as in the first round, but in later rounds, buyers and sellers know what happened in earlier rounds and may use this information to change the prices that they ask or offer.

Some Advice to Traders

Even if you are normally a shy person, let your "trading personality" be more flamboyant. Shrinking violets, though charming in many situations, are likely to miss profitable trading opportunities. To maximize your profits, you should approach trading aggressively. Don't be afraid to shout or gesture for attention. Let people know how much you are willing to pay or the price at which you are willing to sell. When you think that you could get a better price than someone offers you, do not hesitate to propose a price that you like better.

Remember that you would like to "Buy low. Sell high." Demanders make greater profits, the lower the price they have to pay for apples. Suppliers make greater profits, the higher the price they can get for their apples.

Seller Costs will differ from one seller to another, and Buyer Values will differ from one buyer to another, so if someone tells you his Buyer Value or

SAMPLE

Student ID Number _____

Personal Information Sheet

Session 1

In this trading session, you are an *Apple Supplier*. Your *Seller Cost* is $20. If you sell a bushel of apples for price P, your profit is $P - 20$. If you don't sell any apples, your profit is 0.

- -

Session 2

In this trading session you are an *Apple Demander*. Your *Buyer Value* is $40.
If you buy a bushel of apples for price P, your profit is $40 - P$. If you don't buy any apples, your profit is 0.

Seller Cost, don't assume that all other buyers or sellers are the same.[3]

Sometimes students get left out at the end of the market because all their potential trading partners have already traded with someone else. If you think you are getting a good deal, you should probably take advantage of it quickly so that you don't get left out. So long as you haven't yet traded, you should keep an eye on the prices that are posted for other transactions. This may give you some idea of what price to demand or what price to offer in your own negotiations.

Warm-up Exercise

To be completed before you come to class for the first experiment.

Please read the instructions above and look at the sample Personal Information Sheet. Then answer the following questions.

Suppose that a supplier with a Seller Cost of $20 meets a demander who has a Buyer Value of $40.

■ If this supplier sells a bushel of apples to this demander for a price of $35, how much profit will the supplier make? __15__ and how much profit would the demander make? __5__ How much is the total profit obtained by both traders? (Find this by adding the buyer's profits to the seller's profits) __20__

■ What is the *highest* price of apples that would permit both the seller and the buyer to make a profit of $1 or more? __39__ If this price is charged, how much is the sum of buyer's profits plus seller's profits?__ __40__.

■ What is the *lowest* price of apples that would permit both the seller and the buyer to make a profit of $1 or more? __1__ At this price, how much is the sum of buyer's profits plus seller's profits? __58__.

---

[3]When the experiment is over, the instructor will tell you the number of buyers and sellers with each Seller Cost and Buyer Value present in the market. We aren't going to give you this information before the market starts because, in real world markets, buyers and sellers don't usually have this information.

■ More generally, suppose that a seller with Seller Cost C sells a bushel of apples to a buyer with Buyer Value V for a price of P. Then the seller's profit is $P - C$. Write an expression for the buyer's profit. _$P - V$_ Adding these two expressions together, the total profits of buyer and seller are given by _$(P-C) + (P-V)$_ Does the sum of their profits depend on the price?

yes

■ If a buyer and a seller make a deal, the seller will have higher profits the _lower_ (higher? lower?) the price and the demander will have higher profits the _higher_ (higher? lower?) the price.

■ Think about how you will behave the first time that you are a supplier and you start bargaining with a demander. Here are examples of strategies you *might* use.

- Ask the other person to make you an offer and split the difference between your cost and that person's offer.

- Accept the first offer you get that is higher than your cost.

- "Shop around" until you have had at least two offers, then take the better one.

- Look for a price that is at least as good as the average of the prices that have been posted on the blackboard so far.

There are many other strategies you could adopt and there is no single right answer here. You are welcome to change your plan after you have had some experience in the auction. But it is a good idea to have an idea of what you will do at the beginning. Describe the strategy that you plan to start with.

_____

_____

_____

_____

Discussion D1

Supply and Demand

In Search of a Theory

We have a mystery on our hands. In each session of the Apple Market, prices seem to be closing in on certain values. But what determines the values to which prices converge?

It would be really nice to have a *theory* that predicts outcomes, not only for the specific market that we observed experimentally, but for a variety of markets under widely varying conditions. We would like a theory that allows us to answer questions like:

- If everybody's cost of production increases by $10, will the market price increase by $10, by less than $10, or by more than $10?

- Suppose that the government decides to pay $10 to every person who buys a bushel of apples. Such a payment is called a **subsidy** to apple consumption. Will suppliers absorb some or all of the subsidy by increasing their prices, or will demanders get all of the benefits from the $10 subsidy?

- If bad weather reduces the quantity of apples that each producer could supply, what will be the effect on the price of apples and what will happen to total revenue of suppliers?

Economists have just such a theory. It is known as the **supply and demand theory**, or more formally as the **competitive equilibrium theory**. This theory offers answers for the above questions and for many others. These answers are often quite useful and surprising. Of course, a theory that predicts market outcomes will not be much good if these predictions are badly wrong. Therefore it is important and interesting to see whether supply and demand theory does a good job of predicting the outcomes of our experiments. If the theory does well in these experimental environments and continues to do well as we add more elements of realism, then we can put some credence in its predictions for actual markets. If this simple theory does not perform well, then we may have to look for a better theory.

Competitive Equilibrium

In the experimental market sessions, some sellers were able to get higher prices for their apples than others. Some sellers were lucky enough to be offered a relatively high price by the first buyer they ran into. Every buyer would like to get apples as cheaply as possible, but different buyers may have different ideas of how cheaply they will be able to buy apples. To describe everybody's beliefs about the prices they can get and to describe everybody's luck in whom they encounter would be an overwhelmingly complicated task, even for this simple market.

Instead of trying to describe this complex reality in full detail, let's try to make a simplified *model* of competitive markets. The art of good modeling in economics, as in all of science, is to find the "right" simplifications. The model should remove enough complication from the actual situation to allow us to analyze and predict outcomes, but should not remove so much reality that it distorts our picture of the way things really work. We are looking for a manageable model of markets that makes good predictions of the outcomes that we observe in experimental markets and in actual markets of the commercial world. Specifically, we would like to have a model that predicts the average price and the number of transactions in a market using the information that we have about the Buyer Values and Seller Costs of the market participants.

In this experiment, if a supplier sells a bushel of apples for a price higher than her Seller Cost she will make a profit, and if she sells for a price lower than her Seller Cost she will lose money. We define a **supplier's reservation price** for a unit of a good to be the lowest price at which she is willing to sell one unit. In this experiment, the *lowest* price that a supplier is willing to accept for a bushel of apples is her Seller Cost, so that in this case, every supplier's reservation price for a bushel of apples is equal to her Seller Cost.

In this experiment, a demander will make a profit if he buys a bushel of apples for a price lower than his Buyer Value and he will make a loss if he buys a bushel of apples for a price higher than his Buyer Value. We define a **demander's reservation price** to be the highest price that he would be willing to pay to have one unit of the good rather than do without. Since, in this experiment, the most that a demander would be willing to pay for a unit of goods is his Buyer Value, demanders' reservation prices are equal to their Buyer Values.[1] We sometimes refer to a supplier's reservation price as her **minimum willingness-to-accept** and to a demander's reservation price as his **maximum willingness-to-pay**.

One way to simplify this problem is to assume that every demander is offered apples at the same price as all other demanders and every supplier is able to sell apples at the same price as all other suppliers. Especially in the first round of a session in our market experiment, this assumption is not entirely accurate. Some buyers paid higher prices than others and some sellers received higher prices than others. But it is to be expected that those who got stuck paying higher-than-average prices in the first round will think that they may be able to buy for a lower price in later rounds. Similarly, those who sold their apples for a lower-than-average price in the first round are likely to try to get a higher price in later rounds.

If there were just one price for apples, each demander would have to decide whether or not he wanted to buy a bushel of apples at this price and each supplier would have to decide whether or not she wanted to sell a bushel of apples at this price. There is no reason to expect that at an arbitrary price, the number of bushels of apples that demanders want to buy would equal the number of bushels that suppliers want to sell. But, as we will discover, there will be *some* price at which the number of bushels of apples demanded is exactly equal to the number of bushels of apples that suppliers are willing to sell. This price, at which "supply equals demand," is known as the **competitive equilibrium price** and the number of units bought and sold at this price is known as the **competitive equilibrium quantity**.

Supply curves and **demand curves** are the main tools that we use to study competitive equilibrium. The supply curve tells us the total amount of a good that suppliers would want to sell at each possible price. We can draw a supply curve if we know each supplier's reservation price which, in this experiment, is equal to her Seller Cost. In this experiment, where each supplier supplies at most one unit, the number of units that will be supplied at any price P is equal to the number of suppliers who have Seller Costs no

---

[1] As we will see in some later experiments, suppliers' reservation prices are not always the same as their Seller Costs and demanders' reservation prices are not always the same as their Buyer Values.

greater than P.

The demand curve tells us the total amount of a good that buyers would want to buy at each possible price. We can draw this curve if we know each demander's reservation price, which in this experiment is equal to his Buyer Value. In this experiment, the number of units that will be demanded at any price P is equal to the number of demanders who have Buyer Values no smaller than P.

Supply and Demand Curves

Since it is the interaction of suppliers and demanders that determines the outcome in a market, we will find it useful to draw a graph that contains both the supply and demand curves, and to use the resulting graph to find equilibrium prices and quantities.

To learn how to draw supply and demand curves, let us work with a market environment in which there are two types of suppliers and two types of demanders, described as follows:

- There are 10 high-cost suppliers, who have Seller Costs of 25 dollars a bushel.

- There are 20 low-cost suppliers, who have Seller Costs of 5 dollars a bushel.

- There are 15 high-value demanders, who have Buyer Values of 30 dollars for a bushel of apples.

- There are 15 low-value demanders, who have Buyer Values of 10 dollars for a bushel of apples.

This information is summarized in Table D1.1

Table D1.1: Distribution of Types–Example Market

Type of Agent	Number of Agents	Cost	Value
Low-Cost Supplier	20	5	▮▮▮
High-Cost Supplier	10	25	▮▮▮
High-Value Demander	15	▮▮▮	30
Low-Value Demander	15	▮▮▮	10

Making a Supply Table

The information that we have about the distribution of types of agents in the example market can be used to construct a *Supply Table* for this market. The Supply Table shows the number of bushels of apples that suppliers would offer at all possible prices.

In the example market, low-cost suppliers have a Seller Cost of $5 a bushel and high-cost suppliers have a Seller Cost of $25 a bushel. At any price below $5 a bushel, every supplier who sold a bushel of apples would lose money because it costs every supplier at least $5 to produce a bushel of apples. Therefore at prices below $5, nobody would want to supply any apples, so the total number of bushels supplied to the market would be zero. We record this fact in the first line of Table D1.2

Table D1.2: Supply Table–Example Market

Price Range	Amount Supplied
$P < \$5$	0
$\$5 < P < \$25$	20
$P > \$25$	30

Suppose that the price, P, is between $5 and $25. The 20 low-cost suppliers have Seller Cost of $5, so they can each make money by selling a bushel of apples at any price that is above $5. Since high-cost suppliers have Seller Cost of $25, the high-cost suppliers would lose money if they sold apples for any price that is below $25. Therefore at prices between $5 and $25, the 20 low-cost sellers will each want to sell a bushel of apples, but the high-cost sellers won't want to sell any apples. The total quantity of apples that is supplied at prices between $5 and $25 is therefore 20 bushels. This fact is recorded in the second line of the Supply Table.

At prices above $25, all of the high-cost suppliers *and* all of the low-cost suppliers can make money by selling apples. Since there are 10 high-cost suppliers and 20 low-cost suppliers, and since at prices above $25 every supplier wants to supply one bushel, the total amount supplied is 30 bushels. We record this fact in the last line of the Supply Table.

Making a Demand Table

We can construct a *Demand Table* for this market in much the same way. The Demand Table shows the number of bushels of apples that demanders want to buy at all possible prices.

The highest Buyer Value for a bushel of apples is $30. If the price is above $30, no buyer will want to buy any apples. So for all prices above $30, the number of bushels demanded is 0. We record this fact in the first line of Table D1.3.

If the price of apples is between $10 and $30, then all 15 of the high-value demanders can make profits by buying a bushel of apples. But low-value demanders will lose money if they buy apples. So at prices between $10 and $30, the total demand for apples is 15 bushels. We record this fact in the second line of Table D1.3.

If the price of apples is below $10, then both the high-value demanders and the low-value demanders can make a profit by buying apples. There are 15 high-value demanders and 15 low-value demanders, so that total demand for apples at any price below $10 is 30 bushels. We record this information in the bottom line of Table D1.3.

Table D1.3: Demand Table–Example Market

Price Range	Amount Demanded
$P > \$30$	0
$\$10 < P < \$30$	15
$P < \$10$	30

Drawing Supply and Demand Curves

The supply and demand tables will help us draw graphs describing a supply curve and a demand curve. The first step is to draw a pair of axes, with *price of apples* measured on the vertical axis and *quantity of apples* measured on the horizontal axis. This has been done for you in Figure D1.1 below.

Drawing the Supply Curve

A **supply curve** shows the total number of apples that sellers would be willing to sell at each possible price. Price is shown on the vertical axis and quantity (number of units) supplied is shown on the horizontal axis. To determine the quantity that will be supplied at any price, you would first find the price on the vertical axis, then move horizontally across the graph until you reach the supply curve, and then go directly downward to read the

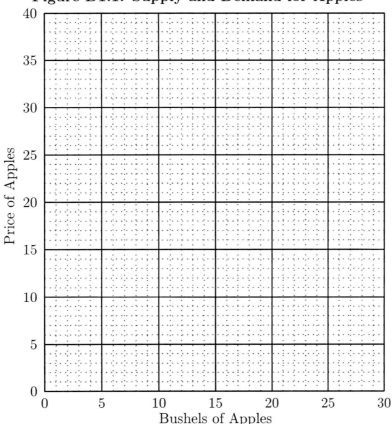

Figure D1.1: Supply and Demand for Apples

quantity supplied. We will make a practice of drawing supply curves in red. (As you will see, your graphs are much easier to read if supply and demand curves are different colors.)

As we see from the Supply Table, at prices lower than $5, the amount of apples supplied will be 0. Thus the supply curve must show that at these prices no apples will be supplied. This means that the supply curve includes a vertical line that follows the vertical axis from the origin $(0, 0)$ up to the point $(0, 5)$ where price is $5 and quantity is 0. Draw this line segment.

At any price greater than $5 but less than $25, the total quantity supplied is 20 bushels. Therefore the supply curve includes a vertical line segment drawn from the point $(20, 5)$ up to the point $(20, 25)$. Add this line segment to your graph.

At prices greater than $25, we see from the Supply Table that the total quantity supplied is 30 bushels. This means that the supply curve includes a vertical line starting at the point $(30, 25)$ and going straight up to the point $(30, \text{one zillion})$. We don't want you to run out of ink drawing one line, so just draw a line segment from the point $(30, 25)$ to the top of the box. (You might want to put an arrow at the top of this line segment to show that it keeps on going.)

Your supply curve so far contains three red vertical line segments. But we haven't yet answered the question of what happens at a price of exactly \$5 or at a price of exactly \$25. At a price of \$5, all of the high-cost suppliers would lose money if they sold any apples. At a price of \$5, the low-cost suppliers won't *make* any money by selling apples, but they won't *lose* any money either. They will just be *indifferent* between selling and not selling. Since at a price of \$5, each of the 20 low-cost suppliers would be satisfied with supplying any quantity between 0 and 1 bushel, we can say that at a price of \$5, suppliers in total would be willing to supply any quantity of apples between 0 and 20 units. We show this fact by adding to the supply curve a horizontal segment at a price of \$5. On the graph, this horizontal segment is a line from the point $(0, 5)$ to the point $(20, 5)$.

At a price of \$25, all 20 of the low-cost suppliers will want to supply, and the 10 high-cost suppliers are just breaking even. At this price, each of the 10 high-cost suppliers is willing to supply any amount between zero and one unit. So at a price of \$25, the total quantity supplied can be any amount between 20 and 30 bushels. This implies that the supply curve includes a horizontal segment at a price of \$25. This horizontal segment runs from the point $(20, 25)$ to the point $(30, 25)$.

Drawing the Demand Curve

Now that you have drawn a supply curve, it is time to draw a **demand curve.** The demand curve shows the total quantity of apples that demanders would like to buy at each possible price. Like the supply curve, the demand curve will consist of vertical and horizontal line segments. You can use the Demand Table to draw the demand curve, much as you used the Supply Table to draw the supply curve. You can probably do this without reading the rest of this section, but in case you get stuck, take a look at these detailed instructions.

According to the Demand Table, at all prices higher than \$30, the quantity demanded is 0. This means that the demand curve contains a vertical segment, running from the point $(0, 30)$ straight up to the top of the graph (and beyond). Draw a vertical line from $(0, 30)$ to the top of the graph (and make a little arrow on the top of it if you wish). We also see from the Demand Table that at prices between \$10 and \$30, the quantity demanded is 15 bushels. So the demand curve contains all points of the form $(15, P)$ where $10 < P < 30$. These points constitute a vertical line drawn from the point $(15, 10)$ to the point $(15, 30)$. Add this line segment to your demand curve.

According to the Demand Table, at all prices lower than \$10, the quantity demanded is 30 bushels. So the demand curve contains a vertical line segment running from the point where price is 0 and quantity is 30 to the point where price is 10 and quantity is 30. Add this line segment to your graph. What remains to be done is to account for the demand when the price is exactly \$30 and when the price is exactly \$10. At a price of \$30, none of the low-value demanders will want to buy. However, all 15 of the high-value demanders will be just indifferent between buying or not buying. At this price, therefore demanders would be just willing to accept any quantity between 0 and 15 bushels. So the demand curve contains a horizontal segment at a price of \$30. This segment runs from the point $(0, 30)$, where no apples are demanded, to the point $(15, 30)$, where 15 bushels of apples are demanded. At a price of \$10, the 15 high-value demanders each definitely want to buy a bushel of apples. The 15 low-value demanders are just indifferent between buying a bushel of apples and not buying any apples. So at this price, demanders in total are willing to take any quantity of apples from 15 bushels to 30 bushels. This means that the demand curve includes a horizontal segment at a price of \$10, running from the point $(15, 10)$ to the point $(30, 10)$.

When you think you have drawn your demand and supply curves correctly, take a look at the supply and demand curves drawn in the Appendix. (But don't peek at this stuff until you have tried to draw the curves on your own.)

Finding Equilibrium Price and Quantity

The **competitive equilibrium price** for a good is the price at which the total amount of the good which suppliers want to sell is equal to the total amount of the good that demanders want to buy. The quantity that is supplied and demanded at the competitive equilibrium price is the **competitive equilibrium quantity**. If you have drawn the supply curve and the demand curve for a good on a graph, how can you find the competitive equilibrium price? Before reading the answer which appears below in small print, see if you can figure it out for yourself.

Answer: Remember that the quantity demanded or supplied at any price is found by locating the price on the vertical axis and reading across until you reach the demand or supply curve. If at some price, supply equals demand, it must be that at this price, the supply curve and the demand curve must be touching each other. Thus to find the competitive equilibrium price, simply

draw the supply curve and the demand curve and find where they cross. If the
two curves intersect at a single point, then you can read across to the vertical
axis to find the competitive equilibrium price and down to the horizontal axis
to find the competitive equilibrium quantity. (Sometimes the demand curve
and supply curve may overlap at more than one point. In this case, there will
be more than one competitive equilibrium price and/or quantity.)

If you look at the supply and demand graph that you drew, you can see
that at any price higher than the competitive equilibrium price, suppliers
want to sell more apples than demanders want to buy. At any price lower
than the equilibrium price, demanders want to buy more apples than suppliers are willing to sell. But at the competitive equilibrium price, suppliers
want to sell exactly as many apples as demanders want to buy.

■   If you have drawn your supply and demand curves correctly, they will
cross each other at exactly one point. At the point where the two curves

cross, the price is \$_____ and the quantity is _____ bushels.

Practice Session–Reading Supply and Demand Curves

You have drawn a supply curve and a demand curve using the numerical
information in a Supply Table and a Demand Table. Now it is time to
practice working the other way around—reading numerical information from
supply and demand curves.

Figure D1.2 is a new supply and demand curve on which you can practice.
To make things a little more exciting, let's suppose that there are not two,
but *three* different kinds of demanders and *three* different kinds of suppliers.[2]
We will ask you some questions which you should try to answer for yourself.

The first set of questions is designed to give you practice in reading
supply and demand curves to determine the quantities demanded or supplied
at various prices.

■   At a price of \$30, suppliers want to supply _____ bushels of apples.

At a price of \$12, suppliers want to supply _____ bushels of apples.

---

[2]If the excitement is too overwhelming, you might want to take a short break, read a
few pages of a text in accounting or political science, and return to this task when you
have calmed down.

Figure D1.2: More Supply and Demand

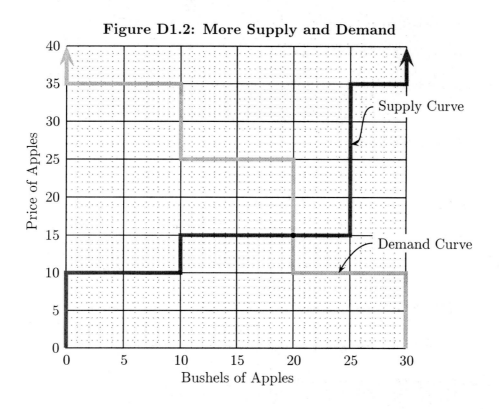

- At a price of $5, suppliers want to supply _____ bushels of apples.

At a price of $40, suppliers want to supply _____ bushels of apples.

- At a price of $30, demanders want to buy _____ bushels of apples.

At a price of $20, demanders want to buy _____ bushels of apples.

- At a price of $5, demanders want to buy _____ bushels of apples.

At a price of $40, demanders want to buy _____ bushels of apples.

- At a price of $15, suppliers are willing to supply any amount of apples

between _____ bushels and _____ bushels.

- At a price of $25, demanders are willing to buy any amount of apples

between _____ bushels and _____ bushels.

You can also use supply and demand curves to determine the *inverse* relation, namely the price at which any specified quantity would be demanded or supplied. For example, we see from the supply curve that the only price at which suppliers would be willing to supply 5 bushels of apples is $10. If the price were lower, suppliers would not want to supply any apples. If the price were higher than $10, they would want to supply more than 5 bushels. (Of course, at a price of $10, they would also be willing to supply any other number of bushels between 0 and 10.)

■ Suppliers would be willing to supply 15 bushels of apples at a price of

$_____.

■ Suppliers would want to supply exactly 10 bushels of apples at any price

between $_____ and $_____.

■ Demanders would be willing to buy 5 bushels of apples at a price of

$_____.

■ Demanders would be willing to buy 15 bushels of apples at a price of

$_____.

■ Demanders would want to buy exactly 10 bushels of apples at any price

between $_____ and $_____.

If, at the current price, the quantity of apples that demanders want to buy is greater than the quantity that suppliers want to supply, we say that there is **excess demand**. If, at the current price, the quantity of apples that suppliers want to sell is greater than the quantity that demanders want to buy, we say that there is **excess supply**.

■ At a price of $30, there is excess _____.

■ At a price of $12, there is excess _____.

■ There is excess supply at all prices higher than $_____ and there

is excess demand at all prices lower than $_____.

■ At a competitive equilibrium price, supply equals demand. In other words, at a competitive equilibrium, there is no excess demand and no excess supply. For the supply and demand curves in Figure D1.2, the competitive

equilibrium price is $_____$.

■ The competitive equilibrium quantity is the number of units bought and sold at the competitive equilibrium price. In this example, the competitive

equilibrium quantity is _____ bushels.

Profits and Consumers' Surplus

The amount of money that someone receives in a transaction is called **revenue**. The amount of money that someone pays out is called **expenditure**. **Profit** is defined to be revenue minus expenditure.

In this experiment, a supplier who sells a bushel of apples for P has revenue P and expenditure equal to her Seller Cost, C. Her profit is the difference between her revenue and expenditure, $P − C$.

A demander who buys a bushel of apples for the price P makes an expenditure of P and receives revenue equal to his Buyer Value V. His profit is the difference between his revenue and his expenditure, $V − P$.

In real-world markets, some goods are used by people who intend to resell them or use them in manufacturing, while other goods are purchased by people who buy them for their own or their family's use and enjoyment. Those who demand goods for their own consumption are known as **consumers**. In experimental markets, we motivate demanders to act like real-world consumers by assigning them Buyer Values which will be paid to them by the market manager if they buy a unit of goods. In real-world markets, there is of course no market manager to make such payments. Instead, consumers receive benefits directly from consuming the goods that they buy.

A demander's **consumer's surplus** from purchasing a unit of some good is defined to be the difference between his reservation price and the price he actually has to pay. In this experimental market, where demanders' reservation prices equal their Buyer Values, a buyer gets a consumer's surplus equal to the difference between his Buyer Value and the price that he pays. This difference is also defined as the buyer's profit. In the experiments in this book, we use the terms *consumer's surplus* and *demander's profit* interchangeably.

Let us now calculate the total profits made by suppliers and demanders in the example market for which you drew supply and demand curves. (Figure

D1.1, page 27.)   First calculate the total profit of all *suppliers*.   In this
example, low-cost suppliers each have costs of $5 per bushel and high-cost
suppliers each have costs of $25 per bushel.   At the equilibrium price of
$10 per bushel, each of the low-cost suppliers can make a profit by selling
a bushel of apples, but the high-cost suppliers would make losses if they
produced.   So each of the 20 low-cost suppliers will want to supply one
bushel and none of the high-cost suppliers will want to supply any apples.
At the equilibrium price of $10, the total amount of apples supplied is 20
bushels.   The total revenue of all suppliers is therefore 20 × $10 = $200.
Each of the 20 low-cost sellers has a Seller Cost of $5.   The total costs of all
the low-cost sellers are therefore 20 × $5 = $100.   The total profit made by
low-cost suppliers equals their total revenue minus their total costs, which
in this case is $200-$100=$100.   At the competitive equilibrium price of $10
per bushel, the high-cost suppliers do not supply any apples so they have
zero revenue, zero costs, and zero profits.   Total profit of all suppliers equals
the total profit of low-cost suppliers plus total profit of high-cost suppliers.
This is $100+$0=$100.

Now we calculate total consumers' surplus of all the *demanders* in the
market.   At the competitive equilibrium price of $10, the high-value deman-
ders, who have Buyer Values of $30, will make a profit by buying apples.
The consumer's surplus of each high-value demander is $30 − $10 = $20.
Since there are 15 high-value demanders, the total consumers' surplus of all
high-value demanders is 15 × $20 = $300.   Each of the low-value demanders has a Buyer Value of $10 for a bushel of apples.   Since the price of
apples is also $10, the low-value demanders who buy apples will have con-
sumer's surplus of $10-$10=0.   (They are neither better off nor worse off
than the low-value demanders who don't buy any apples.)[3]   Since all low-
value demanders receive zero profits, whether or not they buy apples, the
total amount of consumers' surplus received by low-value demanders is 0.
Therefore, the total amount of consumers' surplus made by all demanders
is $300 + 0 = $300.

We also want to measure the *total profit of all market participants*, including buyers and sellers.   This is obtained by adding total profit of suppliers
to total consumers' surplus of demanders.   In the example considered here,
total profit of all market participants is $100 + $300 = $400.

Figure D1.3 shows a useful geometrical way to find total profits from the

---

[3]In this example it turned out that one kind of supplier and one kind of demander
makes a profit.   Later, we will see examples in which all types of suppliers and all types
of demanders make positive profits.

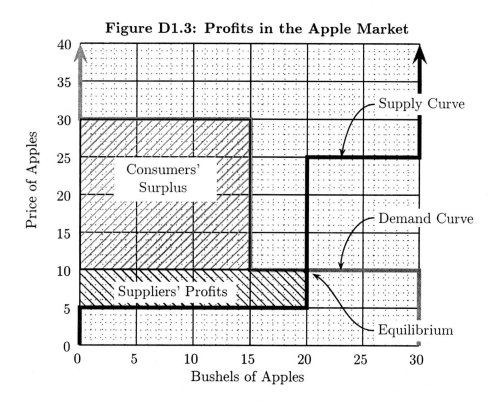

Figure D1.3: Profits in the Apple Market

graph of supply and demand curves. When the price is $10, 20 bushels of apples are sold. Total profits of suppliers are equal to $10 × 20 − $5 × 20, which is the area in the shaded area marked *Suppliers' Profits*.[4] Total consumers' surplus is $30 × 15 − $10 × 15, which is the shaded area marked *Consumers' Surplus*. Total profits of all market participants equals the sum of the two areas marked Suppliers' Profits and Consumers' Surplus. This implies that total profits of all market participants equals the total area between the supply curve and the demand curve to the left of the equilibrium quantity.

---

[4]The area of a rectangle is given by its height times its width. The Suppliers' Profits rectangle is 5 units high and 20 units wide, so its area is 20 × 5 = 100.

Appendix

Mean, Variance, and Standard Deviation

Suppose you have a list of n numbers. Call these numbers $x_1, x_2, \ldots, x_n$. The *mean* or *average* of these numbers is calculated by adding them all together and dividing the result by n. We denote the mean of the list of x's by $\bar{x}$ and hence we write $\bar{x} = \frac{1}{n}(x_1 + x_2 + \ldots + x_n)$. A more elegant way of expressing the same idea is to write

$$\bar{x} = \frac{1}{n} \sum_{i=1}^{n} x_i$$

For example, if we have a list of 5 numbers, 2,7,3,8,10, the mean of this list of numbers is $(2 + 7 + 3 + 8 + 10)/5 = 6$.

Calculating the variance and the standard deviation of a list of numbers is a little more complicated. First you calculate the mean of these numbers. Then you take each of the numbers in the list, subtract the mean, and square the result. Take the mean of all these squares to get the variance. Take the square root of the variance to get the standard deviation. It is customary to use the notation σ^2 for the variance of the list of x's and to denote the standard deviation of this list by σ. Then for a list of numbers $x_1, \ldots, x_n$, we define

$$\sigma^2 = \frac{1}{n} \sum_{i=1}^{n} (x_i - \bar{x})^2.$$

and

$$\sigma = \sqrt{\frac{1}{n} \sum_{i=1}^{n} (x_i - \bar{x})^2}.$$

For example, for the list of numbers, 2,7,3,8,10, we calculate the standard deviation as follows. The mean of these 5 numbers is 6. Then the variance is

$$\sigma_x^2 = \frac{1}{5}\left((2-6)^2 + (7-6)^2 + (3-6)^2 + (8-6)^2 + (10-6)^2\right) = 46/5$$

and the standard deviation is $\sigma = \sqrt{46/5} = 3.033$.

Hints on Drawing the Demand Curve.

The highest value that anybody puts on apples is 30, so we know that at prices above 30, nobody is going to want to buy apples. Therefore you can use your green pen to mark a vertical line extending from the point (0,30) to the top of the box. At prices greater than 10 but less than 30, all of the high demanders, who have values of 30, will want to buy a bushel of apples, but none of the low demanders, who have values of only 10, will want to buy. There are 15 high demanders, so total demand at any of these prices is 15. This means that the demand curve includes a vertical segment running from (15,10) to (15,30). At prices below 10, everybody will want to buy one bushel. There are 30 demanders in all, so that total demand will be 30 bushels. The demand curve, therefore, includes a vertical segment running from (0,30) to (10,30).

At a price of 30, the 15 high-value demanders are just indifferent between buying or not. Total demand could be anything between 0 and 15. Therefore the demand curve includes a horizontal segment running from (0,30) to (15,30). At a price of 10, the 15 high-value demanders will all want to buy one unit. The 15 low-value demanders will be just indifferent between buying and not buying, so at this price, demand can be anything between 15 and 30. Therefore the demand curve includes a horizontal segment running from (15,10) to (30,10).

Figure D1.4: Supply and Demand–Example 1

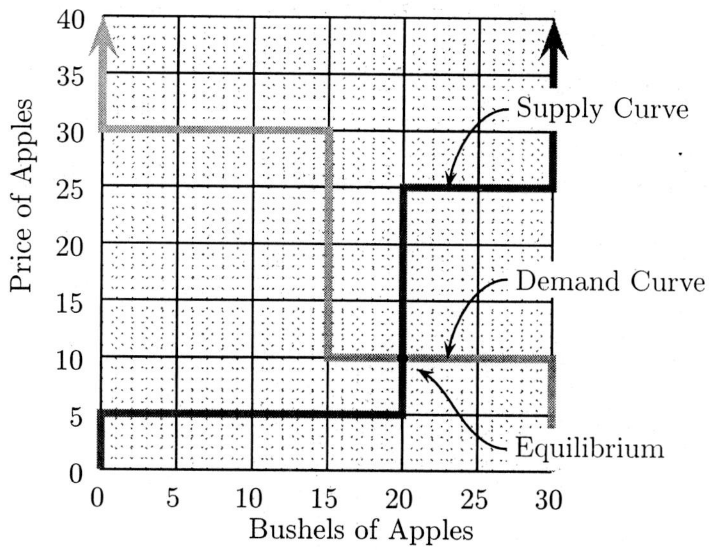

■ ■ Suppose that at the end of trading none of the people who have not traded could make a mutually profitable deal. Try to prove that if this is the case, then the number of trades that were made must be at least as large as the number of trades that are made in competitive equilibrium.

_____

_____

_____

_____

_____

_____

Experiment 2

Shifting Supply

A Village Fish Market

It is early morning at the fish market on a lonely Pacific island. The mist is rising, the gulls are calling, and the fishermen have just returned to the harbor with their catch. A noisy crowd of villagers have come to the fish market to gossip and buy their dinners.

There are no refrigerators on the island and day-old fish will spoil. Since one fish is enough to feed a family for a day, each demander wants at most one fish. Some of the fishermen will have one fish to sell and others will have two or three fish. In the first two market sessions, the fishermen all have zero Seller Costs. In the third market session, each fisherman had to pay $10 for fuel for his fishing boat before he went out fishing the night before. This money has already been spent, and so his total fuel costs will be $10 whether he sells no fish, one fish, two fish, or three fish. (In contrast, in the apple market of our previous experiment, sellers had zero costs if they sold no apples.)

Fishermen have zero Seller Costs in all three market sessions.

The overall distribution of Buyer Values is the same in all sessions, though individual Buyer Values change from one session to another. Because of changes in the weather, the total number of fish caught by the fishermen differs from one session to another.

Instructions

Please read these instructions and work the warm-up exercise before you come to class.

Your personal information sheet will tell you for each session whether you are a fisherman (fish supplier) or a fish demander.

As in previous markets, buyers and sellers must find each other and agree on a price. After each sale, the buyer and the seller bring a sales contract to the market manager. The sales contract records the ID number of buyer and seller, the price and the Buyer Value. (You don't need to fill in a Seller Cost on the sales contract.)

If you are a fish demander and you buy a fish, you will receive your Buyer Value from the market manager. Your profit as a demander is the difference between your Buyer Value and the price you paid for the fish.

If you are a fisherman, you will have either one, two, or three fish to sell. If you have more than one fish, you must find a *different* buyer for each fish that you sell. After you have turned in a contract for the sale of a fish, if you still have some fish left, you can return to the marketplace to seek a buyer for another fish. In the first two rounds, where fishermen have zero Seller Costs, their profits are equal to the total amount of money they get from selling their fish. In the third round, a fisherman's profits is the total amount of money that he gets from selling fish, *minus* the $10 fuel cost.

Warm-up Exercise

■ In the first session of this experiment, suppose that a fisherman catches two fish. He sells one fish for $10 and one fish for $6. How much is his total profit? $_____ Suppose that this fisherman sells the first fish for $10 and is unable to sell the second fish. How much is his total profit?

_____

■ Suppose that you are a fish demander with a Buyer Value of $25, and you see that there are many fishermen still trying to sell fish, but only a few demanders left who have not already bought their fish. Assuming that you want to maximize your profits, at what price would you offer to buy?

_____

■ Suppose that you are a fisherman and you have one fish left to sell. You see that almost all of the fish demanders have already bought their fish, but there are several fishermen still trying to sell fish. The average price of the fish that have already been sold is about $10. Would you expect to be able to sell your fish for $10?_____ If somebody offered you $2 for your fish, would you take the offer?_____ Explain.

_____

■ Suppose that you are a fisherman in the third session, where your fuel costs are $10, and that you have caught only one fish. The best offer that you are made for this fish is $4. What would be your profit (or loss) if

you sell the fish for $4?_____What would be your profit

(or loss) if you don't sell your fish, but let it rot?_____. If you want to maximize your profit from this experiment and you are faced with a choice between selling the fish for $4 or not selling the fish, what

should you do? _____

What Do You Expect to See?

■ What difference do you think the $10 fuel cost will make to the market outcome in Session 3?

_____

■ If fishing conditions improve so that more fish are caught, would you

expect the price of fish to go up or down? _____ Would you expect total profits of *all* fishermen to go up, go down, or stay the same?

_____

_____

_____

Discussion D2

Shifting Supply and Demand Curves

Comparative Statics of Market Changes

In the apple market experiment, we learned to draw supply and demand curves and to find competitive equilibrium prices and quantities. In the fish market experiment, we learned to calculate the expected effects of changes in market conditions on quantity and price, by looking at the supply and demand curves that apply before and after the changes. This simple procedure, which is known as **comparative statics**, is a remarkably powerful tool for predicting the effects of changes in economic variables on prices, quantities, profits, and consumers' surplus.

To carry out a comparative statics analysis of a change in market fundamentals, follow these steps:

- Draw the supply and demand curves that applied before the market change and determine the original competitive equilibrium price and quantity.

- Determine whether the change has altered the demand curve, the supply curve, or both.

- Draw the new supply curve and/or the new demand curve.

- Find the new competitive equilibrium price and quantity and compare them to the initial equilibrium price and quantity.

In the case of our fish-market experiment, we analyzed the effects of a change in fishing conditions that altered the total number of fish caught by fishermen. This change has no effect on the number of demanders or on demanders' reservation prices and, therefore, does not change the demand curve. How about the supply curve? A change in the number of fish caught does not change any fisherman's reservation price for selling a fish, since for a fish that is already caught, he is willing to accept any positive price rather than not sell his fish. But the number of fish that are available at any positive price is equal to the total number of fish that are caught. Therefore an increase in the number of fish caught shifts the vertical segment of the supply curve to the right, and a decrease in the number of fish caught shifts this segment to the left. In the experiment, we traced the effects of such shifts on the equilibrium supply and demand.

In the remainder of this chapter, we will discuss some other examples of comparative statics analysis of shifting supply and demand.

Seasonal Shifts in Demand

Smoothed Supply and Demand Curves

In the examples we have seen so far, the supply curves and the demand curves look like stairways. For a supply curve, the vertical rise in the bottom step of the stairway represents the difference between the lowest Seller Cost, and the second-lowest Seller Cost. The rise in the next step represents the difference between the second and third lowest Seller Costs, and so on up the staircase. In a large population, the supply curve will have many, many of these steps, and each of the steps is likely to be very small. For large populations, it is more efficient, and reasonably accurate, to approximate the supply curve by drawing a smooth curve instead of a staircase. Similar reasoning suggests that the demand curve can also often be approximated by a smooth curve.[1] Here, and in other sections of the book, we will sometimes follow economists' practice of drawing smooth supply and/or demand curves.[2]

---

[1] These smooth supply and demand curves need not be straight lines. But straight line supply and demand curves are nice to use as examples, because they are easy to draw and easy to represent algebraically.

[2] In our experiments, we will continue to work with stair-step supply and demand curves.

A Market for Motel Rooms

Let us think about the economics of motel business in a resort community. Consider a town with 20 small motels, each of which has ten rental units. Motel-keepers in this town have learned that renting a room for a night costs them $20 more than leaving it unoccupied.[3] The market supply curve is drawn in Figure D2.1 below. At prices lower than $20 per night, none of the motel-keepers will want to rent out their rooms, so the supply curve has a vertical segment that runs from the origin (0,0) up to the point (0,20). At a price of $20, all 20 suppliers will be just indifferent between renting or not renting their rooms. Therefore the supply curve includes a horizontal line segment where the price is $20 and the quantity runs from 0 to 200 units. At any price above $20, each of the 20 suppliers will want to supply all 10 of their units. No matter how high the price goes, only 200 units are available, so the supply curve must have a vertical segment that extends from the point where the price is $20 and the quantity is 200 units, all the way up to the sky.

Figure D2.1 shows the demand curves for the months of August and September. The August demand curve crosses the supply curve at the point representing 200 rooms rented at a price of $50 per room per night. In September, as the days get shorter and cooler, everybody's Buyer Value decreases by $20. So, the September demand curve is obtained by shifting the August demand curve downward by $20. The September equilibrium price falls to $30 per night and all 200 rooms continue to be occupied. Thus, the $20 downward shift in demand from August to September reduces room prices by $20, and does not change occupancy rates.

In October and November, as the weather worsens, the Buyer Values continue to decline. Customers' Buyer Values for October are always $20 lower than they are for September. Buyer Values for November are $20 lower than they are for October.

The demand curves for October and November are shown in Figure D2.2. At the October equilibrium, 150 rooms are rented for $20 per night, and 50 rooms remain empty. In November, the demand curve again shifts downwards by $20, but during this month, the *price* does not fall, but remains at $20 per night. The only effect of the demand shift is that it reduces the number of rooms rented from 150 to 50.

---

[3]This $20 cost includes the cost of cleaning the room, washing the sheets, replacing stolen towels, and any other costs that would be avoided if the room were left empty. It does not include the construction cost of the motel, or any other fixed costs that would have to be paid whether the rooms were rented out or not.

Figure D2.1: Supply and Demand in August and September

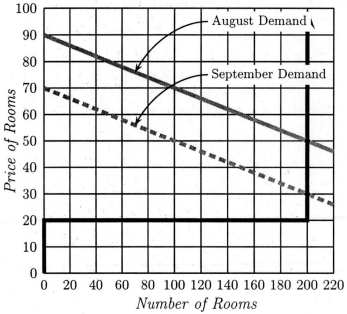

Figure D2.2: Supply and Demand in October and November

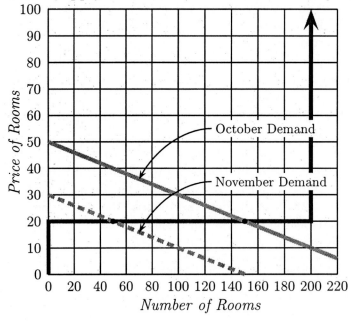

The contrast between the results of the demand shift from August to September and the shift from October to November reveals that a downward shift in demand can have strikingly different effects, depending on the shape of the supply curve over the relevant range of prices. At the equilibrium prices for the months of August and September (Figure D2.1), the supply curve is vertical, so the decrease in Buyer Value causes an equal decrease in price. At the equilibrium prices for October and November, the supply curve is horizontal, so the downward shift in demand from October to November has no effect on price, but reduces the number of units sold.

The demand shift from September to October provides an example of a decrease in demand which lowers *both* the *price* and the *quantity* of rooms rented. Figure D2.3 shows that in September, all rooms are rented at a price of $30. In October, the demand curve shifts down by $20 and the price falls by $10. The number of rooms rented also falls from 200 to 150.

Figure D2.3: Supply and Demand in September and October

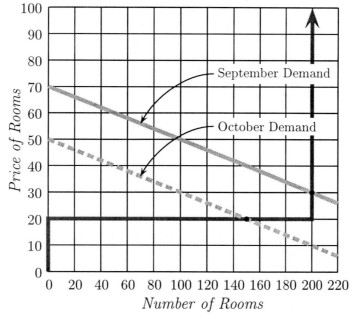

Two Riddles About Supply and Demand

Here are two riddles, each of which seems puzzling at first, but each of which has a very satisfactory explanation. The key to solving these riddles, and many others like them, is to ask: "Which curve shifted, supply or demand?"

- The price of a lift ticket at Michigan's Mt. Brighton ski resort is $20 on weekends and holidays, and $16 on ordinary weekdays. Yet the ski slopes are far busier on weekends and holidays than they are during the week. Does this mean that high prices make people demand more lift tickets?

- In June, supermarkets stock oodles of fresh strawberries, and sell them at low prices. In December, strawberries are rare, and extremely expensive. Does this mean that high prices make strawberry growers supply fewer berries?

For a ski resort, the costs of providing rides on the lifts or space on the slopes is about the same on weekdays as it is on weekends. Therefore, the supply curve does not change very much throughout the week. What shifts is the demand curve. Since Saturday is not a workday or a school day, if the price were the same on both days, more people would buy tickets on Saturday than on Tuesday. Even with lower prices in the midweek, the number of people who are able to take advantage of these low prices may be smaller. Figure D2.4 illustrates supply and demand curves that are consistent with a ski resort having 400 customers on Saturday when it charges $20, and only 200 customers on Tuesday, when it charges $16. As we see in the figure, even though demand curves for any given day slope down, it is possible for both the *quantity* of tickets sold and the *price* of tickets to be lower on Tuesday than on Saturday, because the Tuesday demand curve is different from the Saturday demand curve. The supply curve is the same on both of these days, so that the price-quantity combinations found on Saturday and on Tuesday both lie on the same supply curve.

Unlike skiers' desires for lift tickets, consumers' appetites for fresh fruit do not change significantly from day to day, nor from season to season. What does change in the berry market, and dramatically so, is the *supply* of strawberries. In peak season, local farmers can produce strawberries inexpensively. During other seasons, fruit must be grown in indoor hothouses, or imported from distant sources with high spoilage and shipping costs. As a result, the supply curve for strawberries during peak season is different from the supply curve at other times of the year.

Suppose that in June, when strawberries sell for $1 a carton, a market supplies 200 boxes a day, and in December, when strawberries sell for $15 a carton, the same market supplies only 10 boxes a day. Figure D2.5 shows

Figure D2.4: Supply and Demand for Lift Tickets

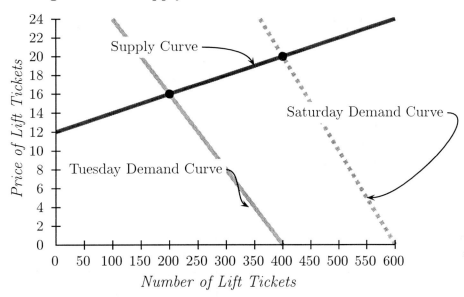

a possible graph of this market. From June to December, the supply curve for strawberries shifts up while the demand curve remains unchanged.

Real-World Investigative Projects

This assignment will be made at your instructor's discretion. Even if your instructor does not ask you to turn in an investigative report, we recommend that you think about what you would do if it were assigned.

We hope that by now you are getting into the spirit of hands-on economics; of observing and analyzing laboratory markets in action. We would like you to apply a similar approach to the real-world "experiments" that go on in everyday commerce. This assignment will allow you to engage your curiosity and investigative skills in looking at the workings of some of the markets that you will find going on around you. Working in groups of two or three is likely to make the project more fun and will allow you to share tasks. We will suggest a few markets that make for interesting investigations, but feel free to make up a project of your own, particularly if you have a good source of information or a special interest in some particular market.

As part of your research, you may decide to talk to some people directly involved in a particular business enterprise. If so, remember that these

Figure D2.5: Supply and Demand for Strawberries

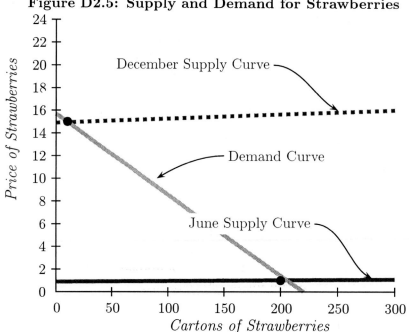

people are not *required* to talk to you. Many will enjoy helping you if you are friendly and interested, but keep in mind that they are doing you a favor.

- **The Ski-Resort Industry.**   Below are some suggestions for researching this project:

  - Research the prices that ski resorts charge for lift-tickets during the week, and on weekends and holidays. You may find this information in ads in ski magazines or in resort brochures from travel agencies and ski shops. For resorts with lodges, also look into the way that room-rental prices vary by month of the year, and between weekends and holidays.

  - Compare patterns of pricing for ski resorts, like those in Michigan and Vermont, which attract primarily locals, with patterns of pricing for resorts, like those in Montana and Utah, which attract a clientele from around the world. (Before gathering the data, would you guess that there is more variation between weekend and weekday rates in the East, or in the Rockies?) Information about ski resort pricing in Europe would be an interesting addition to your data.

— Try to find out how the number of lift tickets sold varies between weekdays and weekends and from month to month throughout the year. You may find some of this information in trade magazines, but your best source will probably be ski resort employees or managers.

— Look for evidence of shifts in supply of and/or demand for lift tickets and lodging at ski resorts from year to year.

— Give a possible explanation for your observations involving shifts in supply curves or in demand curves.

- **Seasonal Demand for Motel Rooms.** You may want to look for information on this topic in motel registers and travel guides like the AAA travel guide, the Michelin travel guide, and the Mobil travel guide. Choose any region, in the U.S. or abroad, for your study. Below are some questions you might try to answer:

  — For your region, how do room rates vary from season to season?

  — How do occupancy rates vary by season? (To answer this question, you may have to look at a trade journal or interview a sample of motel operators.)

  — Do you find greater seasonal variation in prices and/or in occupancy rates for hotels and motels that are in resort areas or for those in urban areas?

  — Try to explain your observations in terms of supply and demand curves.

- **Markets for Fruits, Vegetables and Seasonal Fish.** Choose a perishable food product like sweet corn, strawberries, or fresh peaches that has a relatively short local growing season.

  — Find as much specific information as you can about the seasonal variation of prices for the product(s) that you study. You may find this in newspaper ads or by interviewing someone in the grocery trade or the fruit and vegetable business.

  — Look into the variation of the amount of the product sold throughout the year.

— If you find information about both prices and sales of your product throughout the year, draw a graph with price on the vertical axis and quantity on the horizontal axis. Plot points representing the price-quantity combinations that you observe for different times of the year.

— Whether or not you have enough information to draw a graph relating price and quantity, explain how you would interpret a graph that is drawn in this way. Could the curve that you constructed by plotting price-quantity combinations be a demand curve? Could it be a supply curve?

- **Local Labor Markets for Low-wage Jobs.** Investigate the low-wage job market in the area around your university or in some other city or town where you have good access to information.

  — Compile as large a list as you can of low-wage jobs and the wages being paid for them. Find out what people are earning in the local fast-food restaurants, convenience stores, and coffee shops. You can expand your list as you search. You may find information by looking in help-wanted ads from newspapers, or by asking low-wage workers[4] or employers of low-wage workers.

  — If you find variation among the wages for different low-paying jobs, provide a possible explanation for it. Are the wages higher for nastier or more dangerous jobs?

  — Are some employers having trouble attracting as many workers as they would like? Are these the employers who are paying the lowest wages?

  — Are the wages for the jobs that you investigated greater than the federally-mandated minimum wage?

- **Professional Sports.** Try to document changes in recent years in the earnings of professional athletes in various professional sports. Can you find shifts in supply or demand that might account for these changes?

---

[4] Be discreet about how you ask these questions, if you don't want a greasy cheeseburger flipped in your face.

Part II

Market Intervention and Public Policy

Experiment 3

A Sales Tax

We are back at the Farmers' Apple Market. There is a hint of frost in the air and the leaves are changing colors. Today's market session is a little more complex. Instead of just two types of buyers and sellers, there will be several types of each. This should make shopping a bit more interesting than it was with only two types. A new (and perhaps unwelcome) player, the Tax Collector, also makes his debut.

Instructions

You will be better prepared to participate profitably in this market if you read these instructions and complete the brief warm-up exercise before you come to class.

There will be three market sessions today. In the first session, there are no taxes. In the second session, *suppliers* will have to pay a sales tax of **$15** if they make a sale. In the third session, *demanders* will have to pay a sales tax of **$15** if they buy a bushel of apples. You are likely to play a different role in each of the three sessions, but the overall distribution of buyers and sellers in the market is the same in all three sessions; that is, the total number of buyers with each possible Buyer Value, and the total number of sellers with each Seller Cost, will be the same in all sessions.

Procedures in this market experiment are similar to those used in Experiment 1. In each session you will get a Personal Information Sheet that tells you whether you are a supplier or a demander and reports your Seller Cost or Buyer Value. In each round of a session, you can trade at most one bushel of apples. If you agree on a sale, you and your trading partner should fill in a Sales Contract and bring it to the market manager who will record the transaction and collect any sales tax that is due.

In the second market session, sellers have to pay a sales tax of $15. In this session, if you are a seller with Seller Cost C and you sell a bushel of apples for P, then your profit on the transaction will be $P - $C - 15.

In the third market session, buyers have to pay a sales tax of $15. If you are a buyer with Buyer Value V and you buy a bushel of apples for P, then your profit on the transaction will be $V - $P - 15.

If you make no transactions at all, you don't have to pay a tax and you have no costs or revenue, so your profit is zero.

Warm-up Exercise

■ Suppose that sellers have to pay a sales tax of $15 when they sell a bushel of apples. If a supplier who has a Seller Cost of $5 sells a bushel of apples for $25 to a demander who has Buyer Value of $45, the supplier will make

a profit of $_____and the demander will make a profit (consumer's

surplus) of $_____.

■ Suppose that buyers have to pay a sales tax of $15 when they buy a bushel of apples. If a supplier who has a Seller Cost of $5 sells a bushel of apples for $25 to a demander who has Buyer Value of $45, the supplier

will make a profit of $_____and the demander will make a profit (con-

sumer's surplus) of $_____.

■ Suppose that you are a supplier with Seller Cost of $15 and that sellers have to pay a sales tax of $15 when they sell a bushel of apples. What is the lowest price at which you would not lose money by selling apples?

$_____.

■ Suppose that you are a demander with Buyer Value of $30 and that buyers have to pay a sales tax of $15 when they buy a bushel of apples. What is the highest price at which you can buy a bushel of apples and not

lose money?$_____.

What Do You Expect to See?

These questions ask you to explore your beliefs about what will happen in the experiment before you know the experimental outcome and before you read the discussion in this chapter. After the experiment is done and you have finished the discussion and homework, you can look back to compare your prior answers with what you know when you finish this chapter.

■   In the experimental market, would you predict that the $15 tax paid by sellers in Session 1 will cause the average price paid by buyers to increase by more than $15, less than $15, or just about $15? Explain

_____

_____

_____

■   Do you think that demanders will be better off if sellers pay the tax than if buyers pay the tax? _____

Discussion D3

A Sales Tax

When the government puts a tax on something, there are usually loud complaints from sellers of the taxed good who think that the tax will come out of their profits, and from buyers who think that the tax will be passed on to them in the form of higher prices. Our experimental results suggest that both groups are at least partly right. In this experiment, it appears that whether the sales tax is collected from the suppliers or from the demanders, a sales tax lowers the profits of both.

We are now going to compare the outcome of the experiment with the predictions made by the theory of competitive equilibrium. The beauty of having a general theoretical model like the competitive theory is that it can give us a good idea of what the effects of a sales tax will be, not only under the specific conditions of our experiment, but under a wide variety of possible market environments.

To show how supply and demand curves can be applied to problems of taxation, we work through a supply-demand analysis of a specific environment similar to that in our classroom experiment. As an exercise, you will be asked to draw supply and demand curves for the exact market conditions that applied in the classroom market, and to compare the predictions of the competitive model to the outcomes of the classroom experiments. Finally, you will be asked to explore some other implications of the theory.

Equilibrium without Sales Taxes

Consider a market in which the distribution of Seller Costs and Buyer Values is as given by Table D3.1.

Table D3.1: Distribution of Types of Agents

Seller's Costs	Number in Market	Buyer's Value	Number in Market
3	2	45	2
8	2	40	2
13	2	35	2
18	2	30	2
23	2	25	2
28	2	20	2

Let us begin by drawing the market supply curve and demand curves without sales taxes. The graphs of supply and demand look like stairways.[1] Because we have more different types than we had in our first market experiment, the supply and demand curves will have more steps in them.

The bottom step in the supply-curve stairway is drawn at a price of $3, which is the cost of production for the two lowest-cost suppliers. At prices below $3, the supply is zero. This explains the vertical segment of the supply curve running from (0,0) to (0,3). At a price of $3, these two suppliers are just indifferent between supplying their apples and not supplying their apples, so the supply can be any quantity between 0 and 2. This explains the flat part of the first step of the supply curve, running from (0,3) to (2,3). According to Table D3.1, the second lowest-cost suppliers have costs of $8. At prices between $3 and $8, the lowest-cost suppliers would want to supply, but nobody else would want to, so the supply schedule contains a vertical segment running from (2,3) to (2,8).

The top of the second step in the supply-curve stairway is drawn at a height of $8, the price where supply from the next lowest-cost group of suppliers kicks in. At a price of $8, the two lowest-cost suppliers would surely want to sell apples and the two suppliers with the second-lowest costs would be just indifferent between selling and not selling. So at this price, the supply can be anything between 2 and 4. This gives us the flat top of the second step, a segment running from $(2, 8)$ to $(4, 8)$. In the same way as we drew the first two steps, we add more steps to the supply curve as the price rises and more sellers enter the market. This continues until we have reached a price of $28, at which each of the 12 sellers in the market is willing to supply a bushel of apples. Since every supplier in this market has

---

[1]Functions whose graphs look like this are known to mathematicians as *step functions.*

only one bushel to sell, increasing the price above $28 will not bring in any more supply. Thus, at prices higher than $28, the supply curve is vertical with 12 bushels of apples being provided.

The demand curve is constructed in a similar fashion. At prices higher than $45, nobody wants to buy. At prices between $45 and $40, only the two highest-value demanders want to buy. At prices between $40 and $35, the four highest-value demanders will want to buy, and so on.

Figure D3.1: Supply and Demand with No Sales Tax

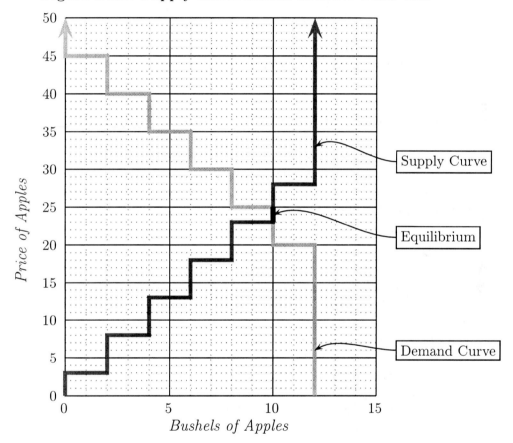

Notice that the supply and demand curves in Figure D3.1 do not cross each other at just a single point, but meet and run together along the interval from $(10, 23)$ to $(10, 25)$ where the number of trades is 10 and the price can be anywhere between $23 and $25.

At prices greater than $25, the supply curve lies to the right of the demand curve, meaning that there are more suppliers wanting to sell a bushel of apples than demanders wanting to buy a bushel of apples. At prices less than $23, the demand curve lies to the right of the supply curve, meaning that there are more demanders wanting to buy apples than suppliers wanting to sell them. But at any price between $23 and $25, there are 10 suppliers who want to sell a bushel of apples and 10 demanders who want to buy a bushel of apples. Therefore, at prices between $23 and $25, "supply equals demand" and the market is in competitive equilibrium. Thus the competitive model predicts that 10 bushels of apples will be sold. Instead of predicting a unique equilibrium price, the theory says only that the price will lie somewhere in the interval from $23 to $25.

Equilibrium When Sellers Pay a Sales Tax

The way to find out the effect of a sales tax on competitive equilibrium prices and quantities is to study the effect of the tax on the supply curve and demand curves.

How does a $15 sales tax, charged to sellers, affect the supply curve? In addition to their production costs, suppliers who sell a bushel of apples have to pay the $15 tax. For example, a supplier who has a Seller Cost of $8 will have a total cost, including taxes, of $8+$15=$23. The effect of the tax is to *increase* the lowest price at which she is willing to sell by $15. The new supply curve is therefore the one that you would draw if each supplier's Seller Cost increased by $15. The new supply curve must be drawn so that the price at which any quantity is supplied is exactly $15 higher than the price at which this quantity was supplied before the tax was imposed. Economists describe this change by saying that the tax "shifted the supply curve up" by $15. In Figure D3.2, the pre-tax supply curve is shown as a solid line. The new supply curve with the tax is the dashed line, obtained by shifting the old supply curve up by $15.

How does this sales tax affect the demand curve? That's easy. Since Buyer Values do not change and buyers do not have to pay any tax, the tax does not change any demander's willingness-to-pay (reservation price) for apples. Therefore the demand curve will be the same as it was without taxes.

Looking at the supply and demand curves in Figure D3.2, we can find the effect of the tax on competitive equilibrium prices and quantities. The equilibrium without a tax is indicated by the darkened interval marked "Old Equilibrium." Without a sales tax, 10 bushels are sold and the price must be in the interval between $23 to $25. The competitive equilibrium with the

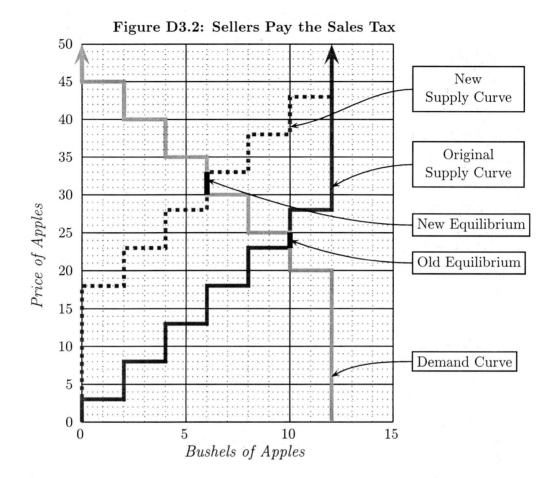

Figure D3.2: Sellers Pay the Sales Tax

tax is marked by the darkened interval marked "New Equilibrium," where
the dashed supply curve meets the demand curve. On this interval, 6 bushels
of apples are sold and the price must be somewhere in the interval between
$30 to $33.

   Thus the sales tax, when collected from sellers, decreases the number of
trades from 10 to 6 and causes the price to rise from a price in the interval,
$23 to $25 to a price in the interval, $30 to $33.

Equilibrium When Buyers Pay the Sales Tax

To find the effect of a sales tax charged to buyers instead of to sellers, we
again ask what happens to supply curves and/or demand curves.

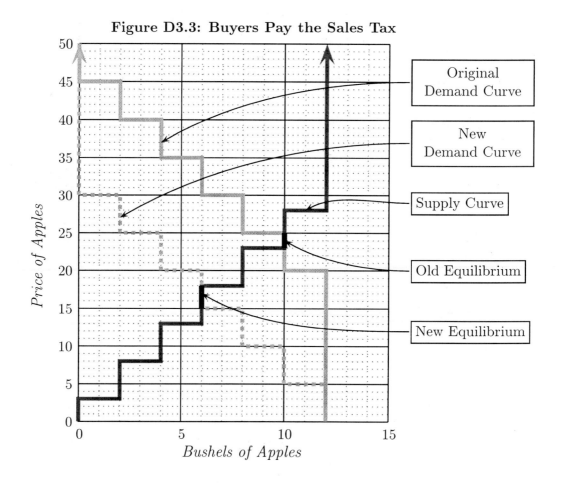

Figure D3.3: Buyers Pay the Sales Tax

How does this sales tax affect the demand curve? A demander who buys a bushel of apples has to pay the seller the agreed-upon price and also has to pay the Tax Collecter $15. For example, a demander with Buyer Value $40 would have to pay a $15 sales tax for every bushel that he buys. If this demander buys a bushel of apples, he would collect $40 from the market manager, but would have to pay the $15 tax, in addition to the price that he would pay to the buyer. Thus the buyer's reservation price (that is, the highest price that he would be willing to pay a seller for a bushel of apples) would be $40-$15=$25. The effect of the tax on a buyer's reservation price is the same as the effect of a $15 decrease in his Buyer Value. This means that the new demand curve will be obtained by "shifting the pre-tax demand curve down" by $15. In Figure D3.3, we show the pre-tax demand curve as a solid line and the post-tax demand curve as a dashed line, exactly $15 lower for each quantity than the original demand curve.

How does this sales tax affect the supply curve? The tax does not change any supplier's Seller Costs, and since sellers do not have to pay any taxes directly to the government, the minimum price that any seller would be willing to accept for a bushel of apples does not change. Therefore the supply curve remains the same as it was without taxes.

We can find the effects of a tax collected from buyers by looking at the supply and demand curves in Figure D3.3. Without a sales tax, 10 bushels are sold and the price must be in the interval between $23 to $25. The competitive equilibrium with the tax is marked by the darkened interval marked "New Equilibrium," where the dashed demand curve meets the supply curve. On this interval, 6 bushels of apples are sold and the price must be somewhere in the interval between $15 to $18. Thus the sales tax collected from buyers decreases the number of trades from 10 to 6 and causes the price to fall, from a price in the interval between $23 to $25 to a price in the interval between $15 to $18.

The Effects of Sales Taxes

Equivalence of Taxes Collected from Sellers and Buyers

Which leads to higher profits for buyers, a sales tax that is collected from sellers, or a sales tax that is collected directly from buyers? At first blush, the answer seems to be obvious. Surely your profits will be higher if somebody else pays the tax than if you pay the tax.

Let us see what happens in the example that we have just discussed. For simplicity, we will assume that in each equilibrium, the competitive price falls exactly in the middle of the range of possible prices. Thus when there is no tax, the price would be $24; when the sellers pay the tax, the price would be $31.50; and when the buyers pay the tax, the price would be $16.50.

Now let us ask which is better for buyers. If sellers pay the tax, the equilibrium price is $31.50 and buyers don't have to pay any tax. If buyers pay the tax, the price is $16.50, but they also have to pay a tax of $15 for each unit they buy. Therefore the total amount that buyers have to pay for a bushel of apples is $16.50 + $15 = $31.50. We see, therefore, that in equilibrium the cost of a bushel of apples, including tax, is the same whether buyers pay the tax or sellers pay the tax.

Now consider the profits of suppliers. If sellers pay the tax, then the equilibrium price is $31.50, but a seller has to pay a tax of $15 for each bushel that she sells, so that after taxes, she receives only $31.50 − $15 = $16.50 per bushel. If buyers pay the tax, the equilibrium price is $16.50. In this case, the seller receives $16.50 per bushel and is not obliged to pay any tax. Thus we see that the after-tax price received by sellers is the same regardless of who pays the tax.

Since the after-tax prices paid by buyers and received by sellers are the same, regardless of from whom the tax is collected, their profits are also the same whether buyers pay the tax or sellers pay the tax. Notice also, that in our example, the total number of transactions is 6 and total government revenue is $15 × 6 = $90. Thus we find that despite apparent differences, *the real effects of a tax are no different, whether the tax is collected from sellers or from buyers.*

How can it be that buyers and sellers get the same profits regardless of who pays the tax? The way this works is that the equilibrium *price* is different depending on who has to pay the tax. The difference between the equilibrium price when sellers pay the tax and when buyers pay the tax turns out to be exactly the amount of the tax. This means that the equilibrium after-tax price paid by demanders, and likewise the equilibrium after-tax price received by suppliers, will be the same regardless of from whom the tax is collected.

Sharing the Burden of a Sales Tax

Who bears the burden of a sales tax? Do sellers simply pass the tax on to buyers, or do sellers absorb the tax and leave the price paid by consumers the same as it would be without the tax? Or is the answer somewhere in between? It turns out that if demand curves are downward sloping and supply curves are upward sloping, the burden of the tax will be shared between buyers and sellers. Without a sales tax, the price received by sellers is the same as the price paid by buyers. With a sales tax, regardless of whether the sales tax is collected from sellers or from buyers, the after-tax price received by sellers falls, and the after-tax price paid by buyers rises. In the new equilibrium, the price paid by demanders will be greater than the price received by suppliers by the amount of the per-unit tax. This means that, in general, the burden of a sales tax is shared between suppliers and demanders.

In the example just considered, without a sales tax there is an equilibrium where suppliers receive $24 per unit and demanders pay $24 per unit. With the sales tax, suppliers receive $16.50 for each unit they sell and demanders pay $31.50 for each unit they purchase. This means that the tax causes the price paid by demanders to increase by $7.50 and the price received by suppliers to decrease by $7.50. Thus the $15 per-unit "burden of the tax" is shared between suppliers and demanders, with demanders bearing a $7.50 increase in the price they have to pay and suppliers bearing a $7.50 decrease in the price they receive per unit.

Tax Revenue, Profits, and Excess Burden

When the government collects a sales tax, total profits of buyers and of sellers will decrease, since the price paid by buyers rises and the price received by sellers decreases. On the other hand, the government gains some revenue, which may be put to use to provide beneficial goods and services both to buyers and to sellers. Is the amount of money that the government collects greater than, less than, or equal to the total loss in profits for buyers and sellers caused by the tax?

The answer to this question is that if demand curves slope down and supply curves slope up, a sales tax will reduce total profits of buyers and sellers by more than the amount of money collected. The difference between the amount of profits lost to buyers and sellers, and the amount of revenue collected by the government is called the **excess burden** of the tax. In general, the reason that a sales tax reduces profits of buyers and sellers by more than the amount of money that the government collects is that the tax prevents some trades that would be profitable for both buyer and seller in the absence of a tax.

Let us try to understand how this works. If a demander with Buyer Value $30 buys from a supplier with Seller Cost $8, they can both make a profit at any price between $8 and $30. Whatever price is chosen, the sum of the buyer's profit and the seller's profit will be $30 − $8 = $22. In this case, since total profits are more than $15, they could still make a mutually profitable trade even if the seller or the buyer has to pay a tax of $15 on this transaction. Their total after-tax profits would be $30 − $8 − $15 = $7. In this case, the $15 loss in buyer's and seller's profits is exactly matched by the $15 gain in tax revenue for the government. But if the demander's Buyer Value exceeds the supplier's Seller Cost by less than $15, there will be no way for the buyer and seller to complete a mutually profitable trade when the tax must be paid by one of them. For example, suppose that a demander has a Buyer Value of $30 and a supplier has a Seller Cost of $18. If there is no tax, they can make a trade that is profitable for both of them and the sum of the seller's profit and the buyer's profit will be $30-$18=$12. But with a tax of $15, there is no way for them to trade with each other and both make a profit. They would therefore not trade, both would make zero profits, and the government would get no tax revenue from them. The net effect of the tax on this transaction is to reduce the total profits of the supplier and demander by $12, while adding nothing to government revenue.

Experiment 4

Prohibition

Illegal Markets

Governments sometimes attempt to regulate trade by taxing certain markets or by enforcing price floors or ceilings. Sometimes they take more dramatic measures, by passing **prohibition laws** that make trade illegal in certain markets. Here are some examples of markets where governments have attempted to enforce prohibition. Perhaps you can think of others.

- In the period from 1920 to 1933, the United States government prohibited the purchase and sale of alcoholic beverages.

- In almost all states in the United States, it is currently illegal to sell alcoholic beverages to minors.

- Federal and local governments in the United States (and many European governments) prohibit the purchase and sale of certain drugs that are believed to be addictive and/or otherwise harmful.

- In many states and countries, gambling is illegal (except through state-sponsored lotteries).

- In most states and localities in the United States, prostitution is illegal.

- It is illegal in most countries to buy or sell animals (or body parts of animals) belonging to endangered species.

- In the 1950's, the sale of yellow-dyed margarine was illegal in the states of Minnesota and Wisconsin.

- In the United States and in many other countries, until relatively recently, it was illegal to perform abortions.

- In the 1980's a law was passed in the United States prohibiting the sale of human body organs to transplant recipients.

- In most countries, it is illegal to buy and sell children for adoption.

- In most countries, including the U.S. since 1863, it is illegal to buy and sell human slaves.

A variety of motives impel governments to pass prohibition laws. Some lawmakers reason that consumers do not realize the harm caused by drugs, alcohol, and gambling. Such lawmakers support prohibition of these goods in hopes of protecting consumers from their own mistakes. Lawmakers who favor endangered species legislation aim to protect the endangered animals from being captured or killed for the market. The prohibition against yellow-dyed margarine in Minnesota and Wisconsin was maintained by political pressure from dairy farmers who feared that the availability of colored margarine would reduce the demand for butter.[1] We leave it to you to speculate about the motives for the other prohibitions mentioned.

Whatever the motives for suppressing certain markets, prohibitions typically fail to *eliminate* trade in the prohibited good. Prohibition of alcohol did not eliminate the marketing and consumption of alcoholic beverages. In the 1950's "oleo-smugglers" would sneak truckloads of colored oleo-margarine into Minnesota and Wisconsin to be sold to eager consumers. The War on Drugs has not eliminated the marketing and consumption of marijuana, crack cocaine, or heroin. Prohibition of gambling and prostitution are only partially effective.

This experiment concerns a partially successful government effort to suppress trade in drugs. In Session 1 of the experiment, trade in the drug market is entirely legal and free from government interference. In Session 2, trade is made illegal. The government cannot prevent all trades, but the police are able to intercept half of the trades and to destroy the confiscated material. In Session 3 (which is optional, depending on available time) the drug trade remains illegal, and the police confiscate half of the drugs that are traded, but instead of destroying the contraband, they resell it to the original buyers at prevailing market prices.

---

[1]Margarine is made primarily from vegetable oils, while butter is made from milk.

Instructions

In this experiment, some participants will be drug suppliers and some will be demanders. Some of the drug demanders will be casual users and some will be addicts. Please read the instructions for all three types.

Suppliers' Instructions

In all sessions of this experiment, suppliers can supply zero, one, or two units of drugs. Suppliers have a Seller Cost of $10 for each unit that they sell. Since each buyer can buy at most one unit of drugs, a supplier who wants to sell two units must deal with two different buyers.

In Session 1, the drug market is free from government intervention. In Session 2, the police intercept some of the sales contracts as they arrive at the market manager's desk. If a seller brings just one contract to the market manager, the police will intercept that sale and seize the drugs. But if a seller finds two buyers and brings both contracts to the market manager, the police will confiscate only one of the two units. (Sellers who want to bring two contracts simultaneously to the market manager will have to get their first buyer to agree to wait around while they find a second buyer.) When a seller brings two contracts to the market manager, the police will randomly select one of the two contracts and confiscate the unit that is sold with that contract. The seller of a confiscated unit will have to pay the $10 Seller Cost and she will also have to pay a $5 fine, but she will not get the money that the buyer agreed to pay. The buyer will not receive the confiscated drugs that he agreed to buy and will not have to pay for them. The sale on the unconfiscated unit will go through as agreed between buyer and seller.

In Session 3, the police confiscate drugs and fine the sellers, just as they did in Session 2, but in this session, the police resell the confiscated drugs. They will sell the confiscated item to the original buyer at the same price that was originally contracted between buyer and seller.

Notice that in Sessions 2 and 3, a seller can never profit from selling just one unit, since that unit is sure to be confiscated, but if the price of the good is high enough, a seller will profit from selling two units, even though there is a fine and one of the two units will be confiscated.

Demanders' Instructions

There are two kinds of demanders in this market:

- Addicts who have a Buyer Value of $30. Addicts who do not buy a unit of the illegal commodity will suffer severe withdrawal systems which result in a *loss* of $20. (In previous markets, buyers who didn't buy anything made zero profits.)

- Casual users who have Buyer Values of $15 and who do not suffer a loss if they are unable to buy the good.

As in previous markets, demanders can buy either zero units or one unit. In Session 2, there is an extra complication for demanders. About half of all sales contracts are intercepted by the police. If a buyer's contract is intercepted, the police will tell him that his seller got caught. When this happens, the buyer does not get the unit that he agreed to buy, but he does not have to pay the amount that he agreed to pay on that contract. When a contract is intercepted, a buyer is free to try to make another purchase from another supplier.

In Session 3, about half the sales are again intercepted by the police. As before, the buyer in a sale that is intercepted does not receive the goods that he contracted for with the supplier, and he does not have to pay the supplier the amount agreed on. But in this session, he has the option of buying a confiscated unit from the police, who resell it at the same price that the original buyer and seller agreed on.

Warm-up Exercise

■ In Session 2, you are a supplier and you agree to sell two units of drugs, each at a price of $40. You bring the contracts to the market manager. The police confiscate one of the units and fine you $5. You have to pay the $10 Seller Cost for each of the two units of output. What are your total

profits?_____

■ In Session 2 you are a supplier. If you sell nothing, your profit (or loss)

is _____. If you sell one unit of drugs for $30, your profit (or loss)

is _____. If you sell two units of drugs, each for $30, your profit (or

loss) is _____.

■ In Session 2 you are a supplier and you sell two units of the prohibited substance, one for $50 and one for $20. Your production costs are $10 per unit and, when the police catch you, they make you pay a $5 fine. If the police confiscate the unit you sold for $20, how much profit (or loss) do you make?_____If the police had confiscated the unit you sold for $50, how much profit (or loss) would you have made?_____

■ You are an addict. You have searched the marketplace and the lowest price at which you can get a unit of drugs is $40. What would your profit (or loss) be if you bought at $40? _____What would your profit (or loss) be if you did not buy any drugs? _____

■ An addict is better off buying a unit of drugs rather than not buying any drugs, so long as the price is lower than _____.

■ You are an addict in Session 2. You agree to buy a unit of drugs for $25. Unfortunately for you, the police confiscate the unit. You go back to the market and you find another seller who offers to sell you a unit for $30. If you buy this unit and the police don't confiscate it, what will be your profits for the round?_____

What Do You Expect to See?

■ Would you expect that making it illegal to sell a drug would cause the street price of that drug to increase or to decrease? _____

■ Do you think that making it illegal to sell a drug would increase or decrease the amount of money spent on this drug: by addicts? _____ _____ by casual users? _____

■ Suppose that the police confiscated drugs whenever they caught a drug seller, but then resold the drugs to users at the going street price. Do you think the amount of the drug consumed would be the same as it would be if the drug were never confiscated?

NAME _____

Lab Report–Experiment 4

Record of Market Transactions

After the experiment, the market manager will inform you of the numbers of suppliers, addicts, and casual demanders who participated. Record this information in Table L4.1.

Table L4.1: Participating Suppliers and Demanders

Participant Type	Number
Suppliers	
Addicted Demanders	
Non-addicted Demanders	

In Tables L4.2 and L4.3, record the prices and Buyer Values for each sale of drugs that was not confiscated. In Table L4.4, record sales of drugs by the police as well as by dealers. In the case of sales by police, record the Sellers' Cost as 0 and the Sellers' Profits as equal to the price.

Table L4.2: Drug Transactions—Session 1, Last Round

(No Prohibition)

Trans-action	Price	Buyer Value	Seller Cost	Buyer's Profit	Seller's Profit	Total Profit
1						
2						
3						
4						
5						
6						
7						
8						
9						
10						
11						
12						
13						
14						
15						
16						
17						
18						
19						
20						
21						
22						
23						
24						
25						

Table L4.3: Drug Transactions—Session 2, Last Round

(Prohibition with Confiscation)

Trans-action	Price	Buyer Value	Seller Cost	Buyer's Profit	Seller's Profit	Total Profit
1						
2						
3						
4						
5						
6						
7						
8						
9						
10						
11						
12						
13						
14						
15						
16						
17						
18						
19						
20						
21						
22						
23						
24						
25						

Table L4.4: Drug Transactions —Session 3, Last Round

(Prohibition with Confiscation and Resale)

Trans-action	Price	Buyer Value	Seller Cost	Buyer's Profit	Seller's Profit	Total Profit
1						
2						
3						
4						
5						
6						
7						
8						
9						
10						
11						
12						
13						
14						
15						
16						
17						
18						
19						
20						
21						
22						
23						
24						
25						

Session 1–No Prohibition

Competitive Equilibrium with No Interference

Before you draw the demand curve for this market, think carefully about an addict's reservation price for drugs, which is the most that he would pay for a unit of drugs. Remember that an addict who gets no drugs suffers a *loss* of $20 and an addict who gets drugs will gain $30.

■ What is the most that an addict would be willing to pay for a unit of

drugs?_____

■ What is the most that a casual user would be willing to pay for a unit

of drugs?_____

■ On Figure L4.1, draw the supply curve and the demand curve that apply under the market conditions of Session 1.

Figure L4.1: No Prohibition–Session 1

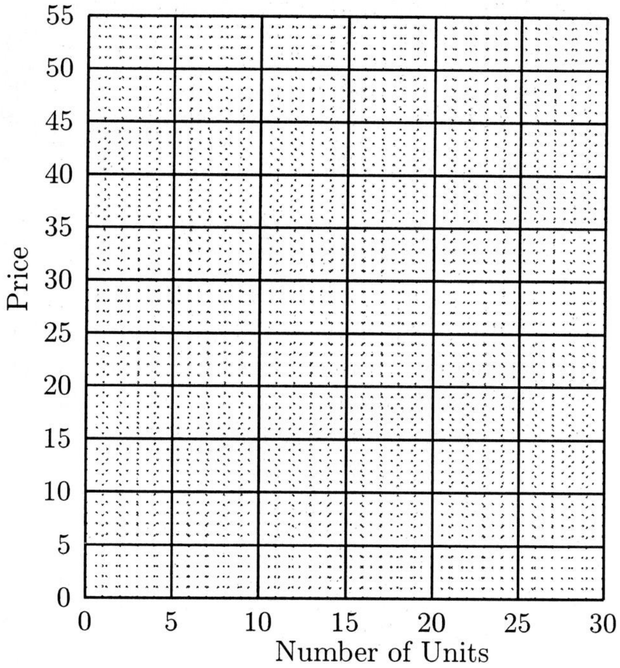

■ In Session 1, the competitive equilibrium price is _____ and the competitive equilibrium quantity sold is _____.

■ In competitive equilibrium for Session 1, would addicts have to pay higher prices than casual users? _____.

Experimental Results in Session 1

■ On Figure L4.1, plot the time path of transactions in Session 1.

■ In the last round of Session 1, the average price paid by addicts was _____ and the average price paid by casual users was _____.

Session 2–Confiscation

Competitive Equilibrium with Confiscation

■ In this session, all Buyer Values are the same as in Session 1, where drugs were legal. Even though some purchases are nullified by confiscation, there is no penalty for buyers. All the buyer has to do is find another seller and make a new agreement. Therefore each buyer's willingness to pay for drugs is the same as when drugs were legal. What does this imply about the relationship between the demand curve when there is no prohibition and the demand curve when there is prohibition?

_____

■ When the sale of drugs is prohibited, the cost to a seller of getting a unit of drugs to market increases because in order to sell a unit of drugs to a buyer, a seller has to produce two units, one of which will be confiscated. Not only does the seller have to pay the cost of producing the confiscated unit, even though it doesn't get to market, but she also has to pay a fine. What is the lowest per-unit price at which a supplier will be willing to sell two units of drugs, knowing that one unit will be confiscated and that she will have to pay a $5 fine for dealing in drugs? _____.

■ On Figure L4.2, draw the demand curve that applies in Session 2. On the same figure, draw the supply curve to show the amount of drugs that would reach the market at each possible price in Session 2.

Figure L4.2: Prohibition with Confiscation–Session 2

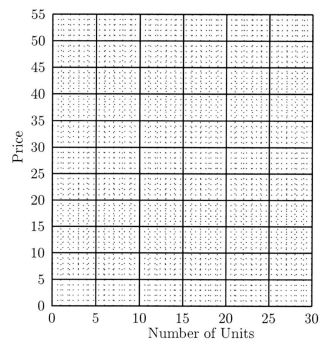

■ In competitive equilibrium for Session 2, the price is _____ and the number of units that reach consumers is _____.

■ In competitive equilibrium for Session 2, the total number of units produced (including the units that were confiscated) is _____

■ How does the government's effort to prohibit drugs change the total number of units consumed by casual users in competitive equilibrium?

_____

■ How does the government's effort to prohibit drugs change the total number of units consumed by addicts in competitive equilibrium?

_____

■ How does the government's effort to prohibit drugs change the total amount of money spent on drugs by all consumers in competitive equilibrium?

_____

Experimental Results in Session 2

■ On Figure L4.2, plot the time path of transactions in Session 2.

■ What was the average price in the last round of Session 2? _____

■ How many units were sold to consumers in the last round of Session 2?

_____

■ In the last round of Session 2, how many units were produced in total (including those that were destroyed by the police)? _____

■ How many units were consumed by addicts? _____

■ How many units were consumed by casual users? _____

■ How much money in total did consumers spend on the prohibited substance in the last round of Session 1? _____ the last round of Session 2? _____

Session 3–Confiscation and Resale

Equilibrium with Confiscation and Resale

In Session 3, as in Session 2, since drug buyers are not penalized, the Buyer Values and reservation prices of demanders are the same as when there was no prohibition. In this session, as in Session 2, a supplier must produce two units of drugs in order to be able to sell one unit to a buyer. One of the two units will be confiscated and the supplier will be fined $5. The main difference between this market session and that in Session 2 is that both of the units of drugs that a supplier produces will eventually find their way to a buyer.

■ In Session 3, a supplier can make a profit selling drugs only if the price is higher than _____. If the price is higher than this, the total number of units of drugs that will be available to consumers is _____.

■ On Figure L4.3, draw the supply curve and demand curve for Session 3.

Figure L4.3: Prohibition with Confiscation and Resale–Session 3

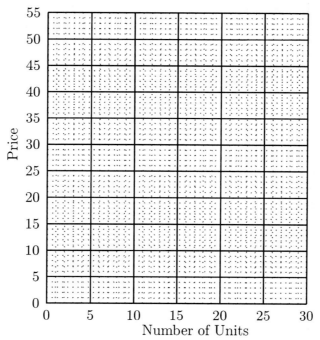

■ The horizontal segment of the supply curve in Session 3 is (higher than, lower than, the same height as) _____ the horizontal segment of the supply curve in Session 2.

■ In Session 3, what is the competitive equilibrium price for drugs? ____

■ In Session 3, what is the competitive equilibrium quantity sold to consumers? _____

■ In Session 3, what is the equilibrium total number of units produced (including the units destroyed)? _____

■ Compare the competitive equilibrium price and quantity consumed when the police resell confiscated drugs with the case where there is no intervention by the government. Explain why prohibition reduces drug consumption even when the police resell all confiscated drugs.

_____

_____

_____

Experimental Results in Session 3

■ On Figure L4.3, plot the time path of transactions in Session 3.

■ In Session 3, what was the average price in the last round?_____

■ In Session 3, how many units were sold to consumers? (Remember to include sales by the police as well as by dealers.) _____

■ In Session 3, how many units were produced in total? _____

■ In Session 3, how many units were consumed by addicts?_____

■ In Session 3, how many units were consumed by casual users?_____

_____

Food for Thought

■ The government's intervention in the drug market shifted the supply curve upward. If the supply curve shifts upward and the demand curve stays stationary, what do you expect will happen to the price of drugs and to the quantity sold?

_____

■ In the experiment we conducted, does the prohibition cause addicts to

reduce their consumption?_____Does the prohibition cause addicts to

spend more or less money on the prohibited substance? _____

■ Suppose that the government prohibits the drug trade because it hopes to discourage addicts from stealing the money needed to buy drugs. Does the policy of prohibition achieve this objective? Explain.

_____

_____

_____

■ What argument(s) would you make in favor of a prohibition on addictive drugs, knowing that any such prohibition will be imperfectly enforced?

_____

_____

_____

■ If the government could find policies that shifted the demand curve for the prohibited substance downward, how would this affect prices and quantities?

_____

■ Suppose the government were considering two alternative policies toward addictive drugs. One policy would shift the demand curve down by some amount and the other would shift the supply curve upward by about the same amount. Which policy do you think would be preferable? Explain.

_____

_____

_____

■ Suggest some policies that would shift the demand curve downwards?

_____

_____

_____

_____

■ For a market with the same Seller Costs and Buyer Values as those in this experiment, suppose that the government decided to legalize trade, but in order to discourage consumption, it put a sales tax on each unit sold. Assuming that the suppliers always complied in paying the tax, how large would the tax have to be in order for the equilibrium price and quantity to be the same as the equilibrium price and quantity for Session 2?

_____

■ If there were no police enforcement of the tax, some suppliers would probably provide the material illegally, without paying the tax. But if the same police effort that is currently devoted to confiscating illegal sales were devoted to punishing suppliers who did not pay their tax, how much tax evasion do you think there would be? Explain.

_____

_____

_____

■ Are there any commodities that are currently legally sold that you think should be prohibited? Explain why.

_____

_____

_____

■ Discuss some commodity (other than drugs) which the government currently makes it illegal to sell. Explain why you think prohibition of this market is either a good idea or a bad idea.

_____

_____

_____

_____

Experiment 5

A Minimum Wage

People are often dissatisfied with the prices that emerge from competitive markets. Farmers think the price of corn is too low. Laborers would like higher wages. Renters want lower rents for their apartments. Borrowers believe that interest rates are too high. Party animals think that beer is too expensive...and so on. Occasionally, governments intervene in markets in the hope of changing market prices in one direction or the other. What is the effect of such intervention?

This lesson concerns government efforts to raise wages by minimum-wage legislation. The good that will be traded in this experiment is "labor." The suppliers are laborers and the demanders are firms. The "price" in this market is the wage rate that firms pay their laborers. In the second and third sessions of this experiment, a **legal minimum wage** is introduced. In the real world, a legal minimum wage is enforced by a law against hiring anyone for a wage lower than a specified amount. In our experiment, the market manager will not honor any contract in which a laborer is paid less than the legal minimum wage.

Instructions

Some participants in this experiment will be laborers and some will be employers. In order to understand the way the market works, you should read the instructions for both types.

Laborers' Instructions

If you are a laborer, you can either take a job or remain unemployed. If you remain unemployed, you will get a payment equalt to the **reservation wage**, listed on your Personal Information Sheet. In the real world, a person's reservation wage represents the lowest wage at which he or she is willing to take a job rather than remain unemployed.[1]

There are two types of laborers. Type A laborers have a low reservation wage and Type B laborers have a higher reservation wage.

In each round of the experiment, if you agree to take a job, you should record your ID number, wage, and reservation wage on your employer's employment record sheet. Your profit will be the wage that you agree to.

If you do not take a job, you should put your identification number and type on the List of Unemployed which is maintained by the market manager, and you will be credited with a profit that is equal to your reservation wage.

Employers' Instructions

In the first two sessions, each employer can hire zero, one, or two laborers. In the third session, each employer can hire up to four laborers. In the first two sessions, if you are an employer, the total value of your output will be 0 if you hire no laborers, $20 if you hire one laborer, and $30 if you hire two laborers. In Session 3, the total value of your output will be 0 if you hire no laborers, $30 if you hire one laborer, $55 if you hire two laborers, $75 if you hire three laborers, and $95 if you hire four laborers. Your profits are equal to the total value of your output, minus the total amount of wages that you pay. In each round, of each session, you will be given an *employment record* on which you should record the ID number and type of each laborer that you hire, as well as the wage that you pay this laborer.

As in previous markets, you can circulate around the trading floor, looking for laborers and trying to make a deal.
Example:

> Suppose that your personal information sheet tells you that the value of your output will be $20 if you hire one laborer and $30 if you hire two laborers. You find somebody who will work for you for $6. You record that person's ID and reservation wage on your employment sheet, and return to the trading floor where you find somebody else who agrees to work for you at a wage of $9. Since you have hired two persons, the value of your output is $30. Your

---

[1] Typically a person's reservation wage is influenced by the amount of unemployment benefits that she could earn if unemployed, the amount or earnings that she could make in self-employed activities, and the value that she places on leisure.

total labor costs are $6+$9=$15. So your profits are $30-$15 =$15. If you had hired only the first laborer and not the second, the value of your output would have been $20, your total labor costs would have been $6, and your profits would have been $20-$6=$14.

A Tip for Employers

A general rule to apply is this: *Hiring one more laborer will increase profits if the amount of money that an additional laborer* adds *to your revenue is more than the amount of money it costs to hire her.*

Warm-up Exercise

The first part of this exercise is designed to help you think about the best strategy to use in the experiment. Please answer these questions before you come to class.

For the next three questions, suppose that you are an employer who can hire either 0, 1, or 2 laborers. If you hire 0 laborers, you will produce no output. If you hire 1 laborer, you will produce $30 worth of output. If you hire 2 laborers, you will produce $50 worth of output.

■ Suppose that you have to pay a wage of $35 for each laborer that you hire, what will your profits (or loss) be if you hire: 0 laborers? _____,

1 laborer? _____, 2 laborers? _____ How many laborers should

you hire in order to maximize profits? _____

■ Suppose that you have to pay a wage of $25 for each laborer hired, what will your profits (or loss) be if you hire: 0 laborers? _____, 1 laborer?

_____, 2 laborers? _____ How many laborers should you hire

in order to maximize profits? _____

■ Suppose that you have to pay a wage of $15 for each laborer that you hire, what will your profits (or loss) be if you hire: 0 laborers? _____,

1 laborer? _____, 2 laborers? _____ How many laborers should

you hire in order to maximize profits? _____

■ Assuming that you have to pay the same wage to each employee, what is the highest wage at which hiring 1 laborer is more profitable than hiring 0 laborers? _____

■ Assuming that you have to pay the same wage to each employee, what is the highest wage at which hiring 2 laborers is more profitable than hiring 1 laborer? _____

■ Suppose that you are a laborer and your reservation wage is $12. You are offered a job at a wage of $10. What will be your profit if you take the job? _____ What will your profit be if you do not take the job? _____

■ Suppose that you are a laborer and your reservation wage is $5. You are offered a job at a wage of $10. What will be your profit if you take the job? _____ What will be your profit if you do not take the job? _____

What Do You Expect to See?

■ Do you think that doubling the legal minimum wage would increase, decrease, or have no effect on the number of people who want jobs but cannot find them? Explain your answer.

_____

_____

_____

■ Do you think that doubling the legal minimum wage would increase, decrease, or have no effect on the total income of employed laborers? Explain your answer.

_____

_____

_____

NAME _____

Lab Report–Experiment 5

Record of Market Transactions

After the conclusion of this experiment, your instructor will supply you with the number of employers and the number of laborers of each type who participated in each session. Copy this information into Table L5.1.

Table L5.1: Distribution of Types of Employers and Laborers

Participant Type	Session 1	Session 2	Session 3
Employers			
Type A Laborers			
Type B Laborers			

■ Your instructor will also supply you with the numbers of unemployed persons of Types A and B for each session. Copy this information into Table L5.2.

Table L5.2: Unemployed Laborers and their Reservation Wages

	Type A's Unemployed	Type B's Unemployed
Session 1		
Session 2		
Session 3		

■   In Table L5.3, record the wages paid by each firm in the last round of Session 1 of the classroom experiment. For each firm, record the wage paid to each laborer that the firm hired and the laborer's type, A or B.

Table L5.3: No Minimum Wage: Session 1–Last Round

Firm ID	Laborer 1		Laborer 2	
	Wage	Type	Wage	Type

■ In Table L5.4, record wages paid by each firm in the last round of Session 2. For each firm, record the wage paid to each laborer that the firm hired and the laborer's type, A or B.

Table L5.4: Binding Minimum Wage: Session 2–Last Round

Firm ID	Laborer 1		Laborer 2	
	Wage	Type	Wage	Type

■   In Table L5.5, record wages paid by each firm in the last round of Session 3. For each firm, record the wage paid to each laborer that the firm hired and the laborer's type, A or B.

Table L5.5: Non-Binding Minimum Wage: Session 3–Last Round

Firm ID	Laborer 1		Laborer 2		Laborer 3		Laborer 4	
	Wage	Type	Wage	Type	Wage	Type	Wage	Type

■ Complete Table L5.6 to determine the amount of profits made by each firm in the last round of Session 1. From Table L5.3, you can find the number of laborers hired and total wages paid by each firm. The value of a firm's output is $20 if it hires one laborer and $30 if it hires two. Subtract total wages paid from the value of its output to find a firm's profit.

Table L5.6: Firms' Employment and Profits–Session 1

Firm ID	Number of Employees	Firm's Total Revenue	Firm's Total Wage Costs	Firm's Profit
Total				

■ Complete Table L5.7 to determine the amount of profits made by each firm in the last round of Session 2. From Table L5.4, you can find the number of laborers hired and total wages paid by each firm. The value of a firm's output is $20 if it hires one laborer and $30 if it hires two. Subtract total wages paid from the value of its output to find a firm's profit.

Table L5.7: Firms' Employment and Profits–Session 2

Firm ID	Number of Employees	Firm's Total Revenue	Firm's Total Wage Costs	Firm's Profit
Total				

■ Complete Table L5.8 to determine the profits made by each firm in the last round of Session 3 of the classroom experiment. From Table L5.5, you can find the number of laborers hired and total wages paid by each firm. The value of a firm's output is $30 if it hires one laborer, $55 if it hires two, $75 if it hires three, and $95 if it hires four laborers. Subtract total wages paid from the value of its output to find a firm's profit.

Table L5.8: Firms' Employment and Profits Round 3

Firm ID	Number of Employees	Firm's Total Revenue	Firm's Total Wage Costs	Firm's Profit
Total				

Effect of a Minimum Wage on Profits and Labor Income

■   In the last round of Session 1, with no minimum wage, total profits of all firms were _____. In the last round of Session 2, with a minimum wage, total profits of all firms were _____. The minimum wage reduced total profits by _____

■   In the last round of Session 1, with no minimum wage, total income of all laborers was _____. In the last round of Session 2, with a minimum wage, total income of all laborers was _____. Did the minimum wage increase, decrease, or leave constant the total income of laborers? _____

_____

■   Was the sum of the total of profits of firms and the total income of laborers larger in the last round of Session 1 (no minimum wage) or in the last round of Session 2 (with a minimum wage)? _____

Competitive Equilibrium Wages and Employment

In this section we will find the competitive equilibrium labor supply and demand curves, and the competitive equilibrium wage and employment level in the absence of a minimum wage. These questions all apply to the distribution of types of agents found in Table L5.1.

Labor Supply Table

■   If the wage offered is less than $5, should laborers with a $5 reservation wage supply their labor or remain unemployed? _____ At wages below $5, would laborers with a $12 reservation wage supply their labor or remain unemployed? _____

■ If the wage offered is between $5 and $12, should laborers with a $5

reservation wage supply their labor or remain unemployed? _____
At wages between $5 and $12, would laborers with a $12 reservation wage

supply their labor or remain unemployed? _____

■ If the wage offered is greater than $12, should laborers with a $5 reserva-

tion wage supply their labor or remain unemployed? _____ At wages
above $12, would laborers with a $12 reservation wage supply their labor or

remain unemployed? _____

■ Fill in Table L5.9 to show the number of laborers willing to work at
possible wage rates. (Hint: You have just determined which types of laborers
will supply labor over each wage range, and from Table L5.1, you know the
number of laborers who participated in the market.)

Table L5.9: Labor Supply–All Sessions

Wage Range	Labor Supplied
Wage < $5	
$5 < Wage < $12	
Wage > $12	

Labor Demand Table

For Sessions 1 and 2, the value of a firm's total output will be 0 if it hires
no laborers, $20 if it hires one laborer, and $30 if it hires 2 or more laborers.
This means that it will not increase its output by hiring more than 2 laborers.
In Session 3, the laborers' reservation wages remain as they were in session
2, but labor is more productive in every firm. The value of a firm's total
output will be 0 if it hires no laborers, $30 if it hires one laborer, $55 if
it hires two laborers, $75 if it hires three laborers and $95 if it hires four
laborers. If it hires more than four laborers, the value of its output will
remain at $95.

■ In Sessions 1 and 2, if a firm must pay a wage greater than $20 per

laborer, how many laborers should it hire in order to maximize its profits?_

_____

■   In Sessions 1 and 2, if a firm must pay a wage greater than $10 and less than $20 per laborer, how many laborers should it hire in order to maximize its profits?_____

■   If a firm can hire laborers at a wage less than $10, how many laborers should it hire in order to maximize its profits?_____

■   Fill in Table L5.10 to show the total number of laborers that employers will want to hire at each possible wage rate in Sessions 1 and 2.

Table L5.10: Labor Demand–Sessions 1 and 2

Wage Range	Amount Demanded
Wage > $20	
$10 <Wage < $20	
Wage < $10	

■   Fill in Table L5.11 to show the number of laborers that employers will hire at each possible wage rate in Session 3.

Table L5.11: Labor Demand–Session 3

Wage Range	Amount Demanded
Wage > $30	
$25 <Wage < $30	
$20 <Wage < $25	
Wage < $20	

Supply and Demand Curves

■   In Figure L5.1, draw the competitive supply curve and demand curve for the labor market in Sessions 1 and 2. (The same supply and demand curves apply in both sessions.) The supply curve shows the number of laborers that are willing to work at each wage, and the demand curve shows the

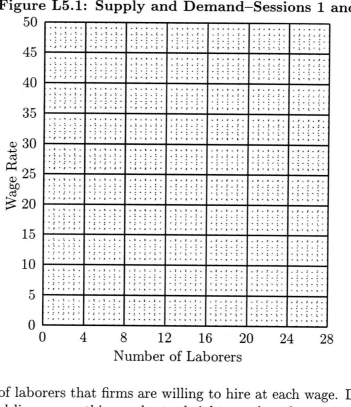

Figure L5.1: Supply and Demand–Sessions 1 and 2

number of laborers that firms are willing to hire at each wage. Draw a blue horizontal line across this graph at a height equal to the minimum wage.

■ The competitive equilibrium wage for Session 1 is _____.

■ In competitive equilibrium for Session 1, the number of laborers employed is _____.

■ In Session 1, at the competitive equilibrium wage, what is the profit maximizing number of workers for a single firm? _____ How much profits would a profit-maximizing firm make? _____

■ In Session 2, at the legal minimum wage, what is the profit maximizing number of workers for a single firm? _____ How much profits would a profit-maximizing firm make? _____

■ For Session 2, compare the number of laborers who are willing to work at the minimum wage to the number of jobs that profit-maximizing firms are willing to offer at this wage.

_____

■ In Figure L5.2, draw the competitive supply curve and demand curve for labor in Session 3 of the classroom experiment. Draw a blue horizontal line across the graph at a height equal to the minimum wage rate.

Figure L5.2: Supply and Demand–Session 3

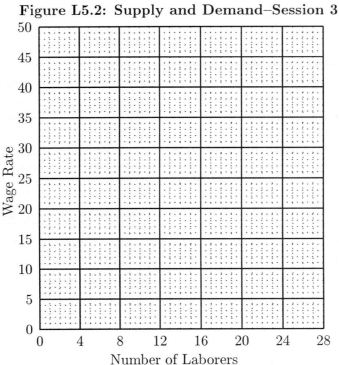

■ In Session 3, at the competitive equilibrium wage, what is the profit maximizing number of workers for a single firm? _____. How much profits would a profit-maximizing firm make? _____

■ If there had been no minimum wage law in Session 3, what would the wage rate have been? _____.

■ In general, what effect do you think a legal minimum wage will have if the legal minimum is lower than the the competitive equilibrium wage? Explain.

_____

_____

_____

Competitive Equilibrium and Experimental Results

■ Complete Table L5.12 to compare the competitive equilibrium prediction about wage rates and number of laborers employed in each session with the predictions made by competitive equilibrium theory.

Table L5.12: Wages and Employment–Theory and Experiment

	Competitive Equilibrium Wage	Average Wage in Experiment	Comp. Eq. Number Employed	Actual Number Employed in Experiment
Session 1				
Session 2				
Session 3				

Discussion D5

Price Floors and Ceilings, Unemployment and Shortages

Price Floors in General

A minimum wage is an example of a **price floor**. A price floor for a good is a legal minimum price such that no one is allowed to buy or sell the good at any lower price. If the price floor is *lower than* the competitive equilibrium price, it will have *no effect* since competition will force prices to rise above the floor. But if the price floor is *higher than* the competitive equilibrium price, then at any legally permitted price the *supply will be greater than the demand*. Figure D5.1 shows the effect of a price floor in a market with smooth supply and demand curves.

Without a price floor, the equilibrium price and quantity are found at the point labeled *A*, where the price is $17.50 and the quantity is 15 units. If there is a price floor of $21, then sellers will want to sell 19 units (at the point *C* on the supply curve) and demanders will want to buy only 11 units (at the point *B* on the demand curve). Since demanders cannot be forced to buy if they don't want to, the total number of units traded at the floor price of $21 is only 11, even though at this price suppliers would like to sell 19 units. The difference between the amount supplied and the amount demanded is known as the **excess supply** of a good. Thus, we see that at a price of $21, there is an excess supply of 8 units (an amount equal to the length of the line segment *BC*).

A price floor set above the equilibrium point presents suppliers with

Figure D5.1: A Price Floor

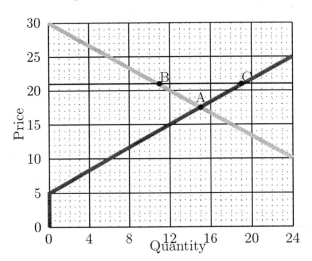

some good news, and some bad news. The good news is that those who can make a sale will receive a higher price. The bad news is that at the higher price, fewer will be able to sell. If the demand curve is very steep, then the bad news will not be very bad, because an increase in price will cause only a slight decrease in the number of units demanded. If the demand curve is very flat, then the bad news will be very bad, because a small increase in the price will cause a big decrease in the number of units demanded.

Involuntary and Voluntary Unemployment

In a labor market, there are two types of unemployment: **involuntary unemployment** and **voluntary employment**. A laborer who is not employed, but would willingly work at the average wage paid to other laborers is **involuntarily unemployed**. A laborer who is not employed and would choose not to work at the average wage paid to other laborers is **voluntarily unemployed**.

Reservation Wages and Opportunity Cost

The lowest wage at which someone is willing to work rather than remain unemployed is known as that person's **reservation wage.** One's reservation wage is also known as one's **opportunity cost** of time. Economists define the opportunity cost of any resource to be the money value of putting that resource to the best alternative use. The opportunity cost of a person's time spent working is the money value that this person puts on using that time in the most profitable alternative use.

Calculating Unemployment and Income Statistics

A laborer who is unemployed and whose reservation wage is lower than the average wage of employed persons is said to be **involuntarily unemployed.** A laborer who is unemployed and whose reservation wage is higher than the average wage of employed persons is said to be **voluntarily unemployed.** Employed laborers receive a payoff equal to the wages that they are paid. The payoff to an unemployed laborer is equal to her opportunity cost or reservation wage. The appropriate measure of the total income of all laborers is therefore the total amount of wages received by employed laborers plus the total of the reservation wages of all unemployed laborers.

On the Effect of a Minimum Wage

The February 4, 1995, edition of *The New York Times* reported that President Clinton was seeking to increase the legal minimum wage from \$4.25 to \$5.15 an hour.[1] The President declared that "the only way to grow the middle class and shrink the underclass is to make work pay." According to National Public Radio, Presidential Assistant Leon Panetta asserted that an increase in the minimum wage would give people an incentive to take jobs instead of collecting welfare benefits.

The Republican Speaker of the House, Newt Gingrich, reacted as follows: "I personally am very skeptical of it, and I think it will kill jobs." According to the *Times*, the House Majority Leader, Dick Armey (who is a former economics professor at the University of North Texas in Denton) intended to fight the increase with "every fiber of his being." The president of the National Federation of Independent Business, a small-business lobbying group, said that the proposal was "a regressive and job-killing scheme which would put a big dent in small-business hiring."

Which of these claims should we believe? It turns out that people on both sides of this argument were at least partially correct. The question of which side gets more partial credit is ultimately empirical rather than

---

[1] Legal minimum wage legislation does not apply to employees of firms in trade and services with sales less than \$250,000, to farm workers working for small farms, or to domestic servants.

ideological. And, as you may have suspected, the empirical matter on which the answer turns is the shape of the labor supply curve.

Losers and Gainers from the Minimum Wage

In our minimum-wage experiment, we found that when a minimum wage was imposed, total employment was diminished. Moreover, **involuntary unemployment** increased by more than employment decreased, because some laborers who were unwilling to work at the old equilibrium wage want to take jobs at the minimum wage.

Some people in the experiment were "harmed" by the minimum wage legislation. The most obvious losers were the firms. The minimum wage forced them to pay higher wages, although the revenue they received from their output did not change. It is not, then, very surprising that the small-business lobby quoted in the *Times* opposed an increased minimum wage.[2] Those laborers who were employed before the minimum wage was introduced, but who could not find jobs at the minimum wage, were also made worse off.

The gainers from the minimum wage increase are the workers who were able to keep their jobs and take advantage of the higher wage rate. If you believe that those who received the minimum wage belonged to the "underclass," but were able to join the "middle class" once they got the new minimum wage, then you will probably think that President Clinton was right.

Leon Panetta presented a less convincing argument. He was probably right in saying that higher wages for unskilled labor would influence some people to work instead of collecting welfare. But an increased minimum wage, even in the most favorable case, is not likely to *increase* the total amount of employment. If employment is to increase, firms must want to hire more labor. But if the wage has increased, firms are going to demand less, not more, labor. If the total demand for labor has not increased, then for every previously unemployed worker who chooses to work after an increase in the minimum wage, at least one previously employed worker will lose her job.

---

[2]Lobbyists do not seem to be bred for truth-telling. You are unlikely to hear a lobbyist say in public that he opposes Proposal X because it reduces the profits of the people who pay him. This is why the guy who is *paid by small business interests* claims he opposes an increased minimum wage because it will harm *labor* by "killing jobs."

Rent Control and Price Ceilings

In the case of minimum wage legislation, sellers (laborers in this case) want the government to enforce a price floor to keep prices high. In other markets, buyers seek laws to keep prices *low*. Sometimes buyers are able to convince a government to establish a **legal price ceiling** on some good. To impose a price ceiling for some good, the government makes it illegal to buy or sell that good at a price higher than the price ceiling. Some governments attempt to control the price of rental housing by imposing a legal maximum monthly rental rate on houses or apartments. During World War II, the United States government imposed price ceilings on many "essential" commodities. During the Arab Oil Embargo of the early 70's, the United States imposed a ceiling on the price of gasoline.

The effects of these price ceilings have been just as the economic models would have predicted. Rent controlled housing has caused, and continues to cause, long waiting lists for renting homes. World War II's price controls resulted in "shortages" of foods, consumer durables, and clothing. Price controls on gasoline led to closed gasoline stations and long lines at the pumps.

Figure D5.2: A Price Ceiling

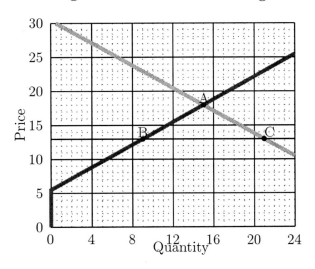

Let us turn to the supply and demand analysis of a price ceiling. Consider the market depicted in Figure D5.2. If there is no price ceiling, the equilibrium price and quantity are found at the point *A*, where the price is $18 and the quantity is 15 units. Suppose that the government enforces a price ceiling of $13. At a price of $13, demanders will want to buy 21 units (at the point C on the demand curve) and suppliers are willing to supply only 9 units (at the point B on the supply curve). While a price ceiling makes it illegal for suppliers to sell the good at a price higher than $13, it *cannot force* them to provide more units than they are willing to supply at this price. Therefore, with the price ceiling of $13, the quantity supplied is only 9 units. The difference between the quantity demanded and the quantity supplied at the ceiling price is known as the amount of **excess demand**. At the ceiling price of $13, there is an excess demand of 12 units. This quantity is represented in the diagram by the length of the line segment BC.

When a good is in excess demand, there is said to be a **shortage** of this good. Demanders who are eager for a unit of the good at this price cannot all find suppliers willing to sell to them. If there were no price ceiling, a demander who could not get a unit at the current price would offer a higher price. The price would get bid up until supply equals demand. But with a price ceiling, the problem of which buyers get the scarce good has to be decided in other ways. Common non-price methods of allocation include long waiting-lines, favoritism towards relatives or friends, under-the-table payments, and brute force.

NAME _____

Home Work–Experiment 5

Calculating Predicted Unemployment Rates

■ Complete Table H5.1 to show the predicted amounts of unemployment and total income of all laborers in competitive equilibrium for Sessions 1, 2, and 3. Total income of all laborers includes the wages earned by employed laborers as well as the total of reservation wages of laborers who remain unemployed.

Table H5.1: Employment and Laborers' Incomes–Competitive Equilibrium

	Employed	Involuntarily Unemployed	Voluntarily Unemployed	Total Income of All Laborers
Session 1				
Session 2				
Session 3				

■ For the distribution of types of employers and laborers present in Sessions 1 and 2, compare the amount of *involuntary* unemployment in competitive equilibrium in Session 1 (where there is no minimum wage) with the amount of involuntary unemployment in Session 2 (where the minimum wage is above the equilibrium wage).

_____

■ For the distribution of types of employers and laborers present in Sessions 1 and 2, compare the amount of *voluntary* unemployment in competitive equilibrium in Session 1 (where there is no minimum wage) with the amount of involuntary unemployment in Session 2.

_____

■ What change does the competitive equilibrium theory predict in total income of all laborers with the change from Session 1 with no minimum wage to Session 2 with a minimum wage?

■ In Session 3, firms' demand for labor was greater than in Session 2. If the demand for labor is as in Session 3 and if the minimum wage law were repealed, what would be the effect on the competitive equilibrium levels of wages, involuntary unemployment, and voluntary unemployment?

■ Complete Table H5.2 to show the employment statistics and total income of all laborers that resulted in our classroom experiments for Sessions 1, 2, and 3.

Table H5.2: Employment and Labor Income–Experimental Outcomes

	Employed	Involuntarily Unemployed	Voluntarily Unemployed	Total Income of All Laborers
Session 1				
Session 2				
Session 3				

■ In the classroom experiment, how did the amount of *involuntary* unemployment change from Session 1 with no minimum wage to Session 2 with a minimum wage?

■ In the classroom experiment, how did the amount of *voluntary* unemployment change from Session 1 with no minimum wage to Session 2 with a minimum wage?

■ In the classroom experiment, how does total income of all laborers change from Session 1 with no minimum wage to Session 2 with a minimum wage?

_____

Minimum Wages–A Conservative's Eye View

With the particular distribution of supplier and demander types used in our market experiment, we found that the minimum wage had only a small effect on total employment. Now we will consider an example with differently shaped demand and supply curves, for which the effect of an increase in the minimum wage rate is more like the effect predicted by Representatives Gingrich and Armey than the effect predicted by President Clinton.

Figure H5.1: Labor Market (Newt's-eye View)

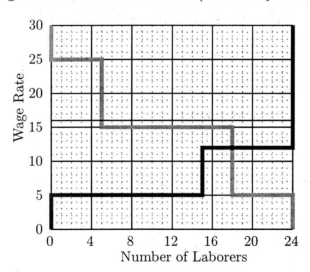

■   If labor supply and demand are as in Figure H5.1 and if there is no minimum wage legislation, what will be the equilibrium wage rate?_____

_____How many laborers will be employed? _____

■   How many laborers will be involuntarily unemployed? _____ How many laborers will be voluntarily unemployed? _____

■   Explain why in this market a minimum wage of $10 would have no effect on employment or on wages.

_____

_____

_____

■   Suppose that a minimum wage of $16 is enforced. At this wage, how many people will want jobs? _____ How many laborers will firms want to hire? _____

■   Assume that the number of workers who find employment when the minimum wage is enforced is equal to the number that firms are willing to hire at that wage. How many jobs are eliminated by the minimum wage?

_____

■   With a minimum wage of $16, how many workers are involuntarily unemployed? _____ How many workers are voluntarily unemployed?

_____

■   How much is the total wage earnings of laborers when there is no minimum wage? _____ How much is the total wage earnings of laborers when there is a minimum wage of $16? _____

■   Does the minimum wage increase or decrease total earnings of laborers? _____ By how much? _____

■   Does the minimum wage increase or decrease total profits of firms? _____ By how much? _____

■ What accounts for the fact that for the demand and supply curves in this exercise the predictions of Representatives Gingrich and Armey are more accurate than those of President Clinton, while for the demand and supply curves that applied in our minimum wage experiment, President Clinton's predictions are more accurate than those of Gingrich and Armey?

_____

_____

_____

_____

_____

Part III

Imperfect Markets

Experiment 6

Externalities

A Polluting Economy

The Isle of Effluvia has many small factories which make beautiful, hand-crafted bronze lawn ornaments, much cherished by Effluvians. The coal-fired furnaces used in these factories produce a fetid grey smoke that leaves a residue of grime all over the island. Effluvians trade only with other Effluvians.

The market for lawn ornaments has suppliers and demanders, much as in our previous experiments, but every lawn ornament that is supplied imposes a pollution cost on all Effluvians. Because of this pollution, trades that benefit both the buyer and seller can cause harm to third parties. Because of these side-effects, unrestricted trade in lawn ornaments leads to an inefficient outcome. This experiment shows that appropriate public policies designed to reduce pollution damage can increase the profits of all Effluvians.

Instructions

You will receive a Personal Information Sheet that informs you whether you are a supplier or a demander and what your Buyer Value or Seller Cost will be in each session. At the beginning of the experiment, the market manager will tell you the amount of damage imposed on everyone by pollution from producing each lawn ornament. If, for example, the market manager announces that producing one lawn ornament causes $1 damage to everyone, and if 15 lawn ornaments are sold, then every participant in the experiment, including those who make no trades, will have to pay a "pollution cost" of $15.

In the first session of this experiment, there is no government interference in the market for lawn ornaments. Buyers and sellers who agree on a price can sign a contract and bring it to the market manager. As in earlier experiments, if a supplier with Seller Cost $C sells a lawn ornament to a demander with Buyer Value $V for price $P, the seller will earn a profit of $(P − C) and the buyer will earn a profit of $(V − P) from the transaction. But in this experiment, everyone in Effluvia, whether they buy, sell, or do not transact at all, will have to pay the pollution cost. If 15 lawn ornaments are sold, and if each lawn ornament that is produced causes $1 worth of pollution damage to every Effluvian, then the profits of each participant in the experiment will be reduced by $15.

In the second session, the market manager imposes a **pollution tax** on sellers. The revenue collected from the pollution tax will be redistributed in equal shares to all Effluvians. In this session, if a supplier with Seller Cost $C sells a lawn ornament to a demander with Buyer Value $V for price $P, and if the tax per lawn ornament is $T, then the seller's after-tax profit from the transaction is $(P − C − T) and the buyer's profit is $(V − P). In addition to any profits that they may make from buying or selling lawn ornaments, every Effluvian will receive an equal share of the government's tax revenue, and every Effluvian will suffer a loss of income equal to the amount of pollution damage imposed on each person by the production of lawn ornaments.

In the third session, a supplier is allowed to sell a lawn ornament only if she has a **pollution permit**. At the beginning of the session, some participants will receive marketable pollution permits along with their Personal Information Sheets. The original owner of a pollution permit can resell this permit to anyone else, but a pollution permit can only be sold once. When a lawn ornament supplier buys a pollution permit, the buyer and the seller of the permit must write their ID numbers and the sales price on the permit. The seller of the pollution permit receives a profit equal to the price at which the permit was sold. Having acquired a pollution permit, a lawn ornament supplier is allowed to sell a lawn ornament to a demander. When a supplier has completed the sale of a lawn ornament, she and the buyer should fill in a sales contract and bring it to the market manager, along with a pollution permit that entitles the seller to supply a lawn ornament.

The lawn ornament seller's total profit from her production activities is the price she receives for the lawn ornament, minus her Seller Cost, minus the price she pays for a pollution permit. The lawn ornament buyer's total profit from a purchase is his Buyer Value minus the price he pays for the lawn ornament. As before, in addition to profits (or losses) that individuals make from transactions, all Effluvians will suffer a loss of profits equal to the amount of pollution damage imposed on each person by the production of lawn ornaments.

Warm-up Exercise

For all questions in this exercise, make the simplifying assumption that your own decision about whether to buy or sell a lawn ornament has *no* effect on the total number of lawn ornaments produced in Effluvia.

■ Suppose that each lawn ornament that is produced in Effluvia imposes pollution costs of $.50 on every Effluvian. If 20 lawn ornaments are sold in Effluvia, each Effluvian will suffer pollution costs of _____. If there are 45 people in Effluvia, the total cost of pollution to all Effluvians is _____

_____.

■ Suppose that in Session 1, a total of 20 lawn ornaments are sold and that each lawn ornament imposes costs of $.50 on all Effluvians. You are a supplier with a Seller Cost of $20 and the best offer you can get for a lawn ornament is $27. If you sell the lawn ornament at this price, your total profit (or loss) in this session will be _____. If you do not sell the lawn ornament, your total profit (or loss) from the session will be

_____. (Don't forget to account for pollution costs.)

■ Suppose that in Session 2, Effluvia has a population of 100 people. Each lawn ornament that is produced imposes a cost of $.20 on each citizen of Effluvia. Suppose that the government imposes a pollution tax of $10 on every lawn ornament produced, and that a total of 40 lawn ornaments are sold. If you make no transactions, you will pay a pollution cost of _____

_____ and your share of the total revenue collected from the tax will be _____, so that your profit (or loss) will be _____.

■ The situation in Effluvia is as described in the previous question. Suppose that a supplier with a Seller Cost of $10 meets a demander with a Buyer Value of $30 and sells a lawn ornament to the demander at a price of $25. Ignoring pollution costs, the supplier's after-tax profit from this transaction will be _____ and the buyer's profit from this transaction

will be _____.

■ In Session 3, suppose that you are a lawn ornament supplier with Seller
Cost of $25 and suppose that you received a pollution permit with your
Personal Information Sheet. The most that anyone will pay you for a lawn
ornament is $32, and the most that anyone will pay to buy your pollution
permit is $10. Should you use your pollution permit to sell a lawn orna-
ment, or should you sell your pollution permit and not produce any lawn
ornaments? Explain.

_____

_____

_____

■ Suppose that in Session 3, Alice who is a supplier with Seller Cost, $15,
buys a pollution permit for $20 from Bill and sells a lawn ornament for $50
to Charlie, who is a demander with Buyer Value, $60. None of these three
people makes any other transactions. A total of 20 lawn ornaments are sold
in Effluvia, each of which imposes a pollution cost of $.20 on all residents.

In this session, Alice makes a profit of _____, Bill makes a profit of

_____, and Charlie makes a profit of _____.

NAME _____

Lab Report–Experiment 6

Record of Market Transactions

■ Before the experiment, the market manager will announce the pollution cost that is imposed on every Effluvian in the production of each lawn

ornament. Record this amount here. _____

■ After trading is completed, the market manager will report the number of suppliers and demanders of each type, and their costs and values. Copy this information into Table L6.1.

Table L6.1: Distribution of Types of Agents

Supplier Type	Seller Cost	Number in Market	Demander Type	Buyer Value	Number in Market
A	28		A	20	
B	23		B	25	
C	18		C	30	
D	13		D	35	
E	8		E	40	
F	3		F	45	

■ In Session 2, the pollution tax charged to each seller of a lawn ornament

was _____

■ In Session 3, the number of pollution permits issued was _____

■ For the last round of Session 1, record the price, Buyer Value and Seller Cost in each transaction in Table L6.2. Complete this table by calculating the buyer's profit and the seller's profit from each transaction. Calculate these profits *without* subtracting pollution costs.

Table L6.2: Transactions in Session 1–Last Round
(No Interference)

Trans-action	Price	Buyer Value	Seller Cost	Buyer's Profit	Seller's Profit
1					
2					
3					
4					
5					
6					
7					
8					
9					
10					
11					
12					
13					
14					
15					
16					
17					
18					
19					
20					
21					
22					

■ In Table L6.3, record the price, Buyer Value and Seller Cost in each transaction of the last round of Session 2. This information will be reported to you by the market manager. Complete this table by calculating the buyer's profit for the transaction and the seller's *after-tax* profit. Calculate these profits *without* subtracting pollution costs or adding redistributed tax revenue.

Table L6.3: Transactions in Session 2–Last Round
(With Pollution Tax)

Trans-action	Price	Buyer Value	Seller Cost	Pollution Tax	Seller's Profit	Buyer's Profit
1						
2						
3						
4						
5						
6						
7						
8						
9						
10						
11						
12						
13						
14						
15						
16						
17						
18						
19						
20						

■ In Table L6.4, record the price, Buyer Value, Seller Cost and the amount that the supplier paid for a pollution permit for each sale of a lawn ornament in the last round of Session 3. This information will be reported to you by the market manager. Calculate each seller's and each buyer's profit. To calculate seller's profits, subtract the seller's Seller Cost and the price the seller paid for a permit from the price the seller got for the lawn ornament.

Table L6.4: Lawn Ornament Transactions in Session 3

(Pollution Permits Required)

Trans-action	Price	Buyer Value	Seller Cost	Price Paid for Permit	Seller's Profit	Buyer's Profit
1						
2						
3						
4						
5						
6						
7						
8						
9						
10						
11						
12						
13						
14						
15						
16						
17						
18						
19						
20						

Profits and Pollution Costs with No Government Interference

■ In Session 1, the total amount of pollution costs imposed on each Effluvian by production of *all* lawn ornaments was _____. (The pollution cost imposed on each Effluvian by production of *each* lawn ornament was announced by the market manager at the beginning of the experiment. Multiply this cost times the number of lawn ornaments produced.)

■ Calculate total profits of buyers and of sellers from Table L6.2 and enter them in Table L6.5. Multiply the total number of persons in Effluvia times the amount of pollution costs imposed on each Effluvian in this market to find the Total Cost of Pollution. Subtract Total Cost of Pollution from the sum of buyers' profits and sellers' profits to find total profits net of pollution costs in Effluvia.

Table L6.5: Profits and Pollution Costs in Session 1

Total Profits of Buyers	
Total Profits of Sellers	
Total Cost of Pollution	
Total Profits Net of Pollution Costs	

Profits and Pollution Costs with a Pollution Tax

■ In Session 2, the total amount of pollution costs imposed on each Effluvian by production of *all* lawn ornaments was _____.

■ In Session 2, the pollution tax assessed on suppliers for each lawn ornament sold was _____. Multiply the pollution tax times the number of lawn ornaments sold to find total tax revenue _____.

■ Use the information in Table L6.3 to calculate the (after-tax) total profits of all buyers and sellers in Session 2, and enter these profits in Table L6.6. Multiply the total number of persons in Effluvia times the amount of pollution costs imposed on each Effluvian to find the Total Cost of Pollution. Add total profits of buyers, total after-tax profits of sellers, and total tax revenue, and then subtract the total cost of pollution, to find total profits and tax revenue net of pollution costs in Effluvia.

Table L6.6: Profits, Taxes and Pollution Damage in Session 2

Total Profits of Buyers	
Total Profits of Sellers	
Total Tax Revenue	
Total Cost of Pollution	
Total Profits and Tax Revenue Net of Pollution Costs	

Profits and Pollution Costs with Pollution Permits

■ In Session 3, the total number of pollution permits issued was ＿＿＿＿＿＿＿

＿＿＿＿＿＿.

■ In Session 3, each person in the market suffered pollution costs of ＿＿＿＿

＿＿＿＿＿＿＿＿＿, and the total amount of pollution costs borne by everyone

in the market was ＿＿＿＿＿＿＿.

■ Use the information in Table L6.4 to calculate the total profits of lawn ornament buyers and sellers in Session 3, and enter these profits in Table L6.7. Add up the prices paid for pollution permits as recorded in Table L6.4, to determine total revenue of permit sellers. Add total profits of lawn ornament buyers, total profits of lawn ornament sellers, and total revenue of permit sellers, and subtract the total cost of pollution, to get total profits net of pollution costs in Effluvia.

Table L6.7: Profits, Permits and Pollution Damage in Session 3

Total Profits of Lawn Ornament Buyers	
Total Profits of Lawn Ornament Sellers	
Total Revenue of Permit Sellers	
Total Cost of Pollution	
Total Profits Net of Pollution Costs	

Discussion D6

Externalities

In previous experiments, a transaction only affected the profits of the buyer and the seller, and not the profits of other participants in the marketplace. In this experiment, every lawn ornament that is sold imposes pollution costs on everybody in Effluvia. When economic activities affect the profits of persons who are not directly involved in the activity, we say that there is an **externality** in the market. If these activities impose *costs* on others, the externality is said to be a **negative externality**. Air and water pollution in manufacturing are conspicuous examples of negative externalities. Highway congestion is another important example of a negative externality. When a driver's car enters an already crowded highway, the addition of this car forces all other drivers to slow down, which costs each of the other drivers a loss of valuable time.

Some economic activities confer *benefits* on people not involved in the activity. These activities are said to produce a **positive externality**. Someone who spends resources on painting her house or planting a beautiful garden benefits her neighbors as well as herself. Someone who acquires education for herself is likely to confer positive externalities, since better educated people are likely to communicate more useful information to those around them, and are also likely to participate more intelligently in public decisions.

Competitive Markets and Externalities

When individuals decide to trade in a competitive market, they are motivated by *their own* costs or benefits, and tend to ignore the costs or benefits that their participation may impose on others. In general, this leads to inefficient outcomes.

An example will help us to understand the reason for this inefficiency. Consider a market with 15 suppliers and 15 demanders of apples. Suppose that for every bushel of apples that is produced, farmers spray insecticide that imposes a negative externality, costing each person in the market $1. The distribution of Buyer Values and Seller Costs in this market is given in Table D6.1.

Table D6.1: Buyer Values and Seller Costs

Seller Cost	Number of Persons	Buyer Value	Number of Persons
15	4	50	5
25	7	30	5
35	4	10	5

Let us draw supply and demand curves for this apple market. Everyone must bear the pollution costs imposed by others, regardless of his or her own decision to buy or sell. Therefore, as with fixed costs in previous experiments, the presence of these costs has no effect on a buyer's willingness-to-pay for apples or on the lowest price that a seller is willing to accept. Therefore the demand and supply curves for apples can be drawn in the same way that we drew demand and supply curves in the absence of externalities.[1] These demand and supply curves are shown in Figure D6.1.

From Figure D6.1, we see that the competitive equilibrium price of apples is $25 per bushel and the competitive equilibrium quantity sold is 10 bushels. As we discovered in Chapter 1, total profits made by buyers and sellers are equal to the shaded area between the demand curve and the supply curve to the left of the competitive equilibrium quantity. In this case, total profits made by buyers and sellers on apple transactions are $190.[2] But this is not the end of the story. Every bushel of apples that is produced imposes a cost of $1 on everybody in the market (whether or not they made a purchase or

---

[1]Almost all of the pollution that an individual experiences is caused by others, rather than by himself or herself, so it is reasonable to make the simplifying assumption that buyers or sellers ignore the effect of their own trading on the total amount of pollution.

[2]You can find this area by breaking up the shaded area into rectangles and adding the areas of these rectangles. One way to calculate this area is as follows: $35 × 4 + $25 × 1 + $5 × 5 = $190.

Figure D6.1: Supply and Demand for Apples

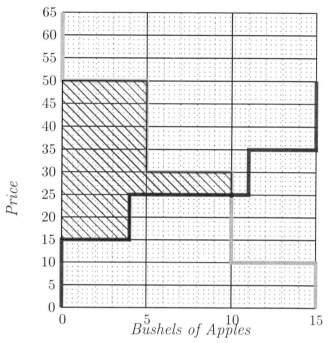

a sale). Since 10 bushels are sold, this means that each of the 30 people in the market has to pay a pollution cost of $10. Therefore the total cost of pollution to people in the market is $10 \times 30 = \$300$. When we subtract the $300 in pollution costs from the $190 in profits made on transactions, we find that the total amount of profit earned by people in this market is -$110! Remarkably, it turns out that total profits are *lower* when people are allowed to trade to a competitive equilibrium than they would be if there had been no trade at all.

How can it be that although everybody who trades makes a profit (or at least no loss) on the trade, total profits of all persons in the market are negative? The answer is that traders take account of their own costs, but do not account for the costs that they impose on others through negative externalities. Consider, for example, a supplier with Seller Cost $25 who sells a bushel of apples to a buyer with Buyer Value $30 for a price between $25 and $30. Both the buyer and the seller make a profit, and the total of the buyer's profit and the seller's profit is $5. But producing this bushel of apples imposed a pollution cost of $1 on each of the 30 people in the market. Although the buyer and seller together make a profit of $5 on the transaction, they impose a negative externality of $30, so that this sale reduced total profits in the market by $25.

One might first think that since total profits are lower in competitive equilibrium than with no trade, the way to maximize total profits is to prohibit all trading in apples. But this turns out not to be the answer. To see why, consider a trade between a demander with Buyer Value $50 and a supplier with Seller Cost $15. Total gains of the seller and buyer from trading are $50 − $15 = $35, and the total costs imposed by the externality are $30. So this trade increases the total total amount of profits in the market by $35 − $30 = $5.

In general, it may be economically efficient for the economy to allow some transactions, even if they impose negative externalities. The transactions that are consistent with efficiency are those in which the total profits to buyer and seller are greater than the total costs imposed by the associated externality. For such trades, the traders would still make a profit even if they had to compensate everyone in the market for the negative externality caused by their trade. On the other hand, trades in which the profits of buyer and seller are smaller than the total amount of externalities caused by these trades result in a reduction in total profits in the economy and are not economically efficient.

While trades between demanders with Buyer Values of $50 and suppliers with Seller Costs of $15 are economically *efficient*, you may well think that they are not *fair*. Why should individuals who make trades that impose negative externalities on others not have to pay their victims for damage done? Is it fair that trading between some individuals leaves others worse off than they would have been if no trades were allowed? We will demonstrate that with a pollution tax like the one in Session 2 of our experiment, it is possible to achieve efficiency while at the same time compensating those who are damaged by negative externalities.

A Pollution Tax to Regulate Externalities

We have seen that in a market with negative externalities and no controls on trader behavior, too many trades are made. One way to improve on this outcome is to introduce a pollution tax, just as we did in Session 2 of our experiment. In this session, sellers were taxed for each unit sold and all participants in the market received an equal share of the tax revenue. The effect of such a tax is that the supplier (at least partially) compensates everyone in the market for the pollution costs that her sales impose on others.

Suppose that the pollution tax on each sale is set equal to the total cost of the negative externalities that the sale imposes. Since the seller must pay the tax, she will be willing to sell a unit of output only if the price she is paid is at least as great as her Seller Cost *plus the tax*. Where the tax equals the total pollution costs imposed by producing one unit, she will sell only for a price that is greater than the sum of her production cost and the total pollution costs that she imposes by producing a unit. [3]

In our previous example, the total cost of externalities generated in the production of a bushel of apples was $30. Suppose that the government imposed a pollution tax of $30, to be collected from the seller for each bushel of apples sold. As we learned in our earlier experiment with sales taxes, the effect of this tax is the same as that of a $30 increase in Seller Costs for all suppliers. The tax would therefore shift the supply curve vertically by $30. This shifted supply curve is shown in Figure D6.2.

In Figure D6.2, we see that the shifted supply curve meets the demand curve where the price of apples is $50 per bushel and the number of bushels sold is 4. These are the competitive equilibrium price and quantity with a $30 pollution tax. Total profits made by buyers and sellers from apple transactions are given by the area between the shifted supply curve and the demand curve. These total profits are $5 × 4 = $20. Since each unit sold is taxed at $30, total tax revenue is $30 × 4 = $120. Since each of the 4 produced units causes $1 worth of negative externalities to each of the 30 persons in the market, the total cost of externalities is $30×4 = $120. To find total profits in the market, we add buyers' and sellers' profits to the amount of tax revenue (which is returned to the market participants) and subtract the total externality costs. Thus we have total profits of $20+$120−$120 = $20.

Let us see how these profits are distributed in the population. The only people who bought apples were four demanders who had Buyer Values of $50 and who paid $50 for a bushel of apples, so all of these buyers made zero profits. The only people who sold apples were four suppliers, who had Seller

---

[3] A careful reader may notice that since 1/30 of the total amount of taxes collected will be rebated to each supplier, the true cost to a supplier of paying a $30 tax is only $29. The same careful reader might also notice that a clever supplier would be aware that her *own* production will cost her $1 in pollution damage, and hence the profits that she gets from selling a unit are $1 less than we have posited in drawing the supply and demand curves. It can be shown that these two effects exactly counterbalance each other, so that the outcome is precisely the same as if each supplier ignored the fact that she would share in the proceeds of the taxes that she paid and also ignored the cost to herself of her own pollution.

Figure D6.2: Supply and Demand With a Pollution Tax

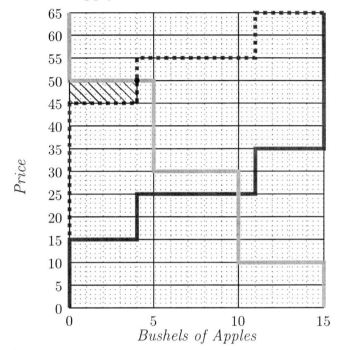

Costs of $15, and who paid a tax of $30. Since they received a price of $50 for their apples and had costs of $15 + $30 = $45, these sellers each made $5 on the transaction. Every participant in the market suffered negative externalities of $4 ($1 from each of the four bushels of apples produced), but everyone got an equal share of the tax revenue. Since there was $120 in tax revenue to be divided among 30 people, each person received $4 as their share of tax revenue; this exactly cancels the $4 costs imposed on each person by the externality. When both the externalities and the divided tax revenue are taken into account, nobody is worse off than they would have been if production of apples had been prohibited, and the four sellers who sold apples are each better off by $5.

In general, total profits in a market will be maximized if each individual takes into account the full externality costs of his or her actions. If a pollution tax on suppliers is set equal to the total cost of the externalities they impose, then the tax serves exactly this purpose. A supplier's total costs will then include all of the costs that her activity imposes on society, the externalities that she generates as well as her own Seller Cost. In the apple market example, if apple producers must pay a $30 tax, they will sell a bushel of apples only if they can get a price that is at least $30 higher than their Seller Costs, which means that they will be able to make a sale only if the buyer's Buyer Value exceeds the seller's Seller Costs by at least the total cost of negative externalities imposed by the production of a bushel of apples.

Marketable Pollution Permits

In Session 3 of the experiment, we tried another method of controlling externalities. Each seller was required to have a pollution permit before being allowed to produce a unit of output. A fixed number of pollution permits was issued, and people were allowed to buy and sell these permits. Since suppliers must present a pollution permit for every unit of output that is produced, the total number of units produced cannot be greater than the number of permits issued.

Given the total number of permits, total profits made by buyers and sellers will depend on which suppliers are using the permits. If pollution permits were not marketable, the only suppliers who would be permitted to sell the good would be the ones who happened to own pollution tickets. If some high-cost suppliers had pollution tickets and some low-cost suppliers did not have pollution tickets, the outcome would be wasteful since output which could have been produced by low-cost suppliers would be produced by high-cost suppliers. If the government authorities know in advance which were the lowest-cost suppliers, they could achieve efficiency by awarding pollution permits only to the lowest-cost suppliers. But it is often difficult for policy-makers to determine who has the lowest costs. A simple way to ensure that pollution tickets will ultimately find their way into the hands of the lowest-cost producers is to allow the holders of pollution tickets to resell them.

To see that marketable permits will ultimately be used by the group of suppliers with lowest Seller Costs, let us consider an example. Suppose that the market price for apples is $50 per bushel and suppose that Supplier A, who has Seller Cost $35, has a permit, while Supplier B, who has Seller Cost $15 does not. If Supplier A uses her permit to sell a bushel of apples for $50, she will make a profit of $15. Supplier B cannot make a sale unless she has a pollution permit, but if she had a permit, she could sell a bushel of apples for $50, which is $35 more than her Seller Cost. Therefore Supplier B would be willing to pay up to $35 for a permit. Since A makes a profit of only $15 from using the permit herself, it must be that both A and B

could increase their profits if A sold her pollution permit to B for any price between \$15 and \$35. This reasoning leads us to expect that if suppliers are free to buy and sell pollution permits among themselves, the permits will eventually fall into the hands of those suppliers with the lowest Seller Costs.

Supply and Demand for Pollution Permits (Optional)

The market for pollution permits will function much like the market for any other good. We should therefore be able to predict the equilibrium price of pollution permits using the tools of supply and demand. The "demanders" in the *permit market* are the suppliers of final goods, who need pollution permits in order to be allowed to produce. In Effluvia, the demanders for permits are the suppliers of lawn ornaments. In our apple market example, the demanders for permits are the suppliers of apples.

Regardless of the price of permits, the total supply of permits to the market is fixed at the number of permits issued by the government. This means that the supply curve for permits is a vertical line.

Plotting the demand curve for permits is a little more complicated. In the case of our apple market example, we need to figure out the amount that each apple supplier would be willing to pay for a pollution permit. This will depend on the number of permits issued. Suppose, that the government issues 4 pollution permits. Knowing this, everyone will realize that only 4 bushels of apples can be brought to market with pollution permits. Looking at the demand curve for apples in Figure D6.1, we see that if the supply of apples is 4 bushels, sellers would be able to sell their apples at a price of \$50 per bushel, but they could not sell any apples for a price higher than \$50. Given that they expect to be able to sell apples for \$50 a bushel, what would suppliers be willing to pay for a pollution permit?

If she had a pollution permit, a supplier with Seller Cost \$15 could sell a bushel of apples for \$50 and would make a profit of \$35. Therefore she would be willing to pay up to \$35 for a pollution permit. With an apple price of \$50, a supplier with Seller Cost \$25 could make a profit of \$25 if she had a pollution permit, and hence would be willing to pay up to \$25 for a permit. By similar reasoning, a supplier with Seller Cost \$35 would be willing to pay up to \$15 for a pollution permit. Therefore the four suppliers with Seller Cost \$15 would be willing to pay \$35, the seven suppliers with Seller Cost \$25 would be willing to pay \$25, and the four suppliers with Seller Cost \$35 would be willing to pay \$15 for a pollution permit. These willingnesses-to-pay imply that the demand curve for pollution permits is as drawn in Figure D6.3.

Figure D6.3: Supply and Demand for Pollution Permits

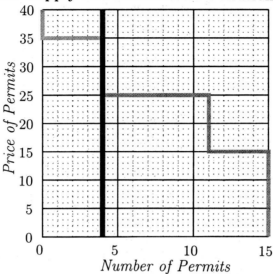

Since the government makes exactly 4 pollution permits available, the supply curve for permits is a vertical line, corresponding to a fixed supply of 4 permits. From Figure D6.3, one can see that when 4 permits are available, the supply curve meets the demand curve along the line segment running from $(4, 25)$ to $(4, 35)$. This means that the market for pollution permits is in equilibrium at any price between $25 and $35 per permit.

The Apple Market with Required Permits (Optional)

In our analysis of the market for permits, we discovered that if four permits are issued, the competitive equilibrium price can be any price between $25 and $35. Let us have a look at supply and demand in the apple market if pollution permits sell for $30. Since every supplier must have a pollution permit costing $30 and must also pay her Seller Costs, the supply curve for apples is obtained by shifting the supply curve that applies when permits are not required upward by $30. This shifted supply curve is shown as the dashed line in Figure D6.4.

The requirement that suppliers must have permits does not affect buyers' willingness-to-pay for apples, so the demand curve for apples remains unchanged. As we see from Figure D6.4, the demand for apples equals the supply of apples when the price is $50 and the number of apples produced is 4 bushels. This is the same equilibrium that we found when we imposed

Figure D6.4: Supply and Demand for Apples With 4 Permits

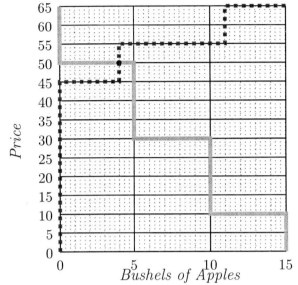

a $30 pollution tax.[4]

A Remark on Information

In order to achieve full efficiency, either with a pollution tax or with pollution permits, the government would need to have far more detailed information about supply, demand, and externalities than it is likely to be able to obtain. In order to set a pollution tax equal to the total cost of the negative externalities generated, the government would need precise information about these costs. In order to issue the right number of permits, the government would need to be able to calculate the economically efficient output in the polluting industry. While full efficiency may not be attainable with available information, it is likely that significant movements in the direction of efficiency can be made by using policies based on approximate information.

If the government knew the demand and supply curves perfectly, it would always be possible to attain the same goals of pollution reduction either by taxing pollution or by distributing a limited number of marketable pollution permits. But if the government is not sure about these curves, then it faces

---

[4]If the price of pollution permits takes any other value in the equilibrium range, which runs from $25 to $35, the supply curve, which is shifted by the amount of the tax, will still intersect the demand curve at an output of 4 bushels of apples. Thus, all permit prices in the equilibrium range will result in the same efficient output of apples.

a choice between setting the tax at a certain level without knowing the resulting level of pollution, or of issuing a fixed number of pollution permits, so it knows the amount of pollution reduction in advance, but does not know the price of pollution tickets, and hence does not know in detail the effects on the price of goods produced. One of the benefits that governments have discovered when they issue marketable pollution permits is that they are able to observe the prices of these permits and thus make better estimates of the costs and benefits of changing air-quality standards.

Positive Externalities

In the lawn ornament experiment and also in the apple market example discussed above, production caused *negative* externalities. What policies do you think would be recommended for an industry that generates *positive* externalities? For example, suppose that lawn ornaments can be produced without pollution and that Effluvians get pleasure from observing the beautiful lawn ornaments in front of each others' houses. Or in the apple example, suppose that apples are produced without insecticides and people enjoy looking at the apple trees. In each case, a market transaction would benefit not only the buyer and the seller, but also people who are not involved in the trade. With negative externalities we found that competitive markets led to too *many* transactions. With positive externalities, it will be the case that competitive equilibrium results in too *few* transactions. In contrast to the case of negative externalities, where a *tax* can be used to enhance efficiency, it turns out that with positive externalities, a *subsidy* can increase total profits by more than the cost of the subsidy. Your home work assignment will include an example of a subsidy.

NAME _____

Home Work–Experiment 6

Competitive Supply and Demand

Session 1–No Government Intervention

■ Use the information in Table L6.1 of your Lab Report to draw demand and supply curves for the market in Session 1 where there is no governmental intervention.

Figure H6.1: Supply and Demand in Session 1

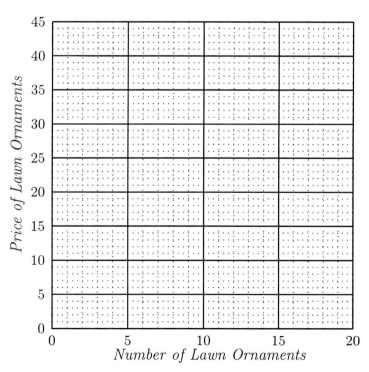

■ In Session 1, in *competitive equilibrium*, the price of lawn ornaments is

_____ and the quantity of lawn ornaments produced is _____.

■ In Session 1, in *competitive equilibrium*, the cost of pollution to each

inhabitant of Effluvia is _____. (Hint: Your instructor has told you
the pollution cost that each lawn ornament imposes on each individual. You
know the number of lawn ornaments produced in competitive equilibrium.)

■ Calculate total profits of buyers and of sellers, total pollution costs, and
total profits net of pollution costs in *competitive equilibrium* for Session 1
and enter these numbers in Table H6.1.

Table H6.1: Competitive Equilibrium Profits and Pollution Cost

Total Profits of Buyers	
Total Profits of Sellers	
Total Cost of Pollution	
Total Profits Net of Pollution Costs	

Session 2–A Pollution Tax

■ The effect of a pollution tax paid by sellers is to increase a supplier's
costs by the amount of the tax. This means that the (supply? demand?)

_____ curve is shifted (up? down?) _____ by the amount of
the tax.

■ In Figure H6.2, draw the supply and demand curves that apply in Session
2, where sellers must pay the pollution tax. Use the information recorded
in your lab report about the distribution of Seller Costs and Buyer Values
and about the amount of the pollution tax.

■ In Session 2, in competitive equilibrium, the price of lawn ornaments is

_____ and the quantity of lawn ornaments produced is _____.

Figure H6.2: Supply and Demand in Session 2

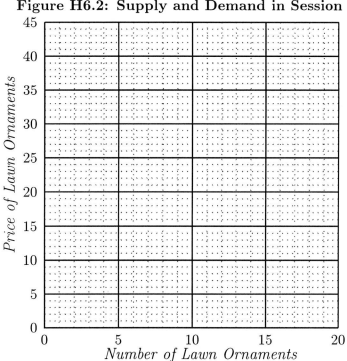

■ Calculate total after-tax profits of all buyers and sellers in competitive equilibrium for Session 2 and enter these profits in Table H6.2. Total tax revenue is equal to the number of lawn ornaments sold times the pollution tax per unit. Add total profits of buyers, total profits of sellers, and total tax revenue and subtract total cost of pollution to find total profits and tax revenue net of pollution costs in Effluvia.

Table H6.2: Profits, Taxes and Pollution Damage in Session 2

Total Profits of Buyers	
Total Profits of Sellers	
Total Tax Revenue	
Total Cost of Pollution	
Total Profits and Tax Revenue Net of Pollution Costs	

Session 3–Marketable Pollution Permits

■ The number of pollution permits issued in Session 3 of the experiment

was _____. Therefore the number of lawn ornaments supplied in Ses-

sion 3 can be no larger than _____.

■ Use the demand curve that you drew in Figure H6.1 to find the price
at which the number of lawn ornaments demanded equals the number of

pollution permits issued. _____ This will be the equilibrium price of
lawn ornaments.

■ Where the price of lawn ornaments is the equilibrium price that you
found in answer to the previous question, enter the amount that sellers with
each Seller Cost would be willing to pay for a pollution permit in the third
column of Table H6.3. Find the number of suppliers with each seller cost
in Table L6.1 of your Lab Report and enter these numbers in the second
column of Table H6.3.

Table H6.3: Suppliers' Willingness to Pay for Pollution Permits

Seller Cost	Number in Market	Willingness to Pay for a Permit
3		
8		
13		
18		
23		
28		

■ In Figure H6.3, use the information from Table H6.3 to draw the demand
curve for pollution permits. On the same graph, draw a vertical supply curve
at the number of permits that were issued in Session 3 of the experiment.

■ The competitive equilibrium price for permits in Session 3 is _____

_____.

Figure H6.3: Supply and Demand for Pollution Permits

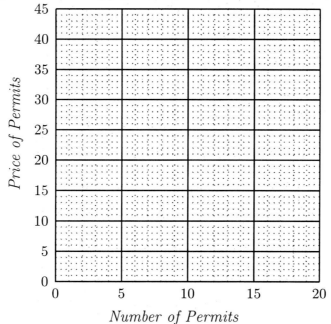

Price of Permits (y-axis)

Number of Permits (x-axis)

Positive Externalities

In our earlier discussion, we analyzed an apple market with negative externalities. Let us now consider a happier story, in which the distribution of Buyer Values and Seller Costs are as in the discussion, but the apple orchard uses no chemical sprays. The beauty and fragrance of the orchard generates *positive* rather than negative externalities. In fact, for every bushel of apples that is produced, everyone in the market gets a *benefit* worth $.50. Since there are 30 people in the market, the total value of the positive externalities generated by apple production is $.50 × 30 = $15.

■ Suppose that the government pays a subsidy of $15 to each supplier who sells a bushel of apples. The government finances this subsidy by requiring everybody in the market, whether or not they bought or sold apples, to pay 1/30 of the total cost of the subsidy. On Figure H6.4, draw the demand curve and the supply curve for apples that would apply if there is no subsidy. Then use a dotted red line to show the supply curve that applies with the subsidy.

■ Without the subsidy, the competitive equilibrium price of apples is ___

Figure H6.4: Supply and Demand With a Subsidy

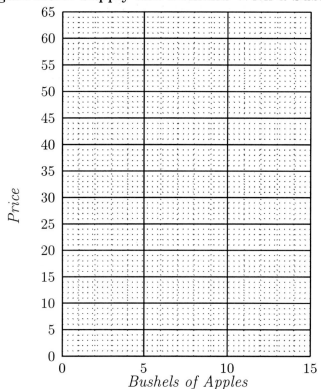

_____ and the competitive equilibrium quantity is _____.

■ Assuming that suppliers ignore the effects of their actions on the tax that pays for the subsidy, draw, on Figure H6.4, the supply curve that applies when the $15 per bushel subsidy is paid to apple sellers.

■ With the subsidy, the competitive equilibrium price of apples is _____

_____ and the competitive equilibrium quantity is _____.

■ Without the subsidy, total profits of buyers and sellers, not counting externalities, are _____ and total profits of all persons in the market, when the value of externalities is _included_, are _____.

■ With the subsidy, total profits of buyers and sellers, including subsidy payments, but not including externalities, are _____. The total amount of subsidy paid is _____. The total value of externalities enjoyed by persons in this market is _____. Calculate total profits of all persons in the market, including the value of externalities, and subtract the amount of taxes that have to be paid to support the subsidy.

_____

■ Explain why it is that the subsidy on apple production increases total profits (including externalities) by more than the cost of the subsidy.

_____

_____

_____

Experiment 7

Monopolies and Cartels

I'll Scratch Your Back

The industry chieftains are gathered in a luxurious hideaway, somewhere in the sunny Caribbean.

The chairman lifts his brandy glass and declares: "It is time to put an end to ruinous competition and price wars. From now on, we will work together. Each firm in our industry will get an output quota. Any firm that produces more than its quota will be severely punished."

"Hear! Hear!" roar his former competitors.

Session 1–The Cartel Sets Output Quotas

A **monopoly** is a market that is served by only one supplier. This supplier is called a **monopolist**. In order to maximize its payoffs, a monopoly should typically supply a smaller amount of its product than the total amount that would be supplied by competitive firms, and it should charge a higher price than the competitive equilibrium price.

A group of firms in the same industry that agree to restrict output in order to raise prices is known as a **cartel**, and such behavior is known as *collusion*.[1] If a cartel can enforce its agreement, each of its members can make higher profits than they would make without an agreement. A cartel will maximize the total amount of profits made by its members if it chooses the same total industry output and the same price that a monopolist would

---

[1] In the United States, cartels are illegal. If the U. S. Department of Justice discovered a meeting of the type described above, it would sentence the persons involved to prison terms.

set. The cartel can then agree to divide these profits among the firms in the industry in such a way that every cartel member gets more profits than it would make without the cartel agreement.

This experiment simulates a market for airline tickets in an imaginary country where the airlines have managed to form a cartel. Five or six members of the class will be designated as ticket suppliers (airlines)[2] and the remaining class members will be ticket demanders.

In all sessions, ticket suppliers will be given Firm Record Sheets on which they should record each customer's identification number and the price charged to that customer.

Ticket Demanders' Instructions

Demanders receive Personal Information Sheets which indicate their Buyer Values for each session. The overall distribution of Buyer Values will be the same throughout all sessions of the experiment. At the beginning of the experiment, the market manager will announce the distribution of Buyer Values in the class and sketch the demand curve on the blackboard.

Demanders should make their purchases according to the following rule. Buy a unit of the good if you can find a posted price that is at least $1 below your Buyer Value, otherwise don't buy. If more than one firm posts a price lower than your Buyer Value, buy from one of the firms that is charging the lowest price. Your profits will be the difference between your Buyer Value and the price that you pay.

Suppliers Instructions

Each ticket-supplying firm can supply as many tickets as it wishes. Each ticket that it sells costs the supplier $5 to produce.

In this session, the suppliers will meet as a *cartel*, to set output quotas for its members. If a 2/3 majority of cartel members agree to a system of quotas, the output quotas will be enforced on all members by the market manager, who will not accept sales by any firm that exceeds the quota assigned to it by the cartel. In addition to assigning quantity quotas, the cartel may also recommend a *price* to be charged by each cartel member. The price recommendation, however, will not be enforced by the market manager.

---

[2]In large classes, the instructor may choose "management teams" of students to play the roles of airline companies. Team members will meet to discuss and try to agree on a team strategy. They send a single representative to the cartel meeting, to vote on cartel agreements.

When the quotas have been set, suppliers are each allocated a location near the blackboard where they can post their prices. Prices must be posted in dollar units, and suppliers are not allowed to change their prices, once they are posted. A supplier can sell any number of units that does not exceed its quota. A supplier's profits are equal to its total revenue minus the cost of producing the number of units that it sells.

Session 2–Can the Cartel Endure Secrecy?

In the previous session, the cartel agreement was enforced by the market manager. In more realistic situations, such outside enforcement may not be available. The cartel may find it very expensive or even impossible to keep track of the activities of its members and to punish overproduction and price-cutting.

In Session 2, the distribution of Buyer Values is the same as in Session 1. Cartel members again meet to discuss quotas and pricing requirements. They can make any agreement they wish. This time, however, the market manager will not enforce the quotas, so that compliance is voluntary.

Firm locations are scattered (if convenient, some firms may be located outside of the classroom.) Suppliers can post prices and can change their posted prices whenever they like. Suppliers are also allowed to negotiate "discounts" with individual buyers. For each sale, the supplier should record the identification number of the buyer and the price at which the sale is made.

Session 3–The Cartel Offers Student Rates

Sometimes a cartel or a monopoly deals with demanders who can be divided into two groups with two different distributions of Buyer Values. When a cartel can determine who belongs to each of these two groups, it may profit by charging different prices to members of the two different groups. This practice is known as **price discrimination**. In Session 3, the cartel finds that students tend to have lower Buyer Values for airline tickets than non-students. It will find it profitable to charge higher prices to non-students than to students.

As before, there are five or six firms and the remaining students are demanders. In this session, as in Session 1, the market manager will enforce cartel agreements.

Demanders' instructions

In Session 3, there are two kinds of demanders, students and non-students. Those demanders who are designated as students will have the words "I AM A STUDENT" printed at the top of their Personal Information Sheets. Although firms will not be allowed to look at demanders' actual Buyer Values, they will be permitted to charge lower rates to demanders who can identify themselves as students. At the beginning of the session, the instructor will report to the class the distribution of Buyer Values among students and among non-students.

A demander will be able to buy either zero or one unit of the good. A demander should buy a unit from a supplier if and only if the supplier's price is the lowest available and is lower than the demander's Buyer Value.

Producer's instructions

As in Session 1, producers meet as a cartel to set production quotas. The cartel will seek to agree on quotas for the number of units each producer can sell to students and the number of units each producer can sell to non-students. Again a 2/3 majority is required for agreements on quotas, and quotas, once agreed to, will be enforced by the market manager. The cartel can also suggest prices to the firms to charge each kind of buyer.

Firms can post separate prices for students and for non-students, and can require customers to show student identification cards in order to qualify for student prices. Prices must be in dollar units and, once posted, can not be changed.

Session 4–Resale by Students

This session can either be run as a "thought experiment" in classroom discussion or it can be acted out in the same way as earlier sessions. The experimental setup is as in Session 3, with one change in the rules. Students will be allowed to buy more than one ticket and, although each student can use only one airline ticket for himself, students can resell tickets to non-students. Cartel members meet to set student prices and non-student prices. Students who resell tickets should report to the market manager, the price at which they resold them and the identification number of the buyer.

Warm-up Exercise

Profit Maximization for a Monopoly

Suppose that the airline ticket market has only one seller, a monopolist that is seeking to maximize its profit. The seller has no fixed costs and it can produce as many units as it wishes at a cost of $5 per unit.

Suppose that the market has 40 demanders with Buyer Values of $21, and 10 demanders with Buyer Values of $16. Assume that demanders will buy a ticket if and only if the price is at least $1 below their Buyer Values.

■ If the monopolist sets its price higher than $20, how many units would it sell? _____

■ If the monopolist set its price at $20, it could sell _____ tickets and its total revenue would be _____. The total cost of producing this number of units is _____, so its total profits would be _____.

■ If the monopolist set its price at $15, it could sell _____ tickets and its total revenue would be _____. The total cost of producing this number of units is _____, so its total profits would be _____.

■ If the monopolist set its price below $15, could total profits be higher than when it sets its price at $15? _____Explain.

_____

_____

_____

■ At what price is total profit maximized? _____ If the monopolist wants to be able to sell at this price, how many units should it produce?

_____

Let the monopolist have the same costs as before, but suppose that the market has 30 demanders with Buyer Values of $21, and 20 demanders with Buyer Values of $16. As before, demanders will buy a ticket if the price is at least $1 below their Buyer Values and otherwise will not buy.

■ If the monopolist set its price at $20, it could sell _____ tickets

and its total revenue would be _____. The total cost of producing this

number of units is _____, so its total profits would be _____.

■ If the monopolist set its price at $15, it could sell _____ tickets

and its total revenue would be _____. The total cost of producing this

number of units is _____, so its total profits would be _____.

■ At what price is total profit maximized? _____ If the monopolist wants to be able to sell at this price, how many units should it produce?

_____

Profit Maximization for a Cartel

For all of the questions in this section, assume that there are 5 firms in an airline cartel, and that each firm has no fixed costs and a $5 variable cost per ticket.

Suppose that the market has 40 demanders with Buyer Values of $21, and 10 demanders with Buyer Values of $16, and that demanders will buy a ticket if and only if the price is at least $1 below their Buyer Values.

■ Total profit for the cartel will be maximized if everyone sets a price of

_____. At this price, a total of _____ tickets would be sold.

■ If cartel members decide to allocate each firm an equal-sized quota of tickets to sell, how many tickets should each be allowed to sell if they want

to maximize their profits? _____ If they choose profit-maximizing equal-sized quotas, what is the highest price at which each cartel member

could sell her entire quota? _____ How much profit would each firm make? _____

Suppose that the market has 30 demanders with Buyer Values of $21 and 20 demanders with Buyer Values of $16, and demanders will buy a ticket if and only if the price is at least $1 below their Buyer Values.

■ Total profit for the cartel will be maximized if everyone sets a price of

_____. At this price, a total of _____ tickets would be sold.

■ Suppose that cartel members decide to allocate each firm an equal-sized quota of tickets to sell. How many tickets should each be allowed to sell

if they want to maximize their profits? _____ If they choose profit-maximizing, equal-sized quotas, what is the highest price at which each

cartel member could sell her entire quota? _____ How much profit

would each firm make? _____

■ Suppose that the market has 31 demanders with Buyer Values of $21, and 20 demanders with Buyer Values of $16. Explain why, in this case, it is not possible to maximize total profits in the industry with equal-sized quotas for everyone. How would you suggest that the cartel might solve this problem?

_____

_____

_____

_____

_____

Student Discounts

Suppose that customers can be reliably identified as students or non-students. Suppose that there there are 30 non-students, all of whom have Buyer Values of $21, and that there are 10 students with Buyer Values of $21 and 10 students with Buyer Values of $16.

The airline market is controlled by a monopoly that has no fixed costs and a $5 variable cost per ticket. The monopolist wants to figure out two things: What is the best price to charge students and what is the best price to charge non-students?

■ If the monopolist charged a price of $20 to students, how many units

would students buy?_____ At this price, what would be the total

amount of profits made from sales to students?_____(Hint:
calculate total revenue from students and subtract the total cost of producing for students.)

■ If the monopolist charged a price of $15 to students, how many units

would students buy?_____ At this price, what would be the total

amount of profits made from sales to students?_____

■ What price to students would give the monopolist the most profits from

the student sector of the market?_____How many units

would be sold to students at this price?_____

■ If the monopolist charged a price of $20 to non-students, how many units

would non-students buy?_____ At this price, what would

be the total amount of profits made from sales to non-students?_____

_____

■ If the monopolist charged a price of $15 to non-students, how many units

would non-students buy?_____ At this price, what would

be the total amount of profits made from sales to non-students?_____

_____

■ What price to non-students would give the monopolist the most profits

from the non-student sector of the market?_____How many

units would be sold to non-students at this price?_____

■   If the monopolist chose its most profitable price for students and its most profitable price for non-students, what would be its total profits from the

two segments of the market?_____Compare these profits with the profits that the monopoly could make if all customers had to be charged the same price.

_____

■   Suppose that a cartel with 5 members could set production quotas for each cartel member to sell to students and non-students. How large would you expect these quotas to be?

_____

_____

_____

What Do You Expect to See?

■   If cartel agreements are enforced by the market manager, would you expect total output of cartel members to be greater, smaller, or about the same as when cartel agreements are voluntary? Explain.

_____

_____

_____

■   Do you think that the sum of firms' profits plus consumers' surplus will

be greater with an effective cartel or with an ineffective cartel?_____

_____

■   Some commodities, like haircuts, surgical operations, and tuition at a university, are difficult or impossible to transfer from one buyer to another. Other commodities, like beer, breakfast cereal, and bananas are easily resold. If a commodity is easily transferable and if a cartel charges some people a higher price than it charges others, what do you think will happen?

_____

_____

_____

NAME _____

Lab Report–Experiment 7

Session 1–The Cartel Sets Quotas

■ In Table L7.1, record the number of demanders of each type who participated in Session 1.

Table L7.1: Distribution of Buyer Types in Session 1

Type of Buyer	Buyer Value	Number of Buyers
High-Value Buyer	$21	
Low-Value Buyer	$16	

What Would Happen Under Competition?

■ Use the information from Table L7.1 to draw the demand curve for airline tickets on Figure L7.1, below.

■ If no quotas are set, firms will not want to produce any output at prices lower than _____ and will want to produce an unlimited amount at prices higher than _____.

■ At a price of _____, each firm would exactly break even on each unit it produced, and would therefore be indifferent between producing any amount between 0 and infinity. This means that the supply curve will be a (horizontal, vertical) _____ line at a price of _____.

■ On Figure L7.1, use a red marker to draw the competitive supply curve for tickets (with no cartel).

Figure L7.1: Competitive Supply and Demand

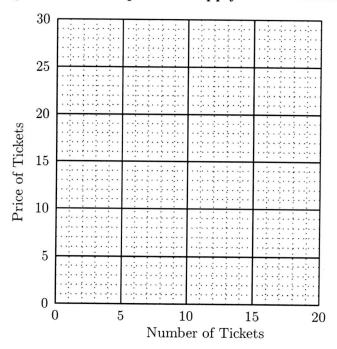

■ If this market were competitive, the competitive equilibrium price would

be _____, the total number of tickets sold would be _____, the

total revenue of all firms would be _____, and the total profits of all

firms would be _____.

Experimental Results in Session 1

■ In Table L7.2, record the price of each sale by each cartel member in the last round of Session 1.

Figure L7.2: Prices and Sales with Quotas Enforced

Seller's ID	Prices Paid By Seller's Customers								Seller's Revenue

■ In the last round of Session 1, total revenue of all cartel members was

_____, total costs of all cartel members were _____, and total

profits of all cartel members were _____.

■ If there had been only one monopoly airline in this market, what would

its profits have been?_____If there had been several firms in the industry and the outcome had been the competitive equilibrium, what would

total profits of all firms in the industry have been?_____

Session 2–Can the Cartel Endure Secrecy?

■ In Table L7.3, record the price of each sale by each cartel member in the last round of Session 2.

Figure L7.3: Prices and Sales with Voluntary Quotas

Seller's ID	Prices Paid By Seller's Customers								Seller's Revenue

■ In the last round of Session 2, total revenue of all cartel members was

_____, total costs of all cartel members were _____, and total

profits of all cartel members were _____.

■ Were total profits in the last round of Session 2 closer to the profits a monopolist would make or closer to the total profits that airlines would make in a competitive market? Why do you think this happened?

_____

_____

_____

Session 3–The Cartel Introduces Student Prices

■ In Table L7.2, record the number of students and non-students of each Buyer Value who participated in Session 3.

Table L7.2: Distribution of Student and Non-Student Buyer Values

Type of Buyer	Buyer Value	Number of Buyers
High-Value Student	$21	
Low-Value Student	$16	
High-Value Non-Student	$21	
Low-Value Non-Student	$16	

■ In Table L7.4, record the price of each sale by each cartel member in the last round of Session 3. Mark sales to students with a ∗.

Figure L7.4: Prices and Sales for Students and Non-students

Seller's ID	Prices Paid By Seller's Customers							Seller's Revenue

■ In Session 3, total profits of cartel members were _____. In this session, a profit-maximizing monopolist could have made total profits of _____.

Session 4–The Resale Market

■ If your class did Session 4 only as a thought experiment, how large would you expect total profits of cartel members to be when students are allowed to resell tickets? If you did Session 4 as an actual experiment, compare total profits of cartel members in Session 4, where resale was possible to Session 3 where resale was not possible.

_____

_____

_____

■ Try to explain why profits were (or would be) different in Session 4 from profits in Session 3.

_____

_____

_____

Food for Thought

■ Can you think of examples of price discrimination that you have seen in real markets?

_____

_____

_____

■ Tickets to movies, sporting events, and museums are sometimes offered at reduced rates to senior citizens and to children. Can you think of any explanation for these discounts that does not involve generosity on the part of ticket suppliers?

_____

_____

_____

■ In some of our experiments, the market manager enforced cartel agreements. In real markets, members of a cartel would have to do their own enforcement. What problems would a cartel face in trying to enforce an agreement? What punishment devices do you think it would be likely to use against defectors?

_____

_____

_____

_____

_____

_____

Discussion D7

Monopolies and Cartels

Monopoly

In previous experiments, we studied markets in which there were many sellers. We were able to make good predictions of market prices and quantities by finding the intersection of the competitive supply and demand curves. The competitive theory does not, however, do a good job of predicting the price and quantity in a monopoly. The reason for this difference can be explained by a simple theory of monopolists' behavior.

Profit Maximization and Demand

The important assumption that we make is that a monopolist takes whatever actions are necessary to maximize its profit. If a monopolist could independently choose both price and quantity, it could make itself very rich indeed. For example, it could sell one unit at a price of eighty billion dollars. In general, however, a monopolist is able to choose *price or quantity* but not both. If you owned the only taxi-cab company in town, you could set a price of $10,000 per ride, but at that price you wouldn't sell very many cab rides. Ordinarily, the number of units that a monopolist can sell will be smaller, the higher the price that it charges. Or, to say the same thing in another way, the more units that a monopolist chooses to sell, the lower the price it will be able to charge for each unit.

The relation between the price that a monopolist charges and the number of units that it sells is determined by the *demand curve*. Remember from previous experiments that the demand curve tells us the number of units demanders will buy at any price. Consider, for example, a monopolist who faces the demand curve drawn in Figure D7.1.

Figure D7.1: A Monopolist's Demand Curve

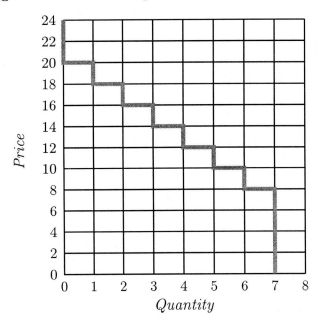

From the demand curve, we can read off the number of units that the monopolist can sell at any price. It cannot sell any output at a price above $20. At a price of $20, it can sell one unit. At a price of $18, it can sell two units, at a price of $16, it can sell three units, and so on. From the same demand curve, we can also read off the best price that it could get as a function of the number of units it sells. That is to say, if it wants to sell exactly one unit, the highest price it can charge is $20. If it wants to sell two units, the highest price that it can charge per unit is $18, and so on. Either way that we read the demand curve, we see that the monopolist can not independently choose both price and quantity, but in choosing one of these variables, is forced to accept the other.

The first two columns of Table D7.1 record each quantity that the monopolist could sell and the highest price at which the monopolist can sell this quantity, given the demand curve in Figure D7.1.

Total Revenue and Marginal Revenue

A monopolist's **total revenue** is the price it charges times the number of units it sells. A monopolist's **marginal revenue** is the increase in total revenue that it gets from selling one more unit. The third column of Table

Table D7.1: Quantity, Price, Costs, and Profits

Quantity Sold	Best Price	Total Revenue	Marginal Revenue	Marginal Cost	Total Cost	Total Profit
0	–	0			0	0
			20	5		
1	20	20			5	15
			16	5		
2	18	36			10	26
			12	5		
3	16	48			15	33
			8	5		
4	14	56			20	36
			4	5		
5	12	60			25	35
			0	5		
6	10	60			30	30
			–4	5		
7	8	56			35	21

D7.1 reports total revenue for each quantity sold. In the fourth column, we record marginal revenue. Notice that we align the entry for marginal revenue *between* the rows corresponding to two different levels of output. If the monopolist increases its sales from zero units to one unit of output, total revenue changes from $0 to $20, so marginal revenue is $20. When it increases sales from one unit to two units, total revenue changes from $20 to $36, so marginal revenue is $16, and so on. When the monopolist increases sales from five units to six units, its total revenue remains at $60, so marginal revenue is $0. Finally when it increases sales from six units to seven units, total revenue *falls* from $60 to $56, and so marginal revenue is -$4.

Marginal Costs, Total Costs, and Profits

The monopolist's marginal cost is assumed to be $5 for every unit produced. We record marginal cost in the fifth column of Table D7.1 and total cost for each quantity of output in the sixth column.

The monopolist's profits are found by subtracting total costs from revenue. These are recorded in the last column of Table D7.1. As we see from the table, the monopolist achieves a maximum profit of $36, which it accomplishes by selling 4 units at a price of $14 per unit.

Marginal Revenue, Marginal Cost, and Profit-Maximization

In the example considered here, it is easy enough for the monopolist to find the most profitable number of units to sell and the corresponding price, simply by calculating profits for each amount of output that can be sold for a positive price. In more complicated and realistic environments, it is often easier for a firm to determine the marginal revenue and the marginal cost of a change in output than to determine total revenues and total costs for all possible quantities. Decision-making is made easier by the fact that information about marginal revenue and marginal cost is sufficient to determine whether small changes in the number of units sold will increase or decrease profits. In particular, we are able to apply the following principle:

The Marginal Principle for a Monopolist. *For any number of units sold, if the marginal revenue from selling one more unit is greater than the marginal cost of producing one more unit, then a monopolist would increase its profits by* increasing *its output. If the marginal revenue gained by selling its last unit is less than the marginal cost of producing its last unit, then a monopolist would increase its profits by* decreasing *its output.*

When a firm is selling the profit-maximizing number of units, it must be that it cannot increase its profits either by increasing or by decreasing its output. Therefore, if a monopoly is maximizing profits, the marginal revenue gained from selling an extra unit must be no greater than its marginal cost, and furthermore, the marginal revenue received from selling its last unit must be at least as great as the marginal cost of producing its last unit.[1]

For example, in Table D7.1, one sees that if the monopoly is selling 3 units of output, its marginal revenue from increasing its output to 4 units is $8, which is greater than its marginal cost of $5. It can therefore increase its profits by selling 4 units rather than 3 units. On the other hand, if the monopoly is selling 5 units, its marginal revenue from selling the fifth unit is $4, which is *less than* its marginal cost of $5. Therefore, it could increase its profits by reducing its output by one unit. When the number of units sold is 4, however, profits cannot be increased either by lowering the price and selling 5 units or by raising the price and selling 3 units.

Comparing Marginal Revenue and Price

If the price that a firm could get for its output did not depend on the number of units it sold, then the extra revenue that it would get from selling

---

[1]Those who are familiar with elementary calculus will recognize that this condition corresponds to the "first-order condition" for a local maximum and that this is a *necessary* conditions for profit-maximization and is not a *sufficient* condition. It may, for example, be that at some quantities, no *small* change would increase profits, but some non-marginal change might do so.

one more unit would be just its price. But if the demand curve for a monopolist's product is downward sloping, then in order to increase its sales, the monopolist has to lower the price that it charges. If the monopolist has to charge the same price for every unit it sells, then lowering its price means that it loses revenue on every single unit sold. Therefore the *marginal revenue* from selling an extra unit is less than the *price* at which that unit is sold. For instance, in the example above, suppose that the monopolist is selling 4 units. If it increases its sales to 5 units, it could sell all 5 units at a price of $12 per unit. But the monopolist's marginal revenue is less than $12, because if it sold only 4 units, it could sell these 4 units at a price of $14 per unit. Thus in order to sell the extra unit, the monopolist has to cut its price on each of the first 4 units by $2. This means that although the monopolist gets $12 for its fifth unit, in order to make this sale it has to reduce the revenue it gets on its first four units by $2 × 4. Therefore its marginal revenue is only $12 − $8 = $4. In general, we have the following useful fact:

Marginal Revenue Is Less Than Price. *If a monopolist sells at a single price in a market with a downward-sloping demand curve, then marginal revenue at any amount of output is always less than the price at which that amount of output can be sold.*

Comparing Monopoly and Competition

We found that the profit-maximizing monopolist in our example would sell 4 units at a price of $12 per unit and would make a total profit of $36. Let us see what would happen if this same market had many competitive firms, each of which could produce the good at a cost of $5 per unit.

The market demand curve would be the same as that in Figure D7.1. What about the supply curve? At prices below the marginal cost of $5, no firm would want to sell any output. At prices above $5, all firms would want to produce as much as possible, so supply would be very large. At a price of exactly $5, firms would be willing to supply any positive amount. The resulting supply curve is a horizontal line at a height of $5, running all the way across the graph, as shown in Figure D7.2.

In Figure D7.2, the supply curve meets the demand curve at a price of $5 and a quantity of 7 units. Since the price is $5 and costs are $5 per unit, firms all make zero profits. At a price of $5, the demander with Buyer Value $20, makes a profit of $15, the demander with Buyer Value $18, makes profits of $13, and so on, down to the demander with Buyer Values $8,

Figure D7.2: Competitive Supply and Demand

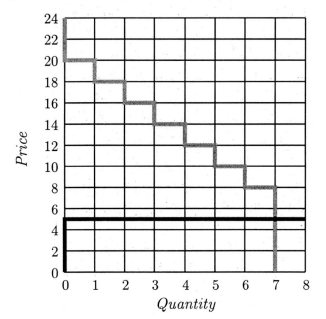

who makes profits of $3. The total amount of buyers' profits (consumers' surplus), which is measured by the area between the demand curve and the supply curve, is $63.

We can now compare the monopoly outcome and the competitive outcome. Table D7.2 shows prices, quantities, and profits for our example, when the market is a monopoly and when the market is competitive with several firms, each with a marginal cost of $5.

Table D7.2: Comparing Monopoly and Competition

	Price	Quantity	Sellers' Profits	Buyers' Profits	Total Profits
Monopoly	14	4	36	12	48
Competition	5	7	0	63	63

Differences Between Monopoly and competition

In general, the following differences are found between a monopoly (where the monopolist must charge the same price for each unit sold) and the outcome in a market with the same demand curve and same marginal costs, but with many competitive firms:

- A profit-maximizing monopolist charges a higher price than the competitive equilibrium price, and sells a smaller quantity than the competitive equilibrium quantity.

- A profit-maximizing monopolist makes greater profits than the total profits that all firms in the industry would make under competition.

- The sum of demanders' profits and suppliers' profits is lower under monopoly than under competition.

Since monopolists charge a price that is higher than the competitive price, it is not surprising that the profits of demanders are lower under monopoly than under competition. What is more interesting is the fact that *total* profits, which are the sum of demanders' profits and suppliers' profits are, in general, higher if the market is competitive than if it is a monopoly. Why is this the case? Wouldn't you think that the buyers' loss from this price increase would be exactly matched by the seller's gain?

The sellers' gain from acting like a monopolist would equal the buyers' loss if the number of transactions did not change when the price rose. In fact, for those demanders who continue to buy from the monopolist, the effect of the monopolist's higher price is simply to reduce the demanders' profits by the same amount as the monopolists' profits increase. The sum of profits of demanders and suppliers from these transactions would therefore be the same under monopoly as under competition. But this is not the end of the story. The monopolist's higher price typically eliminates some trades that would be made at competitive prices. In our example, increasing the price from $5 to $14 eliminates three trades that would have been made under competition. At the competitive price of $5, buyers with Buyer Values $12, $10, and $8 would all have made purchases, and each of these purchases would have been profitable for the buyer and caused no loss to the sellers. At the monopoly price of $14, these three buyers make no purchases, and so neither buyer nor seller makes a profit. Therefore *total* profits of demanders and suppliers are lower with monopoly than with competition.

The monopolist in our example, if it charges the profit-maximizing price of $14, is faced with a tantalizing possibility. There are buyers who still have not bought its output, but who are willing to pay $12, $10, and $8. The monopolist's marginal cost is only $5 per unit. If it could identify these buyers, the monopolist could increase its profits by charging each of them a price of $7, while maintaning a price of $14 to the other buyers. If it did this, the monopolist would sell three more units, for an additional revenue of $21 and its additional costs would be only $15. This was not possible in the discussion so far, because we assumed that the monopolist must charge the same price to all buyers. In the next section we discuss the possibility that the monopolist can increase its profits by charging different prices to different buyers.

Price Discrimination

Perfectly Discriminating Monopolist

Imagine that a monopolist is able to sell at different prices to different customers, and that the monopolist knows each demander's willingness-to-pay. A monopolist who is able to do this is called a **perfectly discriminating monopolist**. How would a perfectly discriminating monopolist behave? The most money that it can extract from any demander would be an amount just slightly less than the demander's Buyer Value. Therefore to maximize its total profit, it should sell the good to all demanders who have Buyer Values greater than its marginal cost, and it should charge each demander a price slightly less than the demander's Buyer Value.

The demand curve from our previous example is drawn again in Figure D7.3. This monopolist could charge just under $20 for the first unit sold, just under $18 for the second, and so on down to the seventh unit which it could sell for just under $8. The monopolist's total revenue would then be slightly less than $20+18+16+14+12+10+8=$98. This is equal to the area of the shaded region in Figure D7.3. Since it is selling 7 units, its total costs would be $35, and its profit would be slightly less than $98-35=$63. (This is equal to the area of the part of the shaded region above the horizontal line which is drawn at a height of $5.) In comparison, recall that a monopolist who must charge the same price to all consumers would charge a price of $14 to everyone, would sell only 4 units, and would make a profit of $36.

Figure D7.3: Discriminating Monopolist's Demand and Costs

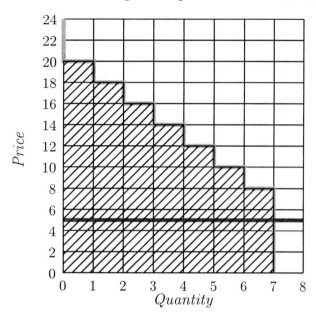

This example illustrates several facts that are true in general for perfectly discriminating monopolists. These facts are summarized as follows:

Perfectly discriminating monopoly. *A perfectly discriminating monopolist:*

- *charges each demander a price just slightly below his Buyer Value.*

- *sells the same number of units that would be sold in competitive equilibrium.*

- *sells more units and makes higher profits than a monopolist who charges a single price.*

- *leaves all demanders with profits of almost zero.*

- *makes profits that are almost as high as the total of demanders' and suppliers' profits in competitive equilibrium.*

Since a perfectly discriminating monopolist makes even more profits than a monopolist who charges a single price, you may wonder why all monopolists don't practice such price discrimination. There are at least two important limitations on a monopolist's ability to charge different prices to different buyers. One of these limitations is the possibility of resale. If a monopolist sells at a lower price to some buyers than to others, then one of the buyers who can get the good cheaply can make profits by buying the good and reselling it to someone who would have to pay the monopolist a higher price. For example, suppose that the demander with Buyer Value $8 buys a unit from the monopolist for $8 and resells this unit to the demander with Buyer Value $20 for $15. If he does so, the buyer with Buyer Value $8 makes a profit of $7, and the buyer with Buyer Value $20 makes a profit of $5, while the monopolist loses the opportunity to sell a unit to the $20 buyer for a price of $20. For this reason, price discrimination is not likely to be successful for commodities, which like clothing or computers, are easy to resell. On the other hand, goods and services like restaurant meals, haircuts, appendectomies, or taxi-cab rides are difficult, if not impossible, for the original purchaser to resell. For such commodities, the possibilities for price discrimination are greater.

Even if a good is not resellable, a monopoly's ability to price discriminate is limited by the fact that although it may have a good estimate of its overall market demand curve, a monopolist is unlikely to know which *individuals* have high willingness-to-pay and which have low. In our example, the monopolist may know that one of the demanders has a Buyer Value of $20, another has a Buyer Value of $18, and so on, but may not know which demander is which. Nor is the monopolist likely to get this information by asking potential customers. Suppose that you are a demander and a monopolist asks you to report your Buyer Value. If you know that the monopolist is going to charge you a price just below your reported Buyer Value, what will your answer be? Buyers would have every incentive to report Buyer Values below their true willingness-to-pay.

Pricing in Separate Markets

Although monopolists are rarely, if ever, able to practice perfect price discrimination, they are sometimes able to separate their demanders into two separate market groups and to charge different prices to members of each market group. For example, book publishers charge different prices for the same book in different countries. Restaurants and movie theaters sometimes charge different prices to senior citizens or students than to other demanders. Software sellers sometimes charge different prices to new customers and customers who own an earlier, less elaborate version of the same product, and so on. In each case, the two different types of demanders can be identified by some publicly observable characteristic, and resale from one type of customer to another is impossible, or at least inconvenient.

If a firm is able to separate its demanders into two separate groups, and if the distributions of Buyer Values in the two groups differ, it is possible for the firm to increase its profits by charging a different price to each group. In order to maximize its profit, it separately determines the most profitable price to charge each group. For example, suppose that the demanders in our earlier example can be separated into two groups, senior citizens and others. Suppose that the three demanders with Buyer Values of $14, $10, and $8, are senior citizens, and the remaining demanders with Buyer Values of $20, $18, $16, and $12, are not senior citizens. Assume that the monopoly is able to identify senior citizens, and the good can not be resold. The most profitable price to charge senior citizens is $10.[2] At this price, the monopolist would sell two units to senior citizens and make a profit of $10 from this segment of the market. The most profitable price for the monopolist to charge other demanders is $16.[3] At this price, the monopolist would sell 3 units to non-senior citizens and would make a profit of $33 from this segment of the market. The monopolist's total profit from the two groups is $10 + $33 = $43. Recall that the monopolist's profit when it must charge the same price to all buyers is $36. Thus we see that price discrimination enables the monopolist to increase its profits.

Cartels

Recall that a *cartel* is a group of firms, all in the same industry, who agree to produce less than they would in a competitive environment in an effort to increase the price of their output. In order to maximize the total profits of its members, a cartel would like to produce the same total quantity and charge the same price as a monopolist. The cartel will also have to work out an arrangement for dividing total profits and a way to coordinate the activities of its members.

Where cartel members all have the same costs of production, one simple way of maximizing total profits is to calculate the profit-maximizing quantity

---

[2] At a price of $14, the monopoly would sell one unit and make a profit of $14 − $5 = $9, at a price of $10, the monopolist would sell two units and make a profit of $2 × $10 − 2 × $5 = $10, and at a price of $8, the monopolist would make a profit of $3 × $8 − 3 × $5 = $9.

[3] At a price of $20, the monopolist would sell one unit and make a profit of $20 − 5 = $15, at a price of $18, the monopolist would sell two units and make a profit of $2 × $18 − 2 × $5 = $26, at a price of $16, the monopolist would sell three units and make a profit of $3 × $16 − 3 × $5 = $33, at a price of $12, the monopolist would sell four units and make a profit of $4 × $12 − 4 × $5 = $28.

for a monopolist, and then give each firm a *production quota* equal to the monopoly output divided by the number of firms in the industry. If all firms produce their quotas, then total output will be the same as the monopoly output, each firm can sell its entire quota at the monopoly price, and all firms will get equal profits. For example, in the market discussed in the previous section, the profit-maximizing output for a monopoly is 4 units, which the monopoly would sell at a price or $14 per unit. If this industry had 4 firms, and the firms agreed to collude, they could assign a production quota of $4/4 = 1$ unit to each firm and recommend a price of $14. So long as each firm stuck to its quota, it would be possible for every firm to sell its single unit of output at a price of $14. Each of the four firms would then make a profit of $9, and total profits of all firms would be $36.

While a cartel agreement would be very profitable for its members, it is not easy to enforce. The problem is that any one firm could gain by violating its production quota and producing more output. Attempts to maintain industry prices by collusive agreements frequently break down because of secret price cuts. To see why, consider the four firms who agreed to production quotas of one unit of output for each firm. Suppose that one of these firms secretly chose to produce 2 units and to offer these units for sale at $12. It would be able to sell these two units for a total revenue of $24 and since its costs are $5 per unit, it would have a profit of $14, which is $5 better than the $9 that it would make if it stuck to the agreement. But when this firm violates its quota, it reduces the profits of all other cartel members. If the other three firms each produce one unit, and the violator produces two units, then total output in the industry is five units, and we see from the demand function that in order for all five units to be sold, the price must fall to $12. The three firms that produced one unit, would therefore each get a revenue of $12 and a profit of $7. But this is not the worst of it. The other firms would realize that they too could gain by cheating on the cartel agreement and the price would soon be driven close to the competitive price. You most likely saw this happen quite dramatically in Session 2 of the experiment.

In most countries, since cartels are illegal, cartel agreements have to be made in secret and certainly can not be enforced by legal contracts. Cartels may still be able to get their members to restrain production by threatening punishment to those who produce too much, but in order to enforce these threats, they would need to observe the output and/or pricing behavior of each cartel member. Thus we are more likely to see cartel behavior when it is easy for firms to monitor each others' pricing and output than when it is difficult to do so.

NAME _____

Home Work–Experiment 7

Price Discrimination

■ Suppose that the monopolist described in the previous discussion is the only barber in a small town. The barber's costs are $5 for each haircut that he gives. He discovers that the only three red-haired people in town have Buyer Values of $18, $12, and $10 (but he doesn't know which redhead has which of these Buyer Values), and that the other four people in town have Buyer Values $20, $16, $14, and $8. He decides to charge different prices to redheads than he charges others. In order to maximize his profits, what

price should he charge redheads? _____ What price should he charge

the others? _____

■ Compare the maximum profits that the barber can make by charging everyone the same price to the maximum profits that he can make by charging a different price to redheads than he charges to others.

_____

■ If the barber price-discriminates between redheads and others in the profit-maximizing way, which people will not get haircuts?

_____

■ If the barber must charge the same price to everyone and chooses his profit-maximizing price, which people will not get haircuts?

_____

■ Assuming the barber is a profit-maximizer, calculate total consumers' surplus (the sum of demanders' profits) when the barber can and can not charge separate prices to redheads.

Monopoly with Linear Demand (Optional)

If you work this problem, you will have a pretty good idea of how monopoly theory extends to the case where the demand curve is a straight line rather than a step function.

Bill Barriers, president of MightySoft Inc, is marketing a new software product, called DoorStops. According to his market researchers, the demand for Doorstops is described by the equation

$$P = \$100 - \frac{1}{1000}X$$

where P is the price charged per copy of DoorStops and X is the number of copies sold. MightySoft has spent \$3,000,000 on developing the product and \$2,000,000 on advertising it. In addition to these fixed costs, it has a variable cost of \$10 for each unit that it sells. Therefore, if it sells X copies of DoorStops, MightySoft's total costs will be $C(X) = \$5,000,000 + \$10X$. At all levels of output, its marginal cost is \$10.

■ From the demand equation, we can see that the demand curve for DoorStops must be a straight line. To draw this curve, all we need to do is to find two points on it and connect the dots. From the demand equation one finds that if $X = 0$, then $P =$_____ and if $X = 100,000$, then $P =$_____.

■ On Figure H7.1, use green ink to draw the demand curve for DoorStops.

■ If the demand curve is a straight line, where the price at which X units can be sold is given by the equation, $P = A - BX$, then when X units are sold, marginal revenue is given by the equation $P = A - 2BX$.[4] The graph of this equation is called the "marginal revenue curve." As you can see from the equation, the marginal revenue curve meets the vertical P axis at the

---

[4]For those of you who know a little bit of calculus, the monopolist's marginal revenue is the derivative of total revenue with respect to output. Total revenue is equal to $R(X) = PX = (A - BX)X = AX - BX^2$, and thus marginal revenue is $R'(X) = A - 2BX$.

same point that the demand curve meets it, and has a slope twice as steep as that of the demand curve. On Figure H7.1, use blue ink to draw the marginal revenue curve.

Figure H7.1: The DoorStop Monopoly

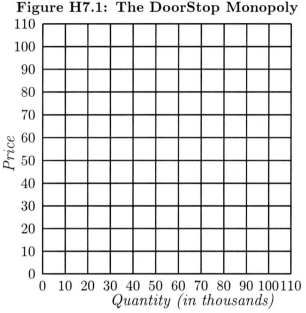

Quantity (in thousands)

■ On Figure H7.1, use red ink to draw a horizonal line, showing a $10 marginal cost at each level of output.

■ On Figure H7.1, label the intersection of the marginal revenue line and the marginal cost line with the letter A. Draw a vertical dotted line from A to the horizontal axis. This line meets the horizontal axis at a point

representing an output quantity of _____.

■ On Figure H7.1, extend the dotted vertical line that you drew through A up to the demand curve. Label the point where this line meets the demand curve B. Draw a horizontal dotted line from B to the vertical axis to

determine the price that the monopolist would charge. This price is _____

_____.

■ When MightySoft sells the profit-maximizing quantity, its total revenue

is _____ and its total cost is _____. Its profit is then _____

_____.

Part IV

Firms and Technology

Experiment 8

Entry and Exit

The Ins and Outs of the Restaurant Business

Have you ever wondered what it would be like to open a restaurant? In this experiment, even if your cooking is so bad that your dog whimpers when you serve it, and even if you are too surly to wait tables, you will have your chance.

In the real world, restaurants, like most other businesses have some costs that are the same, no matter how many units they sell and some costs that depend on the number of units sold. The former are known as **fixed costs** or equivalently as **overhead costs**, and the latter are known as **variable costs**. A firm's **total cost** is the sum of its fixed costs plus its total variable costs.

Examples of fixed costs for a restaurant include the cost of renting the building in which it locates, the cost of kitchen equipment, booths and tables, the cost of advertising, and the cost of employing a chef. A restaurant will have to pay these costs, regardless of how many meals it sells. In contrast, the cost of the ingredients used in meals will vary with the number of meals sold.

In the real world, anyone is free to open a restaurant, but it clearly wouldn't be profitable for everyone to do so. If very few people open restaurants, demand for meals at most restaurants will be high and profits will be high, but if too many people open restaurants, then demand at each restaurant will be lower and competition will cause at least some of them to lose money. In this experiment, we study the way that competitive forces determine the number of restaurants that choose to open.

Instructions

In this market, anybody who wants to open a restaurant can do so. These restaurants are small (intimate, as they say in the restaurant guides). If you open a restaurant, you will be able to serve up to four customers. You will have to pay a *fixed cost* of $20, no matter how many customers you get. In addition to its fixed costs, each restaurant will have a *variable cost* of $5 per customer. A restaurant's *total cost* is the sum of its $20 fixed cost, plus the total of its variable costs for all the meals it sells.

In this experiment, a restaurant will have a total cost of $20 if it sells no meals, $25 if it sells one meal, $30 if it sells two meals, $35 if it sells three meals, and $40 if it sells four meals. We can describe a restaurant's total cost by a **total cost function** $C(n)$ as follows: for n customers, where n is between 0 and 4, total cost is $C(n) = \$20 + 5n$.

Everyone in the class is a potential customer for any of the restaurants in this week's market. Everyone gets a Personal Information Sheet with his or her Buyer Value for each market session. If you chose to buy a restaurant meal, then the market manager will pay you your Buyer Value, so that your profit ("consumer's surplus") from buying a meal will be your Buyer Value *minus* the price you pay for the meal. If you own a restaurant, you will be allowed to buy a meal, either in your own restaurant or in somebody else's. Of course if you buy a meal in your own restaurant, you will count as one of the four customers in your restaurant's serving capacity, and the variable cost of your own meal will be $5, like anyone else's.

Stage 1–To Open or Not To Open a Restaurant?

Each round of each session has two stages. In the first stage, everyone must decide whether to open a restaurant. Before anyone has to make a decision, the market manager will help you to get a rough idea of the distribution of Buyer Values by asking for a show of hands, for each possible Buyer Value. The market manager then publicly asks class members, in succession, whether they intend to open a restaurant. (People with the lowest Buyer Values get first crack at opening restaurants.) When it comes to be your turn to decide, you will know how many people are already committed to opening restaurants. If you choose to open a restaurant, you will be charged $20 in overhead cost, no matter how many meals you sell, and you will be given a customer list, which will have spaces for four names, since you have a "seating capacity" of four customers. If you decide not to open a restaurant, you will have no overhead cost and will not be allowed to sell meals.

Stage 2–Posting Prices and Selling Meals

In the second stage of any round, restaurant operators post prices at which they are willing to sell meals to any buyer (until they fill up their restaurants). These posted prices should be clearly visible to buyers and to other sellers. If it is convenient, each restaurant will be assigned a location next to the blackboard where its owner can post a price.

Customers, after looking at the posted prices, can either choose a restaurant and buy a meal at the posted price or wait for a change in posted prices. Firms can change posted prices only when the market manager allows price changes to be made. The market manager will typically allow three or four occasions for price changes per round, and will always let everyone know when the last opportunity for price changes arises.

When a customer buys a meal at a restaurant, the owner must add the customer's identification number to the restaurant's customer list, along with the price paid by the customer.

Later Rounds of Trading in the First Session

At the end of the first round of trading, the market manager will report the profits of each restaurant. The market manager may also choose to present the market demand curve on the blackboard. After this information has been made available, another round of trading begins.

In all rounds of trading in the first session, customers' Buyer Values are the same as in the first round. In each new round, class members are given another chance to decide whether to enter the restaurant industry. The market manager proceeds exactly as in the first round, asking class members, in the same order as before, whether they intend to open a restaurant. Those who choose to open a restaurant are charged $20 in overhead cost, and those who choose not to open a restaurant have no overhead cost and are not allowed to sell meals. In the second stage of each round, prices are posted and purchases made, just as they are in the first round. At the end of the round, results are made publicly available.

Introducing a Sales Tax

In the second session, the distribution of Buyer Values is the same as in the first session, though Buyer Values of individuals may be different. As in the first session, the market manager asks class members in turn, beginning with those with the lowest Buyer Values, whether they want to open a restaurant. Overhead cost remains at $20. This session though, the government initiates a sales tax of $3 per meal sold, which increases each restaurant's total variable cost to $8 per meal (the original $5, plus the $3 tax). Thus a restaurant that serves n meals will have a total cost, including the sales tax, of $C(n) = \$20 + 8n$. In all other respects, the market procedures are as in Session 1.

Warm-up Exercise

■ Suppose that you have opened a restaurant and find that you can sell up to 4 meals at a price of $15 per meal, but that at any higher price you would be unable to sell any meals. In order to maximize your profit (or minimize your losses), how many meals should you sell? _____ What would be your profit (or loss)? _____

■ Suppose that you have opened a restaurant and find that you can sell up to 4 meals at a price of $7 per meal, but that at any higher price you would be unable to sell any meals. In order to maximize your profit (or minimize your losses), how many meals should you sell? _____ What would be your profit (or loss)? _____

■ Suppose that you have opened a restaurant and find that you can sell up to 4 meals at a price of $3 per meal, but that at any higher price you would be unable to sell any meals. In order to maximize your profit (or minimize your losses), how many meals should you sell? _____ What would be your profit (or loss)? _____

■ If you have already opened a restaurant, what is the lowest price at which you will be willing to sell meals?_____

■ Let $P be the average price at which you expect to sell meals and suppose that you believe you will be able to sell 4 meals at this price. What is the smallest value of P such that you would be willing to enter the industry.

In Session 2, Buyer Values are the same as in Session 1, and hence the demand curve remains the same as before. All firms have to pay a sales tax of $3 for each meal sold.

■ In Session 2, is the sales tax a variable cost or a fixed cost for a restaurant?

_____

■ In Session 2, with the sales tax, a restaurant has variable costs of _____

_____ and fixed costs of _____.

■ In Session 2, if you have already opened a restaurant, what is the lowest

price at which you would be willing to sell meals? _____

What Do You Expect to See?

■ If you wanted to open an additional coffee house in a college town, how would you decide whether it is likely to make money?

_____

_____

_____

■ Suppose that the largest employer in a small industrial city decides to close its local plant and the total number of people employed in the city decreases drastically. What would you expect to be the *immediate* effect on the number of customers in each restaurant, and on the profitability of each restaurant?

_____

_____

_____

■   Suppose that in the small industrial city discussed above, after two or
three years, employment does not recover to its previous levels. What would
you expect to happen to the number of restaurants that are in business?
What would you expect to happen to the number of customers in each
restaurant?

_____

_____

_____

NAME _____

Lab Report–Experiment 8

Record of Market Transactions

■ In Table L8.1, record the distribution of Buyer Values as reported by the market manager.

Table L8.1: Distribution of Consumer Types

Buyer Value	Number of Buyers
24	
18	
12	
8	

To complete Tables L8.2 and L8.3 below, you will need to calculate total revenues and total costs for each restaurant. The total revenue of a restaurant is the sum of the prices that it receives for the meals that it sells.

■ A restaurant's total costs will be _____ if it sells 4 meals, _____ _____ if it sells 3 meals, _____ if it sells 2 meals, _____ if it sells 1 meal, and _____ if it sells no meals.

■   In Table L8.2, record the price received for each meal sold by each restaurant in the first round of Session 1. Then calculate total revenue, total costs, and profits of each restaurant in this round.

Table L8.2: Restaurants' Sales–Session 1, Round 1

Restaurant Owner's ID	Prices Paid By Restaurant Customers				Total Revenue	Total Cost	Profit

■   In Round 1 of Session 1, the number of firms making a profit was _____

_____ and the number of firms making a loss was _____ .

■ In Table L8.3, record the price received for each meal sold by each restaurant in the *last* round of Session 1. Then calculate total revenue, total costs, and profits of each restaurant in this round.

Table L8.3: Restaurants' Sales–Session 1, Last Round

Restaurant Owner's ID	Prices Paid By Restaurant Customers				Total Revenue	Total Cost	Profit

■ In the *last* round of Session 1, the number of firms making a profit was

_____ and the number of firms making a loss was _____.

■ In Table L8.4, record the price received for each meal sold by each restaurant in the *first* round of Session 2. Then calculate total revenue, total costs, and profits of each restaurant in this round.

Table L8.4: Restaurants' Sales–Session 2, Round 1

Restaurant Owner's ID	Prices Paid By Restaurant Customers				Total Revenue	Total Cost	Profit

■ In Round 1 of Session 2, the number of firms making a profit was _____ _____ and the number of firms making a loss was _____.

■ In Table L8.5, record the price received for each meal sold by each restaurant in the *last* round of Session 2. Then calculate total revenue, total costs, and profits of each restaurant in this round.

Table L8.5: Restaurants' Sales–Session 2, Last Round

Restaurant Owner's ID	Prices Paid By Restaurant Customers				Total Revenue	Total Cost	Profit

■ In the last round of Session 2, _____ firms made a profit and _____ firms made a loss.

Discussion D8

Entry and Exit

Realism and the Restaurant Experiment

Though the imaginary restaurants in our experiment are smaller and less complicated than real restaurants, our experimental market illustrates some important features of actual markets, both in retail business and in manufacturing industries.

Features of the experimental restaurant market that mirror actual markets include the following:

- Free Entry into the Industry. In our experiment, anybody is permitted to open a restaurant, and all potential entrants face the same cost structure. This situation corresponds closely to the environment faced by most small businesses.

- Short-Run and Long-Run Decision-Making. Actual firms are able to change some of their business decisions quickly as new information comes in. Other decisions involve long-term commitments, and firms can only change them slowly. For example, a restaurant can quickly decide to order more meat or more vegetables from the wholesalers. It can also change the number of hours its employees work, and can hire or lay off its employees on short notice. By contrast, it can only change the size of the restaurant, or go in and out of business, over a longer period of time. The period during which firms only have time to change some but not all of their business decisions is called the **short run**. The period of time in which all of a firm's business decisions can be changed is called the **long run**. In our experiment, restaurants can change pricing and output decisions during the course of a round (the short run), but they accept their overhead costs at the beginning of a round and can not go out of business and drop these costs, until the next round (the long run).

- Limited Capacity. In our experiment, the restaurants are limited to four customers. In the short run, real firms are restricted in their capacity by the size of their physical plant and by other design features. Often in the real world, capacity limits are more flexible than the limits in our experiment. A firm may be able to produce more output than its plant is designed for. For manufacturing firms, production at above capacity will typically raise costs per unit of output, and may lower quality. For service firms, like restaurants, retail stores, ski resorts or medical clinics, accepting more customers than the plant is designed to accommodate increases congestion and makes the environment less pleasant for customers.

- Fixed Costs. In our experiment, any firm entering the industry must pay a fixed cost that is independent of the amount of output it produces. This is the cost of fixed inputs such as the rental of a building, heating and lighting, which have to be paid so long as a firm stays in business, no matter how many units the firm produces or sells. When overhead costs are nonrecoverable, they are known as **sunk costs**. In our experiment, a restaurant owner has to pay a fixed cost of $20 to open a restaurant. This cost is a sunk cost, since even if the restaurant shuts down, its owner cannot reclaim the $20. In the real world, sunk costs often include advertising, the purchase of specialized buildings and equipment and specialized training for their workers.

- Variable Costs. In our experiment, firms have variable costs of $5 per meal sold. These costs correspond to costs for inputs such as raw materials and labor, for which the number of units used varies with the amount of output produced.

The Short Run and the Long Run

The Short Run

In the short run, a firm has to pay the same amount of fixed costs, no matter how much it produces, and there is not time for new firms to enter the industry. The **short-run industry supply curve** is the industry supply curve obtained when fixed costs can not be changed, and the number of firms in the industry is held constant at the current level. Sometimes, after a firm has invested in fixed inputs, it finds that demand for its output is not as great as it had expected when it made the investment. It may be, then, that the firm can find no way to recover all of its fixed costs. If such a firm finds that at some positive output, its revenue exceeds its *variable* costs, it should minimize losses by continuing production for the short run.

The **short-run equilibrium** for an industry occurs at the price and quantity at which the short-run supply curve meets the demand curve. This is the point at which variable costs per unit are equal to revenue (price) per unit.

The Long Run

An industry is in **long-run competitive equilibrium** if it is in short-run equilibrium and if, in addition, no firms that are in the industry want to exit and no firms that are not in the industry want to enter. An industry that is in short-run equilibrium will not be in long-run equilibrium if some firms are making losses. If firms are not making enough revenue to cover both variable costs and fixed costs, then in the long run some will go out of business as their leases expire and their equipment wears out. An industry that is in short-run equilibrium with firms making very high profits will also not be in long-run equilibrium. If firms are making more than enough to cover both their variable costs and their fixed costs, new firms will be attracted into the industry. Thus, for an industry to be in long-run equilibrium, firms that are in business must not be losing money, and no new firm can be able to make money by joining the industry.

If all of this sounds a little confusing, you will probably find that things are cleared up by looking at an example based on our restaurant experiment.

Short and Long-Run Equilibrium Example

Suppose that there are 32 persons in the market and that the distribution of Buyer Values is as in Table D8.1, below.

Table D8.1: Distribution of Customer Types

Buyer Value	Number of Buyers
24	8
18	8
12	8
8	8

As in our restaurant experiment, each restaurant that opens must pay an overhead cost of $20, each has a capacity of four customers, and each has variable costs of $5 per meal served. The short-run supply curve is determined in Stage 1 of the round by decisions of market participants about whether to open restaurants. The short run lasts one round, and the long run is represented by an entire session of rounds.

In the first round of trading, potential restaurant owners have little information about the demand schedule. It could easily happen that too many restaurants open, so that in short-run competitive equilibrium, many of them lose money. We are going to look at just such a case here. Suppose that in Stage 1, seven people decide to open restaurants. Let us see what would happen in short-run equilibrium.

Short-Run Equilibrium with Excess Capacity and Losses

In the short run, all of the restaurants that have entered the industry must pay overhead costs, no matter how many meals they sell. Since there is nothing a restaurant can do to alter its fixed costs in the short run, it should ignore these costs in deciding how much to supply. It is only the variable costs that determine the lowest price at which a firm is willing to sell a meal. Therefore, overhead costs do not affect the number of meals supplied, or the supply curve, for the short run. The only costs that affect supply in the short run are the variable costs.

The short-run supply and demand curves are drawn in Figure D8.1. At any price above $5, a restaurant gets more than enough to cover variable costs and therefore is willing to sell four meals; at a price of exactly $5, restaurants are just indifferent between selling and not selling; and at a price below $5, restaurants are unwilling to sell any meals. Since 7 restaurants have opened, 28 meals are served at any price above $5. From Figure D8.1, we see that the short-run equilibrium price is $8 a meal, and the number of meals sold is 28. At a price of $8, each firm's revenue ($8 × 4 = $32) exceeds its variable costs ($5 × $4 = $20) by $12, so it is earning $12 towards covering its overhead costs.

Figure D8.1: Short Run with Excess Capacity

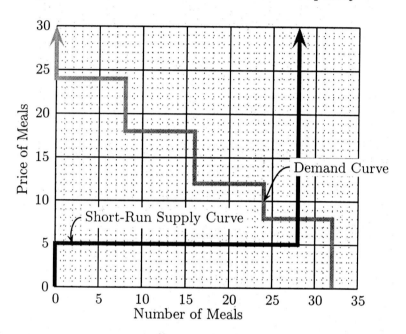

Although the firm should only consider variable costs when deciding how much to produce, we must remember that to calculate a firm's profit, we have to subtract total costs, including fixed costs, from revenue. When fixed cost is $20 and variable cost is $5 per unit, the total cost of producing 4 units is $20 + (5 × 4) = $40. Total cost ($40) exceeds total revenue ($32) by $8, so at this short-run equilibrium each firm in the industry loses $8. (Another way to describe this loss is to say that the $12 excess of revenue over variable cost falls $8 short of covering the $20 fixed cost.) Although each restaurant owner regrets her decision to open, this is the best she can do. For example if she sold no meals, a restaurant owner's revenue and her variable costs would both be 0, but since she still has to pay $20 in fixed costs, she would suffer a loss of $20 rather than just $8.

This outcome would not persist through many rounds of the experiment. In the long run, enough firms would drop out of the business so that the remaining firms would no longer have to operate at a loss.

Short-Run Equilibrium with "Short Capacity" and Profits

Since potential restaurant owners do not have good information about the demand schedule in the first round, it could just as easily happen that too few restaurants open as too many. In this case, those who open restaurants would make positive profits in the short run. Suppose that in Stage 1, five people decide to open restaurants.

Since there are 5 open restaurants, at any price above $5, the number of meals supplied is 20. The supply curve is as shown in Figure D8.2. In this case, the short-run supply curve crosses the short-run demand curve where the price of a meal is $12 and the number of meals sold is 20. Total revenue of each restaurant is $4 \times \$12 = \$48$. Total costs of each restaurant are $\$20 + (4 \times \$5) = \$40$. Restaurant revenue more than covers both variable and fixed costs. Each restaurant is making profits of $8.

Figure D8.2: Short-Run Supply and Demand for Meals

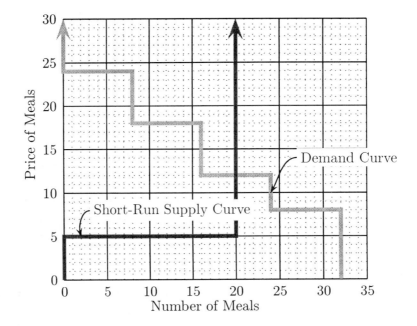

In the long run, these profits are likely to attract additional entrants to the industry. As we will show, there is room for one more person to open a restaurant and make a profit (or at least not lose money). Therefore, this short-run equilibrium is not a long-run equilibrium.

A Long-Run Equilibrium

Suppose that 6 firms enter the industry. Then at any price higher than $5, the quantity supplied is 24. The supply and demand curves in this case are illustrated in Figure D8.3 . The supply curve and the demand curve coincide on the interval where the quantity is 24 and the price is in the range from $8 to $12.

We claim that an outcome where the industry has 6 restaurants and where the price is anywhere between $10 and $12 is a long-run equilibrium. At a price of $10, restaurants have total profits of $(\$10 \times 4) - (\$20 + \$5 \times 4) = \$0$. At any price below $10, firms would make too little money per meal to cover their total costs. At $12, restaurants have total profits of $8. At any price higher than $12, firms would not be able to sell enough meals to break even.

At prices between $10 and $12, everyone who has opened a restaurant makes a profit or at least breaks even, so none of the restaurants will go out of business. You have already seen that if a seventh were to open, all restaurants would lose money, so no new entrants will be lured by potential profits.[1]

We could have found a long-run equilibrium price without going to the trouble of drawing all of these short-run supply and demand curves, by using the following reasoning. In long-run equilibrium, firms must not be losing money. Therefore the price must be at least as great as the **average cost of production**. A firm's average cost is its cost per unit output including both variable and fixed costs. To calculate a firm's average cost, divide its total costs by its number of units output.

In long-run equilibrium, all firms must all be operating in such a way as to minimize their average cost. In this example, a restaurant minimizes its average cost by operating at full capacity and selling 4 meals. When a restaurant sells 4 meals, it has total costs of $20 + (4 \times 5) = \$40$. Its average costs are $10, and so the long-run equilibrium price must be at least $10. If the price is exactly $10, then none of the people who opened restaurants have any reason to drop out and none of the people who did not open restaurants would profit from entering the industry. Therefore $10 (the average cost per unit of output when operating at full capacity) is a

---

[1]Some economists would argue that the only long-run equilibrium price is the zero-profit price of $10, since any price greater than $10 would lure other firms into the industry. But, if a seventh firm entered the industry, each firm would still need to sell all four meals to make a profit, and so together firms would sell more than twenty meals. For demanders to buy more than 20 meals, the price would have to drop to $8, which would drive the revenue of all firms below their total costs, and cause all entrants to lose money.

Figure D8.3: Short-Run Supply and Demand for Meals

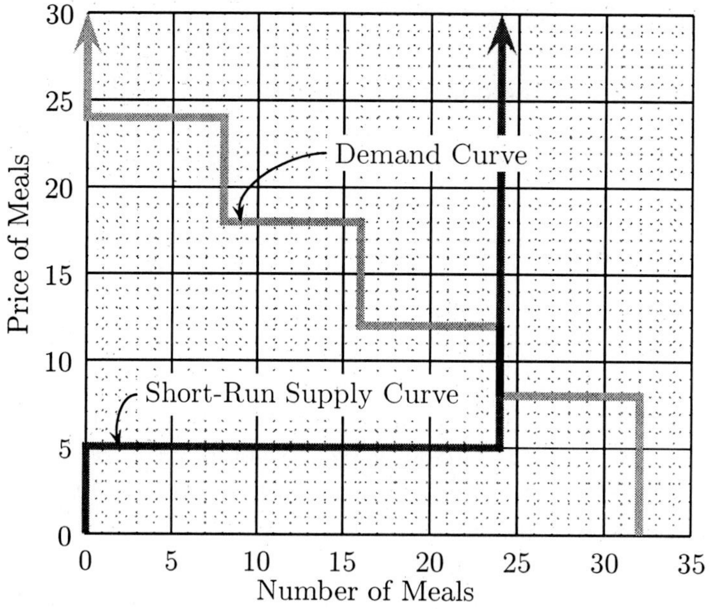

long-run equilibrium price. Long-run equilibrium might also be sustained at prices slightly higher than $10, but if the price rose much higher, new entrants would be attracted by the profits being made.

NAME _____

Home Work–Experiment 8

Short-Run Competitive Equilibrium–Session 1

In each round of Session 1, participants have to decide whether to open a restaurant before they know the prices at which they can sell. The only restaurants that can sell meals in this round are those who initially chose to enter the market. These firms must pay their fixed costs, no matter how many meals they sell. The **short-run supply curve** in any round is the supply curve that applies when the only firms that can produce are those that have already entered the market.

A **short-run competitive equilibrium** for any round of the experiment is the intersection of the short-run supply curve with the demand curve. In short-run competitive equilibrium, if the number of firms in the industry is small all firms will make profit, and if the number of firms is too large, all firms will make losses.

■ In the first round of Session 1, _____ restaurants were opened. On Figure H8.1 use a dashed red line to show the short-run supply curve in the first round of Session 1.

■ In the last round of Session 1, _____ restaurants were opened. On Figure H8.1 use a solid red line to show the short-run supply curve in the last round of Session 1. (Your short-run curves for the first and last round will overlap at least part of the way.)

■ On Figure H8.1, draw the demand curve for restaurant meals and mark the short-run competitive equilibrium prices and quantities for the first and last rounds of Session 1.

■ For round 1 of Session 1, the short-run competitive equilibrium price

was _____. At this price, each restaurant that entered the market

would make a profit (loss) of _____.

■ For the last round of Session 1, the short-run competitive equilibrium price was _____. At this price, each restaurant that entered the market would make a profit (loss) of _____.

Figure H8.1: Short-Run Supply and Demand–Session 1

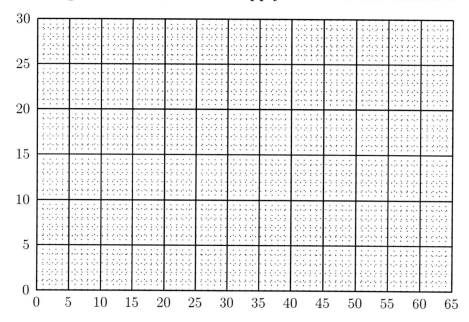

■ Fill out Table H8.1 to compare the actual outcomes in the first and last round of Session 1 with short-run and long-run competitive equilibrium.

Table H8.1: Comparing Theory and Experiment–Session 1

	Average Price	Std Dev of Prices	Number of Meals Sold	Restaurants' Total Profits
R1–Actual Outcome				
R1–Short-Run Equilibrium				
Last Rd–Actual Outcome				
Last Rd–Short-Run Equil.				
Long-Run Equilibrium				

■ Was the outcome in the last round of Session 1 closer to a long-run equilibrium than the outcome of the first round? If so, explain why you think this happened.

_____

_____

_____

Short-Run Competitive Equilibrium–Session 2

■ In the first round of Session 2, _____ restaurants were opened and

in the last round of Session 2, _____ restaurants were opened.

Figure H8.2: Short-Run Supply and Demand–Session 2

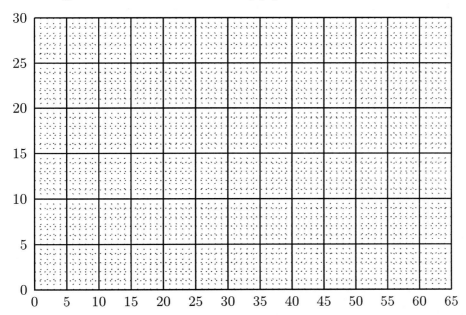

■ On Figure H8.2, draw the short-run supply curve for restaurant meals in Round 1 with a dashed red line, and draw the short-run supply curve for restaurant meals in Round 2 with a solid red line. On the same figure, draw the demand curve for restaurant meals with a green line.

■ In round 1 of Session 2, the short-run competitive equilibrium price is

_____. At this price, each restaurant that entered the market would

make a profit (loss) of _____.

■ In round 2 of Session 2, the short-run competitive equilibrium price is

_____. At this price, each restaurant that entered the market would

make a profit (loss) of _____.

■ Fill out Table H8.2 to compare the actual outcomes in the first and last round of Session 2 with short-run and long-run competitive equilibrium.

Table H8.2: Comparing Theory and Experiment–Session 2

	Average Price	Std Dev of Prices	Number of Meals Sold	Restaurants' Total Profits
R1–Actual Outcome				
R1–Short-Run Equilibrium				
Last Rd–Actual Outcome				
Last Rd–Short-Run Equil.				
Long-Run Equilibrium				

■ Was the outcome in the last round of Session 2 closer to a long-run equilibrium than was the outcome of the first round? If so, explain why you think this happened.

_____

_____

_____

■   What effect does the sales tax have on the long-run equilibrium price?

_____

■   From the experimental results, compare the average price per meal in
the last round of Session 2 with the average price per meal in the last round
of Session 1.

_____

Experiment 9

Measuring Productivity

Paper Airplane Factories

In this experiment, you will make and fly paper airplanes.[1] You will produce
the airplanes in a work group, or **firm.** There will be a series of experiments
in which we measure the effect on output of variations in the number of
workers in a firm. The experiment also illustrates the notions of gains from
specialization of labor, congestion at a work site, and learning-by-doing in
production processes.

There will be no money or grade rewards for performance in this experiment (but lots of glory, if you like glory).

Instructions

Each firm has fixed inputs, consisting of one worktable, one red pen, and one
company truck (a manila folder used to transport unfolded sheets of paper).
From session to session we will vary the amount of labor used. Firms will
be allowed to use as many sheets of paper as they like, but the amount of
fixed inputs will remain unchanged.

In the first session of the experiment, firms each have 5 workers. A
"quality control inspector" (not a member of the firm) will be appointed to
observe the output of each firm and count the number of finished airplanes it
produces. Each firm gets 4 minutes to discuss its organizational plans. Then
production begins. Firms will then be given 3 minutes in which to produce
as many finished airplanes as possible. Members of the most productive firm

---

[1]This experiment was originally developed by Janet Gerson of the University of Michigan. We are grateful to her for sharing her experience.

will be warmly congratulated. The market manager will then calculate the average output of each of the 5-member teams and write the results on the blackboard.

In the second session of the experiment, each firm will have 10 workers. Each firm again gets 4 minutes to organize and 3 minutes to produce. There is a quality-control inspector for each firm, who will report the number of satisfactorily completed planes produced. The market manager will calculate the average product of each of the 10-worker firms and record these average products on the blackboard.

In subsequent sessions, the same exercise will be conducted with firms consisting of 15 workers, and 20 workers.

Product Specifications

A finished paper airplane must meet the following specifications.

- Take an ordinary sheet of paper and tear it once vertically and once horizontally, to make four small sheets of equal size. Planes will be made from these small sheets.

- Each plane must be folded in the way described on the attached instructions.

- The words "Econ Glider" must be written on the underside of each wing, using the company pen. No other pen can be used for this purpose.

- When the above steps are completed, the plane must be given a test flight in the designated test flight area.

- After testing, the plane must be put in a wastebasket designated as the shipping container.

Production Rules

All airplanes that a firm produces must be folded on the firm's worktable. Each sheet of paper used to make an airplane must be obtained from the Stock Clerk by one of the workers, using the company truck. The company truck holds one sheet of paper at a time. The quality-control inspector will count an airplane as finished only if it is produced according to the above specifications, test-flown, and placed in the shipping container. "Goods-in-process" that are not finished at the end of 3 minutes do not count at all.

Warm-up Exercise

■ To prepare for this experiment, you should train yourself to become a (semi)-skilled model airplane fabricator. Follow the instructions listed above as *Product Specification*. Make at least one or two airplanes for practice.[2]

What Do You Expect to See?

■ Would you expect that a firm with 10 workers, working according to the rules of this experiment could produce more than twice as many, less than twice as many, or just about twice as many airplanes as a firm with 5

workers? _____

■ Would you expect that a firm with 20 workers, working according to the rules of this experiment could produce more than twice as many, less than twice as many, or just about twice as many airplanes as a firm with 10

workers? _____

■ What do you think will happen to the average number of planes produced per worker as the number of workers gets large, assuming that a firm can have only one pen, one workbench, and one company truck.

---

[2]Warning! The tips of these airplanes can be sharp. Do not throw them at university administrators or other inflatable objects.

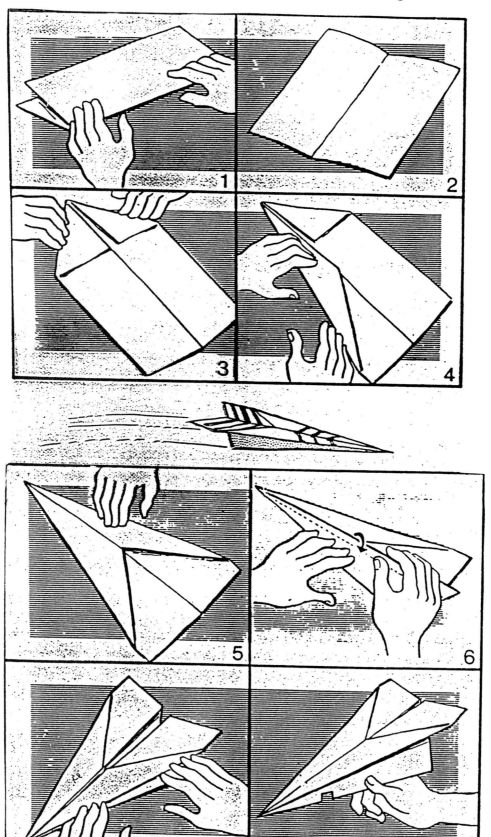

NAME _____

Lab Report–Experiment 9

Production Records

■ For the session with five-worker firms, complete Table L9.1, using the information gathered in the experiment on the output of each of the 5-person firms in a three minute interval.

Table L9.1: Outputs of Five-Worker Firms

	Number of Planes		Number of Planes
Firm 1		Firm 6	
Firm 2		Firm 7	
Firm 3		Firm 8	
Firm 4		Firm 9	
Firm 5		Firm 10	

■ The average number of planes produced by five-worker firms was _____

_____.

- For the session with ten-worker firms, complete Table L9.2.

Table L9.2: Outputs of Ten-Worker Firms

	Number of Planes
Firm 1	
Firm 2	
Firm 3	
Firm 4	
Firm 5	
Average	

- For the session with fifteen-worker firms, complete Table L9.3.

Table L9.3: Outputs of Fifteen-Worker Firms

	Number of Planes
Firm 1	
Firm 2	
Firm 3	
Firm 4	
Average	

- For the session with twenty-worker firms, complete Table L9.4.

Table L9.4: Outputs of Twenty-Worker Firms

	Number of Planes
Firm 1	
Firm 2	
Firm 3	
Average	

Discussion D9

Measuring Productivity

Inputs and Output

Typically a firm will use **labor**, **capital goods**, and **raw materials** as inputs into its production process. A firm's capital goods are the durable assets that it uses in production. These often include a building, tools, machinery, and any other physical inputs that are not used up by the process of production. A firm's raw materials are the materials used up in production. In this experiment, a firm's capital goods include its workspace, the company pen, and the company truck. The raw materials are the sheets of paper made into airplanes. In this experiment, the amount of capital goods is held constant as the amount of labor and raw materials used is varied.

Using the data from this experiment we can measure the **total output**, **average product of labor**, and **marginal product of labor** for each firm, and we can observe the way that these quantities change as the number of laborers per firm is varied.

The average product of labor in a firm is obtained by dividing the number of completed airplanes by the number of workers. For sessions in which more than one firm is producing, we can calculate the average output per worker in the average firm, by calculating the average product of labor in each firm and then calculating the average of these average products.

The marginal product of labor for a firm is defined to be the extra output that the firm gets for adding one extra worker. The marginal product of the first worker that a firm hires is the difference between the firm's output with 1 worker and its output with 0 workers. Thus the marginal product of the first worker is the same as the average product of the first worker. The marginal product of the second worker, however, is not necessarily the same as the average product of the first and second workers. The average product is the total output of both workers divided by two, while the marginal product of the second worker is the difference between the firm's output with two workers and its output with one worker.

Instead of increasing the size of a group by one worker at a time, our experimental design increases the size of a group by five workers at a time. Adding workers in larger increments averages out variations due to differences in workers' skill levels, and also makes it possible to complete our experiment in a reasonable amount of time. Because we proceed by increments greater than 1, we have to adapt the standard definition of marginal productivity. By definition, marginal productivity is the extra output that one firm with a given number of workers gets from adding one more worker (of average skill). What we will calculate is the extra output per worker that we get by adding 4 or 5 workers at a time. For example, if a group with 15 workers produces 45 airplanes and a group with 20 workers produces 55 airplanes, then the additional 5 workers increases output by 10 units. Our measure of the marginal product per additional worker when there are 15 workers is (55-45)/5=2.

NAME _____

Home Work–Experiment 9

Average Product and Marginal Product

■ In the first line of Table H9.1, use the information from your lab report to fill in the average number of planes built by firms with 5, 10, 15, and 20 workers.

■ Fill in the second line of Table H9.1 by calculating the average product of labor for each firm of a given size and then calculating the average of these average products of labor for all firms of that size.

■ Fill in the third line of Table H9.1 by calculating an estimate of the marginal product of labor for firms of each size by the method described in the discussion section above. (Average your estimates of marginal product across all firms of the appropriate size)

Table H9.1: Number of Workers and Output

Number of Workers	5	10	15	20
(Average) Output Per Firm				
Average Product of Labor				
Marginal Product of Labor				

■ Which group sizes, if any, had greater average output per worker than the average output of a firm with one worker?

_____

■ As output increases, how does average product change?

_____

■   As output increases, how does marginal product change?

_____

■   Why do you think that average product fell (or, if it didn't in your experiment, why might it have fallen) when the firms got very large?

_____

_____

_____

■   Estimate the total amount of output that one firm could produce using the same plant and equipment that all of our firms had, but with an additional 200 workers? 500 workers?

_____

■   With the largest group that we tried, how large do you think output would have been had the group been provided with two worktables, two company pens, and two company trucks? Explain.

_____

_____

_____

Specialization and Learning by Doing

■ Give some examples of the division of labor and the specialization of tasks that you observed during the market experiment.

_____

_____

_____

■ You were given only a short time for organizing the work groups or practicing. What do you think would have happened to productivity if these groups continued to work together for several sessions of 3 minutes?

_____

_____

_____

■ Did someone in your firm become a leader, or firm manager? If your firm did, was this helpful? If not, would stronger leadership have helped?

_____

_____

_____

■ You may have noticed some variation in the skill levels of the workers. In an industry where firm managers get to pick workers, the best workers might be hired first. How would this affect marginal productivity as more workers are added?

_____

_____

_____

■   In the later rounds of airplane building, people will have more experience than they had in the earlier rounds. How could this effect lead to misleading results? How might you improve the experimental design so as to better separate learning-by-doing effects from the effects of the size of the firm on output?

_____

_____

_____

_____

_____

_____

Experiment 10

Comparative Advantage and Trade

Two Island Economies

If you get a very large World Atlas, and stare very carefully with a high-quality magnifying glass, you may be able to spot the outline of Ricardo Island, a speck in the mid-Atlantic. Ricardo Island is divided between two countries, Richland, on the north end of the island, and Poorland, on the south. Poorland has twice as many people as Richland.

Inhabitants of Ricardo Island produce and consume only two goods, bread and fish. Every islander insists on consuming bread and fish in fixed proportions–one unit of bread for every unit of fish. In any round of trading, the payoff to an islander is $10 times the *minimum* of the number of units of fish and the number of units of bread that he or she acquired in that round. For example, consider an islander who has 7 units of fish and 4 units of bread at the end of trading. Since the minimum of 7 and 4 is 4, she will get a payoff of $10 \times 4 = 40.

Everyone who lives on the island has 20 hours of labor time which can be divided between producing fish and producing bread. In Richland, it takes a person 1 hour to produce a unit of fish and 1.5 hours to produce a unit of bread. In Poorland, life is harder. It takes 3 hours to produce a unit of fish and 2 hours to produce a unit of bread.

Session 1–Economies without Trade

In the first session of this experiment, there is no trade, either within or between countries. The amounts of bread and fish that each individual holds at the end of the session are the amounts that he or she produced. As a participant in the experiment, you will be asked to choose an allocation of your 20 hours of time between producing fish and producing bread, then to write your decisions on a slip of paper, along with your ID number and turn it in to the market manager.

You should prepare for this session by working out the best strategy for inhabitants of each country before you come to class. After the slips have been turned in, we will discuss the best allocations of time in each country and the resulting payoffs.

Session 2–Free Trade Between Countries

In this session, it is possible for anyone in either country to make trades with anyone in the other country.

In this session, you must decide how to allocate your 20 hours of time between producing fish and bread. Before you make your decision about what to produce, you may want to look around for possible trading partners and discuss the terms at which you would trade. When you have decided on your time allocation, go to the market manager, who will give you fish tickets and/or bread tickets, representing the number of units of fish and bread that you produced. To simplify trading, the market manager will not give you tickets for fractional units of bread or fish, but will round down to the next smaller whole number of units.

After you have received your fish and bread tickets, you can make trades with anyone living in either country. To make a trade, simply exchange tickets with someone who is willing to make a deal with you. Trade in fractional tickets is not allowed, but fractional "prices" can be achieved by, for example, trading 2 units of fish for 1 unit of bread, or 2 units of fish for 3 units of bread.

When you have completed trading, record the number of units of fish and of bread that you are left with, and compute your payoff. Recall that your payoff is $10 times the minimum of the number of units of fish and the number of units of bread that you have at the end of trading. When trading has ceased, the market manager will survey the group to determine whether there is anyone who still has extra units of fish that are not matched by units of bread, or extra units of bread that are not matched by units of fish. We will also explore the patterns of specialization in each country and discuss the profitability of alternative decisions on the allocation of time between producing bread and fish.

When the first round is completed, we will conduct a second round of Session 2. (Tickets acquired in the first round are of no use in the second round and should be discarded.) Once again, you must decide how to allocate time between producing fish and producing bread, and when you receive your tickets you can trade them with anyone willing to trade. When you have finished trading, calculate your payoff for this round. If the market manager declares this to be the last round of the session, staple the tickets that you hold at the end of trading to your scoresheet, record your final holdings and your payoff for this round on your scoresheet, and turn in the scoresheet and tickets to the market manager.

Warm-up Exercise

■ If you live in Richland, how many hours would it take you to produce 6 units of bread and 11 units of fish?_____ If you live in Poorland, how many hours would it take you to produce 4 units of bread and 3 units of fish?_____

■ If you live in Richland, how many hours would it take you to produce B units of bread and F units of fish?_____

■ If you live in Poorland, how many hours would it take you to produce B units of bread and F units of fish?_____

■ Write an equation, involving the variables B and F, that states that it is possible for a Richlander to produce B units of bread and F units of fish in 20 hours. _____

■ Write an equation, involving the variables B and F, that states that it is possible for a Poorlander to produce B units of bread and F units of fish in 20 hours. _____

■ If you are a Richlander, you can produce any combination of B and F such that $1.5B + F = 20$. If you can not make any trades, explain why, in order to get the largest payoff, you should choose B and F so that $1.5B + F = 20$ and $B = F$.

_____

_____

_____

_____

■ Find the amounts of B and F that a Richlander who cannot trade should produce in order to maximize payoff.

_____

■ Find the amounts of B and F that a Poorlander who cannot trade should produce in order to maximize payoff.

_____

What Do You Expect to See?

■ Since the inhabitants of Poorland are less productive with both goods than the inhabitants of Richland, can they possibly gain anything by trading with Richlanders? Explain.

_____

_____

_____

■   Do you think that if there is free trade with Richland, Poorlanders will be made even poorer by trading with Richland?

_____

■   Do you think that the citizens of Richland are likely to be impoverished by trading with the low-wage country, Poorland?

_____

NAME _____

Lab Report–Experiment 10

An Economy without Trade

■ Suppose that there is no trade either within or between countries. In order to maximize her payoff, a Richlander should produce _____ units of bread and _____ units of fish. In order to maximize his payoff, a Poorlander should produce _____ units of bread and _____ units of fish.

■ Suppose that everyone produced the quantities that maximize their payoffs in the absence of trade, and suppose that on Ricardo Island trading is permitted between people who live in the same country but not between people living in different countries. Would any two people living in the same country benefit by trading with each other? _____

■ When there is no international trade, the highest payoff that a Richlander can achieve is _____, and the highest payoff that a Poorlander can achieve is _____

■ When there is no international trade and people choose their output so as to maximize their payoffs, Richlanders will produce (more fish than bread, more bread than fish, or the same amount of bread as fish) _____ and Poorlanders will produce (more fish than bread, more bread than fish, or the same amount of bread as fish)?_____

Economies with Free Trade

■   In Tables L10.1 and L10.2, for the last round of Session 2, record for
each inhabitant of Richland and Poorland respectively, the number of units
of fish and bread produced and the final holdings of fish and bread after
trade. Calculate each Richlander's payoff as the minimum of his or her final
holdings of bread and final holdings of fish.

Table L10.1: Output and Payoffs in Richland

ID	Fish Produced	Bread Produced	Final Fish Holdings	Final Bread Holdings	Payoff

Table L10.2: Output and Payoffs in Poorland

ID	Fish Produced	Bread Produced	Final Fish Holdings	Final Bread Holdings	Payoff

■   In Table L10.3, record the average payoffs that Richlanders and Poor-landers received in Session 2 with free trade, and the largest payoff they could receive in Session 1 when there is no international trade.

Table L10.3: Payoffs With and Without Trade

	Average Payoff with Free Trade	Maximum Payoff with No Trade
Richlanders		
Poorlanders		

■   Is free trade better or worse than no trade for citizens of Richland?

_____ for citizens of Poorland? _____

■   In Table L10.4, record the total amount of bread and of fish produced and consumed in Richland and in Poorland. (The amount consumed is the amount that people have at the end of trading.)

Table L10.4: Production and Consumption

	Bread Produced	Bread Consumed	Fish Produced	Fish Consumed
Richland				
Poorland				

Table L10.5: Exports and Imports

	Bread Imported	Bread Exported	Fish Imported	Fish Exported
Richland				
Poorland				

■   If a country consumes more of a good than it produces, then the difference between its consumption and its production is its **imports**. If a country produces more of a good than it consumes, then the difference between its production and its consumption is its **exports**.   Record the amount of goods exported or imported from each country in Table L10.5.

■ Which country exports bread and imports fish?_____ Which coun-

try imports bread and exports fish? _____

■ If the bread-exporting country exported twice as much bread as the
amount of fish it imported, we would say that the average price of a unit of
fish was 2 units of bread. More generally, the average price of fish relative to
bread is the ratio of the number of units of bread exported to the number of
units of fish imported by the country that exports bread and imports fish.
In this experiment, what was the average price of fish relative to bread?

_____

■ Suppose that a citizen of Richland can either produce her own bread or
can get bread in a roundabout way by producing fish and then trading for
bread at a price of 1 unit of bread for a unit of fish. Would it be better for
the Richlander to produce her own bread or to specialize in fish and then
trade? Explain.

_____

_____

_____

■ Who can produce more bread in an hour, a Richlander or a Poorlander?

_____ Which country produces bread when there is free international

trade? _____ Does this mean that free international trade is inefficient? Explain.

_____

_____

_____

■   What do you think determines which country will specialize in fish and which will specialize in bread when there is free international trade?

_____

_____

_____

Discussion D10

Comparative Advantage and Specialization

"It is the maxim of every prudent master of a family, never to attempt to make at home what it will cost him more to make than to buy.... What is prudence in the conduct of every private family, can scarce be folly in that of a great kingdom. If a foreign country can supply us with a commodity cheaper than we ourselves can make it, better to buy it of them with some part of the produce of our own industry, employed in a way in which we have some advantage.... By means of glasses, hotbeds and hot-walls, very good grapes can be raised in Scotland, and very good wine can be made of them at about thirty times the expense for which equally good can be bought from foreign countries. Would it be a reasonable law to prohibit the importation of all foreign wines merely to encourage the making of claret and burgundy in Scotland?" (Adam Smith, *The Wealth of Nations*, Book IV, Chap. II).

The Free-Trade Debate

In his elegant, eighteenth-century prose, Adam Smith, the founder of modern economics, explained the principle whereby individuals or nations with differing abilities can gain by specialization and trade. This idea has been a centerpiece of economic thinking ever since. Indeed, the design for this experimental market is borrowed from an example in a book published in

1817 by the English economist, David Ricardo, *Principles of Political Economy and Taxation*. Ricardo called his two countries England and Portugal, and his commodities were wine and cloth.[1]

Adam Smith and David Ricardo were active participants in a national debate over English trade policy. Smith and Ricardo favored elimination of existing high tariffs on the importation of grain to England. Their arguments did not prevail during their lifetimes. However, in 1846, the British government repealed the Corn Laws and over the next few years, removed most of England's tariffs on imported goods. This enabled England to specialize in manufactured goods and to import cheap food from abroad.

Most present-day economists favor free international trade, for essentially the reason that Smith and Ricardo proposed, the benefits from specialization according to comparative advantage. Anyone who reads the newspapers or listens to political debates will be aware that economists' way of thinking about these matters has not won universal agreement. One of several semi-popular books espousing a contrary view is *The New Protectionism*, by Tim Lang and Colin Hines, who advocate restricting global free trade in favor of greater "regional self-sufficiency."

> "Trade liberalization hopes to bring more trade, yet more international trade brings more of the problems the world needs less of: threats to the environment, uneven spread of unemployment, and widening gaps between rich and poor, both within societies and between societies." (page 3)

> "Thus, the basic thesis of free trade is that instead of being self-sufficient, each one should specialize and produce what it is best at and can produce most cheaply, i. e. the things in which it has a 'comparative advantage' ... This theory runs into difficulty where one country can produce products more cheaply than others, and has no incentive to trade, or where a country has little or no comparative advantage in anything." (page 21)

Of course, our experimental trading economy, which was designed to illustrate the principle of comparative advantage, is far simpler than any modern economy. While this experiment suggests a strong, mutually-beneficial force exerted by free international trade, it is certainly possible that the simplifications made cause us to overlook harmful side-effects of trade. A large

---

[1]Ricardo's contemporary, Robert Torrens, observed that in Ricardo's example, international trade would be mutually beneficial even if one of the two countries were better at producing *both* goods.

literature in economics is devoted to more general and realistic approaches to the question of the benefits and costs of international trade.

Production Possibilities and Trade

Individual and Production Possibility Sets

The set of output combinations that a person or group can produce is known as the **production possibility set** for that person or group. In Richland, as described in our experiment, the production possibility set for a single person consists of all possible combinations of fish and bread that the person can produce in 20 hours. Recall that it takes a Richlander 1 hour to produce a unit of fish and 1.5 hours to produce a unit of bread. The amount of time required to produce F units of fish and B units of bread is therefore $F + 1.5B$ hours. In 20 hours, it would be possible to produce any combination of F units of fish and B units of bread such that $F + 1.5B = 20$. The set of combinations of goods that an individual or group can produce without wasting any output is known as the **production possibility frontier**. In Richland, this is the set of combinations F and B such that $F + 1.5B = 20$. Let us assume that a Richlander could also waste some output, in which case the production possibility set includes every output combination such that $F + 1.5B \leq 20$.

It is instructive to graph a typical Richlander's production possibility set and production possibility frontier. This is done in Figure D10.1, where the amount of bread is shown on the horizontal axis and the amount of fish on the vertical axis. The production possibility frontier consists of all of the points satisfying the equation $F + 1.5B = 20$. Recall from high school algebra that $F + 1.5B = 20$ is the equation for a straight line. To graph a straight line, you only need to find two points on the line and connect them with a straightedge. To find one point on this line, suppose that a Richlander spends all of her time producing fish and no time producing bread. Then she will have $F = 20$ units of fish and $B = 0$ units of bread. This is the point labelled A on Figure D10.1. To find another point on this line, suppose that she spends all of her time producing bread and no time producing fish. Then she will produce $B = 20/1.5 = 13.33$ units of bread and 0 units of fish. This is the point labelled B. The dark line on the graph, connecting the two points A and B, is the line with equation $F + 1.5B = 10$ and thus represents a Richlander's production possibility frontier. A Richlander's production possibility *set* consists of all $F \geq 0$ and $B \geq 0$ such that $F + 1.5B \leq 20$. This set is represented by the shaded triangle in Figure D10.1.

Figure D10.1: A Richlander's Production Possibility Set

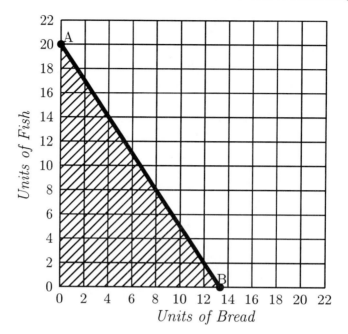

Before you read further, turn to your homework pages and do the first part of the assignment, which asks you to draw a Poorlander's production possibility frontier and production possibility set.

We can also draw a production possibility set for the whole country of Richland. Suppose, for example, that Richland has 10 inhabitants. Then for any possible output combination that one individual could produce, the entire country could produce 10 times as much of each good. Thus the national production possibility set for Richland looks like one of the individual production possibility sets, but scaled up by a factor of 10. Figure D10.2 shows the production possibility set for the country of Richland.

Let us now draw a national production possibility set for Poorland. Recall that in our experiment, Poorland has twice as many people as Richland. For this example, assume that Poorland has 20 people. Then the national production possibility set for Poorland is like the production possibility set for one Poorlander, but scaled up by a factor of 20.

Figure D10.2: Richland's National Production Possibility Set

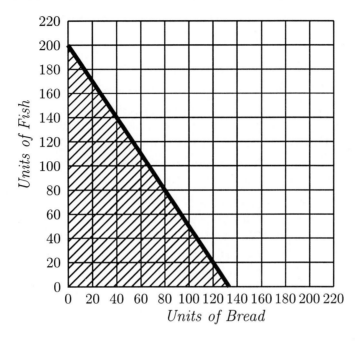

Figure D10.3: Poorland's National Production Possibility Set

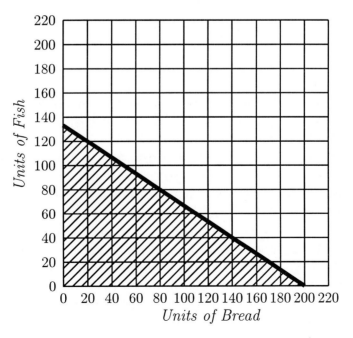

Choice of Outputs with No International Trade

Recall that when no trade is allowed, the payoff to each inhabitant of Ricardo Island is proportional to the minimum of the number of units of fish and the number of units of bread that he or she produces. Therefore, when there is no trade, each person maximizes his or her payoff by producing equal amounts of fish and bread. As you discovered in the warm-up exercise for this experiment, it is possible to find the best output for a Richlander or a Poorlander by solving two equations in two unknowns. One of these equations is the equation that describes the person's production possibility set and the other one is the equation that states that outputs of fish and bread are equal.

It is instructive to find this solution geometrically. Figure D10.4 displays the diagonal line with equation $F = B$ as well as the production possiblity frontiers for Richland and Poorland. A Richlander's production possibility frontier intersects the line $F = B$ at the point $(8, 8)$, which we have labelled R, and a Poorlander's production possibility frontier intersects the line $F = B$ at the point $(4, 4)$, which we have labelled P. Thus in the absence of trade, a Richlander will produce 8 units of fish and 8 units of bread and receive a payoff of \$80, and a Poorlander will produce 4 units of fish and 4 units of bread and receive a payoff of \$40.

Absolute and Comparative Advantage

In our experiment, it takes a Richlander an hour to produce a unit of fish and 1.5 hours to produce a unit of bread, and it takes a Poorlander 3 hours to produce a unit of fish and 2 hours to produce a unit of bread. A Richlander can produce more of either good in an hour than can a Poorlander. In an hour, a Richlander can produce 3 times as many units of fish and $1\frac{1}{3}$ times as many units of bread as a Poorlander. Although in absolute terms, Richlanders are better at producing both goods, their advantage in producing fish is greater than their advantage in producing bread. It is useful to define some terms that express these differences in a clearcut way.

A person's **productivity** in producing a good is the number of units of the good that she can produce per unit of time. Person 1 is said to have **absolute advantage** over Person 2 in the production of a good if she has higher productivity than person 2 in producing that good. In an economy with two goods, A and B, Person 1 is said to have **comparative advantage** in Good A if the ratio of Person 1's productivity in producing Good A to

Figure D10.4: Consumption and Production

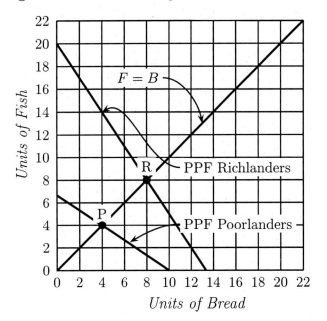

her productivity in producing Good B is greater than the ratio of Person 2's productivity in producing Good A to Person 2's productivity in producing Good B. If Person 1 has comparative advantage in Good A, then it follows from simple algebra that Person 2 has comparative advantage in Good B. Thus we see that even if one person has *absolute* advantage over another in all goods, it is impossible for one person to have *comparative* advantage over another in all goods.

Example:

> In our experiment, the productivity of a Poorlander in producing fish is 1/3 and in producing bread is 1/2. The productivity of a Richlander is 1 in producing fish and $1/1.5 = 2/3$ in producing bread. Richlanders, therefore, have absolute advantage in the production of both fish and bread. The ratio of a Richlander's productivity in producing *fish* to her productivity in producing *bread* is $1/(2/3) = 3/2$. The ratio of a Poorlander's productivity in producing *fish* to his productivity in producing *bread* is $(1/3)/(1/2) = 2/3$. Since $3/2 > 2/3$, we see that a Richlander has comparative advantage over a Poorlander in producing fish. The ratio of a Richlander's productivity in producing *bread* to her productivity in producing *fish* is $(2/3)/1 = 2/3$. The ratio of a Poorlander's productivity in producing *bread* to his productivity in producing *fish* is $(1/2)/(1/3) = 3/2$. Since $2/3 < 3/2$, we see that a Poorlander has comparative advantage over a Richlander in producing bread.

International Production Possibility Set

We have drawn production possibility sets, both for individuals and for the countries of Richland and Poorland. When international trade is allowed, it is useful to study the **international production possibility set** that depicts possible combinations of total outputs of fish and bread for all of Ricardo Island. This production possibility set will be drawn on Figure D10.5 below.

To draw the international production possibility set, let us first find the greatest amount of bread that could be produced in the two countries if no fish were produced. If everyone specialized in bread and produced no fish, each Richlander could produce $20/1.5 = 13.33$ units of bread and each Poorlander could produce $20/2 = 10$ units of bread. We have assumed that there are 10 Richlanders and 20 Poorlanders. Therefore, if everyone specializes in bread, total output will be $10 \times 13.33 + 20 \times 10 = 333.3$ units of bread and 0 units of fish. Therefore the point $(333.3, 0)$ is on the international production possibility frontier. This point is labelled B.

Figure D10.5: International Production Possibility Set

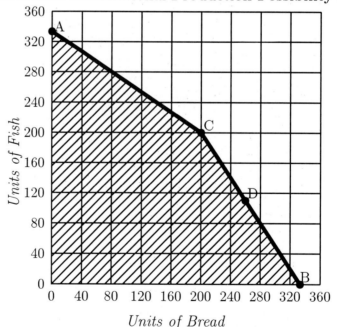

Next let us find the greatest amount of fish that could be produced if everyone specialized in fish. Each Richlander could produce $20/1 = 20$ units of fish and each Poorlander could produce $20/3 = 6.66$ units of fish. The total output of fish would therefore be $10 \times 20 + 20 \times 6.66 = 333.3$. The point $(0, 333.3)$ on the utility possibility frontier is labelled A.

Now let us find output combinations where some of each good is produced. If everyone specializes according to comparative advantage, then Richlanders will spend all their time producing fish and Poorlanders will spend all of their time producing bread. Each Richlander would produce 20 units of fish and no bread, and each Poorlander would produce 10 units of bread and no fish. Since there are 10 Richlanders and 20 Poorlanders, total production of fish would be $10 \times 20 = 200$ and total production of bread would be $20 \times 10 = 200$. Thus the point $(200, 200)$ is also a possible output combination. We label this point C.

Output combinations along the line segment CB can be produced if all Poorlanders specialize in bread and if Richlanders divide their time between producing fish and bread. For example, suppose that Poorlanders produced only bread and that all Richlanders spend 11 hours producing fish and 9 hours producing bread. Each of the 20 Richlanders would then produce 11 units of fish and 6 units of bread. Richlanders' total output of fish would be $10 \times 11 = 110$ and their total output of bread would be $10 \times 6 = 60$. Poorlanders would produce a total 200 units of bread and no fish. This means that the total output of bread in the two countries would be $200+60 = 260$, and the total output of fish would be 110. The point $(260, 110)$ lies on the line segment CB and is labelled D. Similarly, outputs along the line segment AC can be achieved by having all Richlanders specialize in fish and having Poorlanders divide their time between producing fish and bread.

The international production possibility frontier for the two countries located on Ricardo Island turns out to be the broken line ACB. Assuming that it is always possible to waste any amount of either good, the international production possibility set is the shaded area consisting of all the points on or below ACB.

Equilibrium with Free International Trade

As in the simpler models that we studied in earlier experiments, we will look for competitive equilibrium prices, such that supply equals demand. In this experiment, we have two prices to work with, the price of bread and the price of fish, and we have to make sure that in equilibrium the quantity supplied equals the quantity demanded, both for fish and for bread.

In competitive equilibrium, individuals must make decisions both about what to produce and about what to consume. We can think of each individual making these decisions separately. First, acting as a producer, an individual decides how to allocate her time between producing bread and fish. Her income will equal the total value of the output she produces. In the second stage, as a consumer, she takes the income that she earned from production and uses it to buy the combination of bread and fish that gives her the highest payoff of all the bundles that she can afford at the competitive prices.

Let us investigate whether prices of $1 per unit of fish and $1 per unit of bread are equilibrium prices. Recall that it takes a Richlander 1 hour to produce a unit of fish and 1.5 hours to produce a unit of bread. Since it takes her longer to produce a unit of bread than a unit of fish, and since the price of bread is the same as the price of fish, she will maximize her income by spending all of her time producing fish. This means that a Richlander will produce 20 fish and earn an income of $20. It takes a Poorlander 3 hours to produce a unit of fish and 2 hours to produce a unit of bread, so he will maximize his income by spending all of his time producing bread, in which case he produces 10 units of bread and earns an income of $10. Therefore if the prices of fish and bread are both $1 per unit, each of the 10 Richlanders will produce 20 units of fish and no bread, and each of the 20 Poorlanders will produce 10 units of bread and no fish. It follows that the total supply of fish is 200 units and the total supply of bread is 200 units.

Now let us examine the demand for bread and fish at these prices. Each Richlander has an income of $20. Since her payoff is proportional to the minimum of her consumption of bread and fish, she will choose to buy equal amounts of bread and fish, and to spend her entire income. She accomplishes this by buying 10 units of fish and 10 units of bread, which will cost her a total of $20. Each Poorlander has an income of $10. Poorlanders, like Richlanders, seek to spend their entire incomes, while buying equal amounts of fish and bread. The best combination that a Poorlander can afford is 5 units of fish and 5 units of bread. Since there are 10 Richlanders and 20 Poorlanders, the total amount of fish demanded is $10 \times 10 + 20 \times 5 = 200$, and the total amount of bread demanded is $10 \times 10 + 20 \times 5 = 200$. But as we have seen, at prices of $1 for each good, the supply of each good is also 200. It follows that there is a competitive equilibrium in which the price of bread and the price of fish are both $1 per unit. At these prices, residents of each country specialize completely in the commodity in which they have comparative advantage.

Prices of $1 per unit for both goods are not the only prices at which there is a competitive equilibrium. Notice that demand and supply in this market depend only on the *ratio* of prices and not on their absolute sizes. Thus at prices of \$2 per unit for each good, there would also be a competitive equilibrium, with each Richlander and each Poorlander consuming exactly the same amount of each good as at prices of \$1 for each good.

In fact, it is possible to show that any prices p_f for fish and p_b for bread, such that $2/3 < p_f/p_b < 3/2$ will be competitive equilibrium prices. To see this, note that at all such prices, Richlanders will specialize in fish and Poorlanders will specialize in bread, so that total supplies will still be 200 units of fish and 200 units of bread. A little more work will show that at any of these prices, the total amount of fish demanded and the total amount of bread demanded will each be 200 units.

NAME _____

Home Work–Experiment 10

Production Possibilities for Poorlanders

■ The equation for a Poorlander's production possibility frontier is _____

_____ .

■ If a Poorlander spends all 20 hours producing fish and produces no bread, how many units of fish can the Poorlander produce? _____ If a Poorlander spends all 20 hours producing bread and produces no fish, how many units of bread can the Poorlander produce? _____

Figure H10.1: A Poorlander's Production Possibility Set

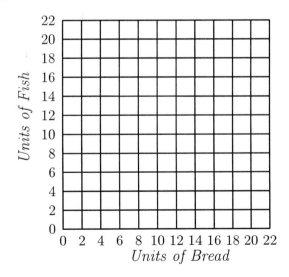

■ Draw and label the production possibility frontier for a Poorlander on Figure H10.1 and shade in the production possibility set.

Specialization and the International Production Possibility Set

Throughout this section, assume that Richland has 10 inhabitants, Poorland has 20 inhabitants, and the individual production possibility sets in Richland and Poorland are as previously described.

■ If every inhabitant of Ricardo Island produces the combination of fish and bread that maximizes his or her payoff in the absence of trade, then

each Richlander would produce _____ units of fish and _____

_____ units of bread. Each Poorlander would produce _____ units

of fish and _____ units of bread. The total amount of fish produced on

Ricardo Island would be _____ units, and the total amount of bread

produced would be _____ units.

■ On Figure H10.2, plot the point representing total outputs on Ricardo Island when there is no trade and each individual produces to maximize his or her payoff. Label this point N. Is the point N on the international

production possibility frontier?_____

■ The point C in Figure H10.2 corresponds to the output when everyone specializes according to comparative advantage; that is, Richlanders produce only fish and Poorlanders produce only bread. Suppose that instead, Richlanders produced only bread and Poorlanders produced only fish. Each

Richlander would produce _____ units of bread, and the total amount

of bread produced on Ricardo Island would be _____ units. Each

Poorlander would produce _____ units of fish, and the total amount

of fish produced on Ricardo Island would be _____ units.

Figure H10.2: International Production Possibility Set

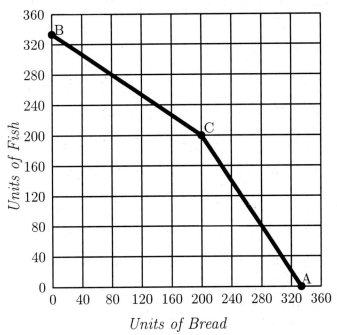

■ Plot the point on Figure H10.2 that corresponds to total output when Poorlanders specialize in fish and Richlanders specialize in bread. Label this point D. Is the point D on the international production possibility frontier?

_____

■ If Richlanders spend all of their time producing fish and if Poorlanders each spend 6 hours producing fish and 14 hours producing bread, the total

amount of fish produced on Ricardo Island will be _____ units and

the total amount of bread produced on Ricardo Island will be _____ units. Plot the point corresponding to this output combination on Figure H10.2 and label this point E. Is the point E on the international production

possibility frontier?_____

Free International Trade Versus No Trade

If it is possible for two people, by trading with each other, to achieve an outcome that is better for each of them than any outcome that either could achieve without trading, we say that **mutual gains from trade** are possible between these two people.

■   On Ricardo Island, are mutual gains from trade possible between two people who live in the same country?_____

■   On Ricardo Island, are mutual gains from trade possible between two people who live in different countries?_____

■   Why are the answers to the previous two questions different from each other?

_____

_____

_____

■   Compare the payoffs to Richlanders and Poorlanders on Ricardo Island when there is no trade and when there is free international trade with bread and fish being traded at one unit of bread per unit of fish.

_____

■   In the passage from *The New Protectionism* which was quoted previously, we found the following remark.

> "This theory (the theory of comparative advantage) runs into difficulty where one country can produce products more cheaply than others, and has no incentive to trade, or where a country has little or no comparative advantage in anything."

Comment on this assertion.

_____

_____

_____

Part V

Information, Auctions, and Bargaining

Experiment 11

Adverse Selection

A "Lemons" Market

If you have ever purchased a used car from a stranger, you probably have worried about whether she was telling you the whole truth about the car. Perhaps you thought: "The seller knows a lot more about her car than I do. If the car is any good, why does she want to sell it?"

Today's experiment simulates a used-car market. There are two kinds of used cars in the market, bad used cars (commonly known as "lemons"), and good used cars. Used-car owners sell their cars to car dealers.[1] Dealers are unable to tell the difference between good cars and lemons.[2] Sellers, on the other hand, have lived with their cars and know very well whether their car is a lemon or not.

Instructions

Used Car Owners (Suppliers)

In all sessions of this experiment, if you are a used-car owner, you will be assigned an **owner's reservation price** for your car. An owner's reservation price for an object is the smallest price that the owner would accept for the object. Thus if you are a used-car owner, you will want to keep the car unless you are offered at least your reservation price. You should be willing

---

[1] Although people usually associate car dealers with the role of sellers, in this experiment they function as buyers purchasing cars for resale.

[2] Some macho buyers may kick the tires and lift up the hood. They may even talk about fuel pumps and suspension systems, but this is all for show.

to sell to the person that makes you the highest offer that is greater than your reservation price.

Understandably, if you own a good used car, you will have a higher reservation price than if you own a lemon. In this experiment, if you own a good used car, your reservation price will be $1600. If you own a lemon, your reservation price will be $0. Regardless of which type of car you own, your profit in the experiment will be the price you get for your used car minus your reservation price.

Used-Car Dealers (Buyers)

Some people are willing to pay more for used cars than these cars are worth to their current owners. In fact, there is a large number of people who are willing to pay $500 for a car that is known to be a lemon and $3500 for a car that is known to be good. These consumers are not directly represented by participants in the experiment, but their willingness-to-pay determines the Buyer Values of the dealers. Dealers will discover the quality of each car that they buy shortly after they buy it, and they are required by law to reveal this quality to consumers. Dealers can resell good used cars for $3500 and lemons for $500 each.

Session 1–Monopolistic Used-Car Dealers

This session contains a thought experiment, in which you decide what price to offer for used cars. Before you come to class, read through these instructions. Then work the Warm-Up exercises, which will help you to understand the most profitable actions to take in this session.

Imagine that you are the only used-car dealer in town. All used-car owners in your town must either sell their used cars to you or keep them. At the time you buy a used car, you cannot tell whether it is a good used car or a lemon. However, between the time you buy the car and the time you resell it, you will find out whether the car is a lemon or a good car. You will resell all of the cars that you buy. You can resell lemons for $500 and good cars for $3500.[3] Your profits are equal to the revenue you get from reselling cars minus the total amount of money you pay for cars. You must post a price at which you are willing to purchase all used cars that are brought to you. Buyers will bring their cars to you if the price you post is higher than their reservation prices.

---

[3]In your town, used-car dealers (unlike the initial owners) are required by law to reveal the actual quality of their cars to their customers.

We consider two alternative situations. In Situation A, in your town there are six good used cars and six lemons. In Situation B, in your town there are four good cars and eight lemons. On a slip of paper, write your name or identification number, the price that you would offer for used cars in Situation A, and the price that you would offer for used cars in Situation B. We will collect your slip of paper and record the profits that you make, given your pricing decision.

Session 2–A Competitive Used-Car Market

In this session, the used-car market is competitive, and car buyers interact with sellers. Most class members are used-car owners (sellers). Half of the car owners have good used cars and half of them have lemons. If you are a used-car owner, the market manager will show you a card that tells you what kind of car you have. The market manager will not show your card to anybody else, and will not give you any document that you can use to prove what kind of car you have.

Some class members are used-car dealers. If you are a dealer, you will be given some blackboard space on which you can post the price that you are willing to pay for used cars. You can change your posted prices at any time. You can buy as many used cars as people are willing to sell to you. When you buy a car, you should record the seller's identification number on your Record of Purchases. At the time of the purchase, you do not know which cars are good and which are lemons.

At the end of trading, dealers will bring their Records of Purchases to the market manager. The market manager will calculate the average value of all used cars purchased by all dealers. You will then receive revenue equal to the number of used cars that *you* bought, times the average value of used cars purchased by *all* dealers. For example, suppose all dealers combined purchase a total of 10 good used cars and 5 lemons. The average value of these cars is

$$\frac{(\$3500 \times 10) + (\$500 \times 5)}{15} = \$2500.$$

A dealer who bought 3 used cars will receive a total revenue of $\$2500 \times 3 = \$7500$. The dealer's profits are then $7500 *minus* the total amount she paid for the 3 cars that she bought.

Session 3–A Used-Car Market with More Bad Cars

Session 3 is conducted exactly like Session 2, except that in this session, only 1/3 of the used cars are good and 2/3 of the used cars are lemons.

Session 4–Quality Certification (Optional)

In this session, half of the used cars are lemons and half of the used cars are good. Used-car owners have cards that tell whether their cars are lemons or good cars. Used-car dealers can ask to see an owner's card before buying a used car and can offer different prices to sellers depending on whether they show a card that says "good car." When a used-car owner sells a used car to the dealer, the dealer records the seller's identification number on the dealer's Record of Purchases. If the seller shows the dealer a "good car" card, the dealer marks an asterisk next to the price. If the seller shows the buyer a "lemon" card, the dealer should put two asterisks next to the price. If the seller shows no card, the dealer should put no mark by the price.

Warm-up Exercise

■ Suppose that, as in Session 1, you are a monopoly car dealer in a town where six used-car owners have good cars and six have lemons. What is the lowest price at which you could get lemon-owners to sell you their cars? ___

_____ Would the owners of good cars sell their cars at this price?

_____ What will your profit be if you offer this price? _____
(Hint: How much revenue could you get from buyers if you had six lemons for sale, but no good cars?)

■ In Session 1, what is the lowest price at which everybody, including owners of good used cars, will sell their cars to you? _____ What will your profit be if you offer this price? _____

■ In Session 1, if there are six good used cars and six lemons in your town, what price should you offer for used cars in order to maximize your profits?

_____

■ In Session 1, suppose that you know that the used-car owners in your town have four good cars and eight lemons. What is the lowest price you could offer to get the lemon-owners to sell you their cars? _____ What will your profit be if you offer this price? _____ What is the lowest price you could offer to get all owners to sell their cars to you? _____

What will your profit be if you offer this price? _____

■   In Session 1, if there are four good used cars and eight lemons in your town, what price should you offer in order to maximize your profits? _____

_____

NAME _____

Lab Report–Experiment 11

Session 1–Monopolistic Used-Car Dealers

■ In Session 1, what was the profit-maximizing price for a monopolist to offer for used cars when there are equal numbers of good and bad cars in town? _____

■ Given that he is the only buyer in town, why would the monopolist not increase his profits by dropping the price that he pays per car down to $1?

_____

_____

_____

■ In Session 1, what is the profit-maximizing price for a monopolist if used-car owners in his market area have twice as many lemons as good used cars? _____

■ Would a monopolist make money or lose money if it set a price high enough to attract the good cars, when used-car owners have twice as many lemons as good used cars?

_____

Session 2–Competing Used-Car Dealers

■ In the last round of Session 2, how many good used cars did dealers

purchase? _____ How many lemons did dealers purchase? _____

_____ (The instructor will supply you with this information at the end
of this session.)

■ In the last round of Session 2, what was the average value to dealers of

the used cars purchased by dealers? _____

■ Use Table L11.1 to list the prices paid for cars by each of the used-car
dealers in the last round of Session 2. Add the prices in each row to find
total expenditures by each dealer.

Table L11.1: Prices Paid by Dealers—Session 2

Dealer ID	Prices Paid									Total

■ What is the average price for which cars sold in the last round of this

session? _____

■ In the first three columns of Table L11.2, fill in each dealer's identification number, total expenditures, and number of cars purchased. In the
fourth column, enter the average value of all cars purchased by all dealers
in the market (which you calculated above). In the fifth column, enter the
value of each dealer's purchases, which is calculated by multiplying number
of purchases times the average value of used cars purchased. In the last column, subtract each dealer's total expenditures on used cars from the value
of his purchases to determine the dealer's profits.

Table L11.2: Used-Car Dealers' Purchases and Profits—Session 2

Dealer ID	Total Expenditures	Number of Purchases	Average Value	Value of Purchases	Dealer's Profits

Session 3–Competing Used-Car Dealers with More Lemons

■ In the last round of Session 3, how many good used cars did dealers purchase? _____ How many lemons did dealers purchase? _____

_____ (The instructor will supply you with this information at the end of this session.)

■ In the last round of Session 3, what was the average value to dealers of the used cars that they purchased? _____

■ In Table L11.3, list the prices paid for cars by each of the used-car dealers in the last round of this session. Add the prices in each row to find total expenditures by each dealer.

■ What is the average price for which cars sold in the last round of this session? _____

■ In the first three columns of Table L11.4, fill in each dealer's identification number, total expenditures, and number of cars purchased. In the fourth column, enter the average value of all cars purchased by all dealers in the market (which you calculated above). In the fifth column, enter the value of each dealer's purchases, which is calculated by multiplying the number of purchases made by this dealer times the average value of used cars

Table L11.3: Prices Paid by Dealers—Session 3

Dealer ID	Prices Paid									Total

purchased. In the last column, subtract each dealer's total expenditures on used cars from the value of his purchases to determine the dealer's profits.

Table L11.4: Used-Car Dealers' Purchases and Profits—Session 3

Dealer ID	Total Expenditure	Number of Purchases	Average Value	Value of Purchases	Dealer's Profits

Session 4–Good Car Cards Displayed

■ In Table L11.5, below, record the sales and purchase prices in the last round of Session 4. Put an asterisk by the price if the seller displayed a "good car" card to the buyer. Put a double asterisk if the seller displayed a "lemon" card to the buyer.

Table L11.5: Prices Paid by Dealers—Session 4

Dealer	Prices Paid									Total

■ What was the average price paid to sellers who showed "good car" cards?

_____ What was the average price paid to sellers who showed "lemon" cards? _____ What was the average price paid to sellers who did not show any card? _____

Discussion D11

Adverse Selection and Moral Hazard

Markets with Asymmetric Information

Our experimental used-car market is an example of a market with **asymmetric information.** This means that people on one side of the market know things that people on the other side of the market do not. Asymmetric information might not seem like it would be a serious problem for markets. Surely the people who have information unavailable to others could share it. The problem, as you may have guessed, either from real-world experience or from the experimental market, is that the people with information may benefit from hiding it or misrepresenting it. Talk is cheap. If a buyer offers a higher price to those who say they have good cars than to those who say they have lemons, lemon owners will want to say they have good cars. In the design of all sessions except Session 4 of our experiment, there is nothing to prevent them from doing so.[1]

Adverse Selection

Asymmetric information often leads to a market problem that is known as **adverse selection.** Adverse selection occurs in a market when buyers or sellers would, on average, be better off trading with someone selected at

---

[1] In real life, even if you don't value the truth for its own sake, lying to those you deal with regularly will hurt you. If your acquaintances find you out in one lie, they will mistrust you in the future. In an arm's length business encounter with someone whom you are not likely to meet again (like a stranger to whom you sell a used car) this constraint on behavior is missing.

random from the population than with their actual trading partners. A classic example of adverse selection occurs in used-car markets. As we saw in our experiments, from a population of good and bad used cars, it may be that in equilibrium, only bad cars come onto the market. When this happens, if a used-car buyer thinks that the used cars on the market reflect the average quality of used cars in existence, he will be sadly mistaken.

The problem of adverse selection also applies to insurance markets. The customers that are most likely to want insurance are the people who face the highest risks, but these are the people that insurance companies would least like to have as customers.

Here are some examples:

- The people who want to buy collision insurance for their cars are those who drive a lot and are most likely to have accidents.

- The people who are most eager to buy health insurance are those who have most reason to think they are going to have expensive illnesses.

- The people most likely to buy life insurance are those who have reason to believe that they are likely to die young.

- An **annuity** is a promise to pay somebody a fixed amount every year until he or she dies. The people who are most eager to buy annuities are those who have reason to believe that they will live for a long time.

Insurance companies are well aware that their customers will, on average, be worse insurance risks than a randomly-selected member of the population. Accordingly, instead of basing their estimates of the risks they face on statistics for the population as a whole, they base them on statistics for *insured* people in previous years.

Moral Hazard

Another problem of asymmetric information, similar to adverse selection, is known in the insurance industry as **moral hazard**. Adverse selection occurs when your trading partners have less favorable *characteristics* than the population at large. Moral hazard occurs when the *actions* taken by your trading partners are less favorable for you than the actions of the average member of the population. Some examples of moral hazard are the following. People who have fire insurance will not mind having a fire as badly as people without fire insurance. People who have insurance against auto theft are likely to take fewer precautions against having their car stolen than people who do not have insurance. People with unemployment insurance may search less intensely for jobs. Workers whose performance is not monitored may shirk. Construction contractors whose work is not closely inspected may do shoddy work, the flaws of which do not become apparent until after they are paid.

With moral hazard, as with adverse selection, the problem is that people on one side of the market know something that the people on the other side do not. Moral hazard is sometimes called the case of **hidden action**. With moral hazard, one side of the market is not able to observe the actions taken by the people they deal with. In the examples of adverse selection, car buyers don't know the kind of car they will be getting, and insurance companies don't know the type of person they are insuring.

Where moral hazard is a problem, the market participant without information tries to monitor performance of the participant with information, and to make this performance part of the terms of the contract. Fire insurance companies have inspectors who observe precautions taken by their large industrial customers. Auto theft insurers may give discounts to customers who have anti-theft devices on their cars. Unemployment insurance runs out after a few weeks of unemployment. Firms try to monitor their workers' performance. People that hire contractors often hire inspectors to observe that construction proceeds according to specifications. Because monitoring is expensive and usually imperfect, even with monitoring, the problem of moral hazard remains a serious one.

Demand and Supply in a Lemons Market

Demand and supply analysis can help us to predict the outcome in a market where there is adverse selection as in our used-car experiment.

Since suppliers know the quality of their own used cars, the supply curve can be constructed in much the same way that we drew supply curves for previous experiments. But drawing a demand curve requires more care. At first glance, it may seem impossible to draw an appropriate demand curve for a lemons market. Demanders cannot observe the quality of a car before they buy it. The amount that a demander is willing to pay for a used car depends on the demander's beliefs about the average quality of used cars on the market. But, as we discovered in the experiment, the average quality of used cars on the market depends on the price, which in turn depends on demand. So how can we draw a demand curve?

In order to determine equilibrium in a lemons market, we need to introduce a new idea, the idea of **self-confirming beliefs**. Self-confirming beliefs have the property that if people hold these beliefs and act on them, the consequences of their actions will be consistent with these beliefs. We illustrate the idea of self-confirming beliefs by considering two examples of lemons markets that are similar to the markets in our experiment.

Example 1

Suppose that the current owners of good used cars have a reservation price of $700 for their cars, and the current owners of lemons have a reservation price of $200 for theirs. Assume that in this market there are a total of 5 good used cars and 15 lemons. At prices below $200, even the owners of lemons would want to keep their used cars, so no used cars would be sold. At prices between $200 and $700, the lemon owners would all want to sell their used cars, so that at these prices 15 used cars would be supplied, all of which would be lemons. At prices above $700, all used-car owners would want to sell their used cars, so that all 20 used cars in the market would be supplied. We can draw a supply curve for used cars on Figure D11.1. It will be useful to remember that if only 15 used cars are supplied, they will all be lemons, but if 20 used cars are supplied, 15 will be lemons and 5 will be good used cars.

A Case of Mistaken Beliefs

Let there be 25 potential used-car buyers, each of whom is willing to pay $1200 for a good used car and $400 for a lemon. Before they purchase a used car, buyers are not able to tell whether it is a good used car or a lemon. Let us first draw the demand curve that would apply if buyers believed that all used cars, the 5 good cars as well as the 15 lemons, will be offered for sale. If this is the case, 1/4 of the used cars for sale will be good and 3/4 will be lemons. Therefore buying a used car is like buying a lottery ticket where you have a probability of 1/4 of winning $1200 (the Buyer Value of a good used car) and a probability of 3/4 of winning $400 (the Buyer Value of a lemon). We will assume that a buyer's willingness to pay for a lottery is the "expected value" of the lottery. The **expected value** of a lottery is equal to a weighted average of the possible amounts of payoff, where the weight placed on each possible amount of payoff is the probability that the payoff is equal to that amount. In this example, the expected value of a used car is $\frac{1}{4} \times \$1200 + \frac{3}{4} \times \$400 = \$600$. This expected value is equal to the *average*

Figure D11.1: Lemons Market IA

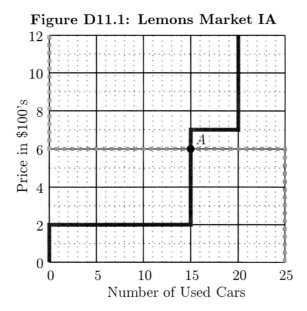

value of used cars to buyers if all used cars reach the market.

Now we can draw the demand curve for used cars, *given that buyers believe that all used cars will come on the market.* At prices above $600, no demanders would want to buy a used car, at prices below $600, all 25 demanders would want to buy a used car, and at a price of $600 all demanders would be indifferent between buying a used car or not. This means that the demand curve looks like the dashed line in Figure D11.1, with a horizontal segment at a height of $600. With these beliefs, the supply curve intersects the demand curve at the point A, where the price is $600 and the number of used cars supplied is 15.

But now we see that the belief that all 20 used cars would come to the market is *not* self-confirming. When demanders act on this belief, they discover that they are mistaken, since the only cars that came to market are the lemons. The mistaken belief that all 20 used cars would reach the market is costly to the buyers since, although they paid $600 for used cars, they are sure to get lemons, which are only worth $400 to them. Demanders who may have started trading with the belief that all used cars would come to market would want to revise their views after this experience.

A Case of Self-Confirming Beliefs

Suppose that all demanders believe that the only used cars that will reach the market are lemons. Since a lemon is worth \$400 to a buyer, the demand curve for demanders with this belief will look like the dashed line in Figure D11.2. When demanders hold these beliefs, the supply curve intersects the demand curve at the point B, where the price is \$400 and the number of used cars supplied is 15. The 15 used cars that are supplied are all lemons, which confirms the pessimistic belief of demanders that all used cars that reach the market are lemons. The belief that all used cars on the market are lemons is therefore self-confirming, since when demanders act on this belief, the market result is consistent with this belief.

Figure D11.2: Lemons Market IB

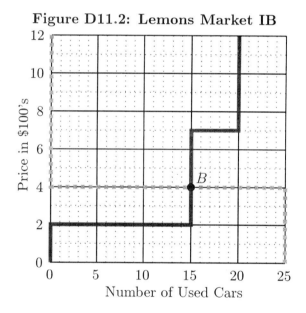

In this example, the only self-confirming belief for demanders turns out to be that only lemons will reach the market. We will next look at an example in which a higher proportion of the used cars in the hands of original owners are good used cars and consequently the belief that all used cars, including the good ones, will reach the market is self-confirming.

Example 2

Optimistic, Self-Confirming Beliefs

As before, current owners of good used cars have a reservation price of $700 for their cars, and current owners of lemons have a reservation price of $200. In this market, however, there are 10 good used cars and 10 lemons. The supply curve for used cars is drawn on Figure D11.3. Remember that if only 10 used cars are supplied, they will all be lemons, but if 20 used cars are supplied, half will be lemons and half will be good.

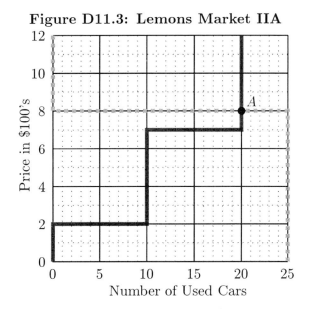

Figure D11.3: Lemons Market IIA

As in the previous example, there are 25 used-car buyers, each of whom is willing to pay $1200 for a good used car and $400 for a lemon. Suppose that all buyers believe that all used cars, including the good ones, will be offered for sale. If this is the case, half of the used cars for sale will be good and half will be lemons. In this case, the expected value of a used car is $\frac{1}{2} \times \$1200 + \frac{1}{2} \times \$400 = \$800$. Therefore, if buyers believe that all used cars will come onto the market, each buyer is willing to pay up to $800 for a used car. The demand curve would look like the dashed line in Figure D11.3, which includes a horizontal line at a height of $800.

Given these beliefs, supply equals demand at a price of $800. Since $800 is greater than the $700 reservation price of the original owners of good used

cars, all 20 used-car owners want to sell their used cars. The demanders'
belief that all used cars will reach the market is self-confirming. That is,
when all demanders act on this belief, their belief is confirmed by the market
outcome.

But this is not quite the end of the story. Remarkably, when half of
the used cars are good and half are lemons, there are *two different* sets of
self-confirming beliefs. The pessimistic belief that all used cars that reach
the market are lemons also turns out to be self-confirming.

Pessimistic, Self-Confirming Beliefs

Suppose that all demanders believe that the only used cars that reach the
market are lemons. Since a lemon is worth $400 to a buyer, the demand
curve for demanders with this belief would look like the dashed line in Figure
D11.4. With these beliefs, the supply curve intersects the demand curve at
the point B, where the price is $400 and the number of used cars supplied
is 10. The 10 used cars that are supplied are all lemons, which confirms the
demanders' belief that all used cars that reach the market are lemons.

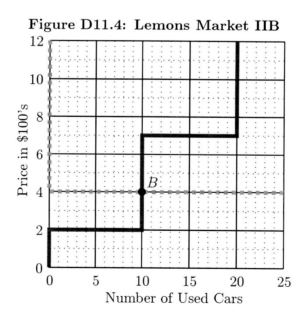

Figure D11.4: Lemons Market IIB

A Remark on Multiple Equilibria

In Example 2, we see that there are two different sets of self-confirming beliefs. One set of self-confirming beliefs occurs when everyone believes that half of the used cars on the market are good and half are bad. The other set of self-confirming beliefs occurs when everyone believes that the only used cars that will reach the market are lemons. Either of these two sets of beliefs will be confirmed by market experience if everyone acts on them.

The possibility of there being more than one equilibrium is fairly common in economic models of markets, and especially in models with asymmetric information. This lack of uniqueness is, perhaps, frustrating, since it means that we can not always make sharp predictions with the theory. On the other hand, it is enlightening to discover that there are plausible situations in which two different sets of beliefs can lead to dramatically different outcomes, both of which are self-confirming. Perhaps this helps to explain how it is that strikingly different systems of beliefs about economic and social matters can survive over long periods of time in different parts of the world.

NAME _____

Home Work–Experiment 11

Session 2–Competing Used-Car Dealers A

Equilibrium With Optimistic Beliefs

■ In Session 2 of the experiment, the original owners have _____

good used cars and _____ lemons. This means that the fraction ___

_____ of all used cars held by original owners are good, and the

fraction _____ are lemons.

■ In Session 2, owners of lemons are willing to sell their used cars at any price above $0. Owners of good used cars are willing to sell their used cars at any price above $1600. At prices between $0 and $1600, the number of

used cars that will be for sale is _____. At prices above $1600, the

number of used cars that will be for sale is _____.

■ To a dealer, a good used car is worth $3500 and a lemon is worth $500. Let V_1 be the expected (average) value to dealers of a used car that comes on the market if dealers believe that all used cars will be sold by their original

owners. Then $V_1 =$ _____.

■ On Figure H11.1, draw the supply curve for used cars in Session 2.

■ Since there are a large number of potential buyers for used cars, if everyone believes that the original owners of all used cars will sell them, then the demand curve for used cars must include a horizontal line running all the way across the graph in Figure H11.1, at a height equal to the expected value V_1. On H11.1, draw the demand curve for used cars, assuming that all buyers have this belief.

Figure H11.1: Supply and Demand for Used Cars

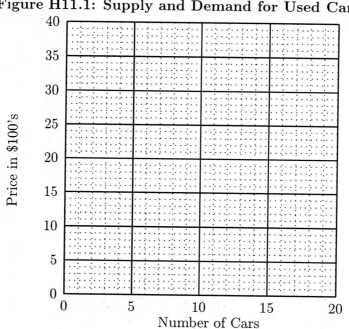

■ Given these beliefs, at what price does the number of used cars supplied equal the number demanded? _____ At this price, how many used cars are sold? _____ Is this consistent with the demanders' belief that all owners of used cars will sell them? _____ Is the belief that all used-car owners will sell their used cars a self-confirming belief? _____

Equilibrium With Pessimistic Beliefs

■ Suppose that car dealers believe that the only cars that suppliers will sell are lemons. Then the expected value of a used car to a dealer is the price he can get for a lemon, which is _____. The demand curve therefore contains a horizontal line across Figure H11.2 at a height of _____.

■ On Figure H11.2, draw the supply curve and the demand curve that apply if used-car dealers all believe that original owners will only sell their lemons.

Figure H11.2: Supply and Demand for Used Cars

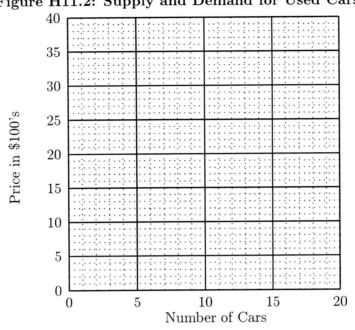

■ With these beliefs, at what price does supply equal demand? _____

_____At this price, how many used cars are sold? _____ Is this consistent with the demanders' belief that only lemons will be available in the used-car market? _____ Is the belief that only lemons will be available in the used-car market a self-confirming belief? _____

Comparing Experimental Outcome with Theoretical Predictions

■ In the last round of Session 2 of the experiment, what was the average price for which used cars actually sold? _____

■ Was the outcome close to an outcome that was consistent with self-confirming beliefs? _____ If so, what beliefs were these?

■   If we held more rounds in this session, what changes, if any, would you expect to see in the average price paid for used cars?

_____

_____

_____

Session 3–Competing Used-Car Dealers B

Equilibrium With Optimistic Beliefs

■   In Session 3 of the experiment, owners of lemons are willing to sell their used cars at any price above $0. Owners of good used cars are willing to sell at any price above $1600. At prices between $0 and $1600, the number of used cars that will be for sale is _____. At prices above $1600, the number of used cars that will be for sale is _____.

■   In Session 3, the original owners have _____ good used cars and _

_____ lemons. This means that the fraction _____ of all used cars held by original owners are good, and the fraction _____ are lemons.

■   To a dealer, a good used car is worth $3500 and a lemon is worth $500. Let V_1 be the expected (average) value to dealers of a used car that comes on the market if dealers believe that all used cars will be for sold by their original owners. Then $V_1 =$ _____.

■   On Figure H11.3, draw the supply curve for used cars in Session 3.

■   Since there are a large number of potential buyers for used cars, if everyone believes that the original owners of all used cars will sell them, then the demand curve for used cars must include a horizontal line running all the way across the graph in Figure H11.3, at a height equal to the expected value V_1. On H11.3, draw the demand curve for used cars, assuming that all buyers have this belief.

Figure H11.3: Supply and Demand for Used Cars

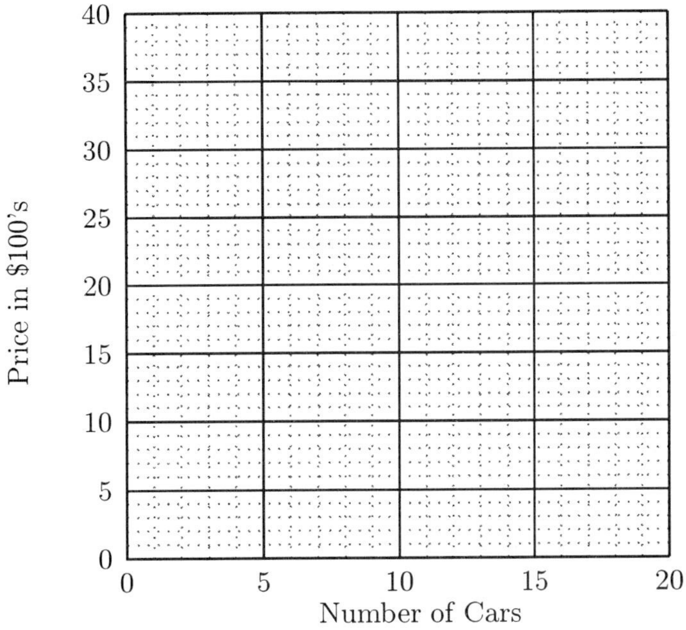

■ Given these beliefs, at what price does the number of used cars supplied equal the number demanded? _____ At this price, how many used cars are sold? _____ Is this consistent with the demanders' belief that all owners of used cars will sell them? _____ Is the belief that all used-car owners will sell their used cars a self-confirming belief? _____

Equilibrium with Pessimistic Beliefs

■ Suppose that car dealers believe that the only cars that suppliers will sell are lemons. Then the expected value of a used car to a dealer is the price he can get for a lemon, which is _____. The demand curve therefore contains a horizontal line at a height of _____.

■ On Figure H11.4, draw the supply curve and the demand curve that apply if used-car dealers all believe that original owners will only sell their lemons.

Figure H11.4: Supply and Demand for Used Cars

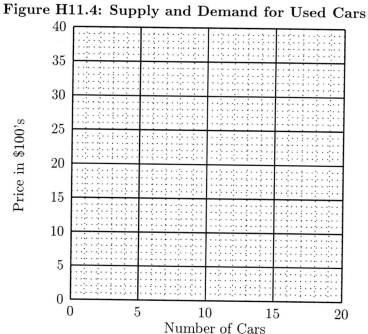

■ With these beliefs, at what price does the number of cars supplied equal

the number demanded? _____ At this price, how many used cars are

sold? _____ Is this consistent with the demanders' belief that only

lemons will be available in the used-car market? _____ Is the belief
that only lemons will be available in the used-car market a self-confirming

belief? _____

Comparing Experimental Outcome with Theoretical Predictions

■ In the last round of Session 3 of the experiment, what was the average

price for which used cars actually sold? _____

■ Was the outcome close to an outcome that was consistent with self-confirming beliefs? _____If so, what beliefs were these?

_____

■ If we held more rounds in this session, what changes, if any, would you expect to see in the average price paid for used cars?

_____

_____

_____

Session 4–Certification of Good Cars

■ In this session, every used-car owner had a certificate that she can display, stating whether she has a good used car or a lemon. What is the most a dealer would be willing to pay for a car from somebody who showed a good

car certificate?_____ What is the most a dealer would be willing to

pay for a car from somebody who showed a lemon certificate? _____

■ If you were a dealer, what is the most you would be willing to pay a seller who refused to show you a certificate? Explain.

_____

_____

_____

■   On Figure H11.5, draw the demand curve and the supply curve for used cars that are certified to be good.

Figure H11.5: The Used-Car Market

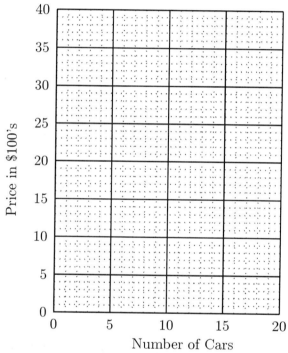

■   What would be the competitive equilibrium price for used cars that are certified to be good? _____

■   What was the average price actually paid in the experimental market for used cars that are certified to be good? _____

■ On Figure H11.6, draw the demand curve and the supply curve for used cars that are not certified to be good.

Figure H11.6: Lemon Market

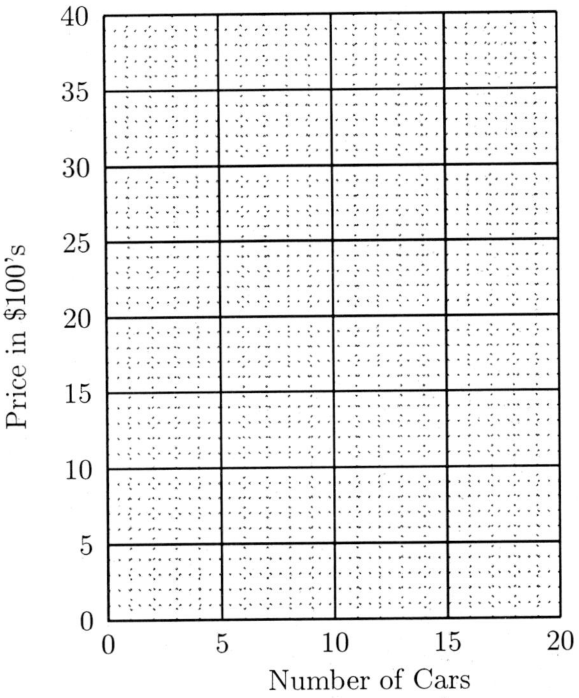

■ What would be the competitive equilibrium price for used cars that are

not certified to be good? _____

■ What was the average price actually paid in the experimental market

for used cars that are not certified to be good? _____

Food for Thought

Suppose that a company offers "grade insurance" that works as follows. For each course in which you get a grade below a C, the insurance company pays you $500. Before offering the insurance policy for sale, the insurance company looks over the transcripts of university students and finds that on average 10% of all grades given are below a C. Explain why the insurance company would be incorrect in assuming that it would only have to pay claims on about 10% of its policies. Explain how adverse selection and moral hazard would each affect this market.

Experiment 12

Auctions

The wind is blowing briskly and the clouds gather overhead as you park your car along the road near the hand-lettered sign, **AUCTION TODAY**, and walk to the old farmhouse at the end of the driveway.

You have come to the auction intending to buy some antique furniture for your new house. You shoulder your way through the crowd and examine several items that seem likely to be of interest.

A few minutes later, the auctioneer arrives. He announces: "There is more than one way to skin a cat and there's more than one way to sell a house full of jun...er antiques. Today we are going to use four different kinds of auctions."

An English Auction

The auctioneer walks over to a small chest of drawers and says, "Just to get warmed up, we will sell this little beauty in an ordinary auction, the kind that experts call an **English auction**."

In an English auction, the auctioneer solicits an opening bid from some-body in the group. Then he asks if anyone has a higher bid. Anyone who wants to bid should call out a new price that is *at least* $1 higher than the previous high bid, or should give the auctioneer a nod when the auctioneer requests a bid. (In order to move things along more quickly, the auction-eer may try to solicit larger jumps in the bidding when it appears that the current bid is likely to be well below the final sales price.) The bidding continues until all bidders but one have dropped out. The highest bidder gets the object being sold for a price equal to the final bid.

In this auction, different people will have different Buyer Values for the chest of drawers. Your Buyer Value is the two-digit number consisting of the last two digits of your social security number. For example, if your social security number is 362-58-5283, your Buyer Value is $83. Your profit, if you are the high bidder, is your Buyer Value minus the price that you bid. Everyone else in the group will get zero profits in this session.

In order to allow several people to participate actively in the auction, we will divide the class into three or four groups and run separate English auctions in each group. When each group completes its auction, the auctioneer will record the top bid and calculate the winning bidder's profits. The auctioneer will also survey each group to determine the two highest Buyer Values in the group.

A Dutch Auction

Having sold the chest of drawers, the auctioneer moves on to the next item for sale, a family portrait in a gilded frame, and says, "This masterpiece will go to the lucky person who makes the highest bid in a **Dutch auction**."

In a Dutch auction, the auctioneer starts with a price that he knows is higher than anyone's Buyer Value and lowers the price gradually until some buyer signals a bid. The first buyer to bid gets the object at the price the auctioneer called just before the bid was made. In English-speaking countries, where the Dutch auction is used, the auctioneer counts downward until someone shouts "Mine!" Accordingly, the Dutch auction scheme is sometimes called "mineing."

Your Buyer Value for the family portrait is found by subtracting the last two digits of your social security number from 100. For example, if your social security number is 362-58-5283, your Buyer Value is $(100-83) = $17.

As before, the class will be divided into groups. The auctioneer will sell a family portrait with gilded frame to each group by means of a Dutch Auction. The auctioneer will count backwards from 100 until someone calls "Mine." The first person who calls "Mine" will get the family portrait for the last price counted out by the auctioneer. This bidder's profit will be the price she paid minus her Buyer Value. Everyone else in her group will get zero profits. When each group completes its auction, the auctioneer will record the winning bid and calculate the winning bidder's profits. The auctioneer will then survey the group to determine the two highest Buyer Values in the group.

A Sealed-bid, First-price Auction

The auctioneer next moves to an old bedstead. "This family heirloom can be yours. The owners are willing to let it go to the winner of a **sealed-bid, first-price auction**."

In a sealed-bid, first-price auction, bidders write their bids for the object and their names or identification numbers on slips of paper, and deliver them to the auctioneer. The auctioneer examines the bids and sells the object to the highest bidder at the price that he or she bid. Ties can be settled in various ways. In some auction markets, a coin is tossed. In some markets, the bid is awarded to the bidder standing closer to the auctioneer. We will use the method commonly used in Japan to settle ties, which is to play a game of stone-paper-scissors (*Jan Ken Pon* to the Japanese).

Your Buyer Value for the antique bedstead is given by the fourth from last and third from last digits of your social security number. For example, if your social security number is 362-58-5283, your Buyer Value will be $52. Write your bid, your Buyer Value, and your identification number on a sheet of paper and hand the paper in to the auctioneer.

The auctioneer will randomly divide the bid sheets into three or four separate piles, representing different groups of buyers. From each group, the largest bid will be selected and a bedstead will be sold to the highest bidder at the highest bidder's bid price. For each group, the market manager will record the bids and Buyer Values of the top two bidders, the profits made by the highest bidder, and the two highest Buyer Values in the group.

A Sealed-bid, Second-price Auction

The auctioneer now moves along to admire a hand-painted chamberpot. "I am going to sell this elegant gem by means of a **sealed-bid, second-price auction**."

As in a first-price auction, bidders write their bids for the object and their names or identification numbers on slips of paper, and deliver them to the auctioneer. The auctioneer opens the bids and sells the object to the highest bidder, but at the *price bid by the second-highest bidder*. If there is a tie for top bid, the winner of a game of stone-paper-scissors between the two tying bidders get the object at the price at which the top bidders tied.

Your Buyer Value for the chamberpot is given by subtracting the number made up of the fourth from last and third from last digits of your social security number from 100. For example, if your social security number is

362-58-5283, your Buyer Value will be $(100 - 52) = \$48$. Write your bid, your Buyer Value, and your identification number on a sheet of paper and hand the paper in to the auctioneer. The top bidder in each group will make profits equal to his or her Buyer Value minus the second-highest bid in that group. Everyone else earns zero profits.

The auctioneer will randomly divide the bid sheets into three or four piles, representing different groups of buyers. From each group, the highest and second-highest bid will be selected and a chamber pot will be sold to the highest bidder at the *second-highest* bid price. For each group, the auctioneer will record the bids and Buyer Values of the top two bidders, the profits made by the highest bidder, and the two highest Buyer Values in the group.

Warm-up Exercise

Preparation for the English Auction

■ Suppose that an object is sold by English auction, your Buyer Value is $85, and the other participants have Buyer Values of $40, $50, and $60. How much would you expect to have to pay in order to get the object?

_____

■ In an English auction, what bidding strategy would you recommend?

_____

_____

_____

Preparation for the Dutch Auction

■ In a Dutch auction, would it ever be profitable to say "Mine!" when the price is higher than your Buyer Value? _____

■ Would it ever be profitable to say "Mine!" when the price is equal to your Buyer Value? _____

■ Suppose that the auctioneer has reached a price that is lower than your Buyer Value. What is the advantage of waiting for him to count still lower and what is the risk if you wait for him to count lower?

_____

_____

_____

Preparation for the Sealed-Bid, First-Price Auction

■ In a Sealed-bid, first-price auction, would it ever be profitable to submit a bid that is higher than your Buyer Value? _____ Would it ever be profitable to submit a bid that is equal to your Buyer Value? _____

■ Do you think the best bid for you to make in a sealed-bid, first-price auction should be higher than, lower than, or the same as the price at which you would say "Mine!" in the Dutch auction if nobody has yet done so? Explain.

_____

_____

_____

Preparation for the Sealed-Bid, Second-Price Auction

In this auction, you will get the object only if you are the top bidder, but the amount that you pay for it, given that you are the top bidder, does not depend on your bid, but on the bid made by the second-highest bidder. If you are not the top bidder, your profits for this auction are zero.

■   Suppose that your Buyer Value is \$10 and that the highest bid made by anyone else is \$8. How much profit will you earn if you bid \$7?_____ What if you bid \$9? _____ What if you bid \$10? _____ What if you bid \$11? _____ What if you bid \$13?_____

■   Suppose that your Buyer Value is \$10 and that the highest bid made by anyone else is \$10.50. How much profit will you earn if you bid \$7?_____ _____ What if you bid \$9?_____ What if you bid \$10? _____ What if you bid \$11? _____ What if you bid \$13?_____

■   Suppose that your Buyer Value is \$10 and that you do not know the bids that will be made by others. If you bid \$8, could it ever happen that you would make *less* money than you would have made if you had bid \$10?

_____If so, give an example of bids by others that would make this happen.

_____

■   Suppose that your Buyer Value is \$10 and that you do not know the bids that will be made by others. If you bid \$8, could it ever happen that you would make *more* money than you would have made if you had bid \$10?

_____If so, give an example of bids by others that would make this happen.

_____

■   Suppose that your Buyer Value is \$10 and that you do not know the bids that will be made by others. If you bid \$12, could it ever happen that you would make *less* money than you would have made if you had bid \$10?

_____If so, give an example of bids by others that would make this happen.

_____

■ Suppose that your Buyer Value is $10 and that you do not know the bids that will be made by others. If you bid $12, could it ever happen that you would make *more* money than you would have made if you had bid $10?

_____If so, give an example of bids by others that would make this happen.

_____

■ Do you think that the best bid to make in this auction is greater than, less than, or equal to your Buyer Value?

_____

NAME _____

Lab Report–Experiment 12

An English Auction

■   In Table L12.1, record the requested information for each auction group in the English auction.

Table L12.1: Outcome of English Auction

	Group A	Group B	Group C	Group D
Highest Bid				
High Bidder's Buyer Value				
High Bidder's Profits				
Highest Buyer Value				
Second-Highest Buyer Value				

■   With the English auction, record the difference between the highest bid and the second-highest Buyer Value for each group: Group A _____;

Group B _____ ; Group C _____ ; Group D _____.

■   If you knew the highest Buyer Value and the second-highest Buyer Value of participants in an English auction, and if you knew that bidding always proceeded in increments of $1, what would you predict the highest bid to be?

_____

■   In an English auction, if everyone bids intelligently, will the object necessarily be sold to the person with the highest Buyer Value? _____

■ In the experimental English auction, was the chest of drawers sold to the person in each group with the highest Buyer Value?_____

A Dutch Auction

■ In Table L12.2, record the requested information for each auction group in the Dutch auction.

Table L12.2: Outcome of Dutch Auction

	Group A	Group B	Group C	Group D
Winning Bid				
Winning Bidder's Buyer Value				
Winning Bidder's Profits				
Highest Buyer Value in Group				
Second Buyer Value in Group				

■ With the Dutch auction, record the difference between the highest bid and the second-highest Buyer Value for each group: Group A _____;

Group B _____; Group C _____; Group D _____.

■ In a Dutch auction, if everyone bids intelligently, will the object necessarily be sold to the person with the highest Buyer Value? Explain.

_____

_____

_____

■ In the experimental Dutch auction, was the family portrait sold to the person in each group with the highest Buyer Value?_____

■ In this experiment, do you think that participants in any of the groups acted irrationally, given the information available to them when they made their decisions? Explain why or why not.

_____

_____

_____

■ In which groups, if any, would the seller have gotten a higher price if the family portrait had been sold in an English auction rather than a Dutch auction (assuming that in the English auction, everyone bids intelligently)?

_____

A Sealed-bid, First-price Auction

■ In Table L12.3, record the requested information for each auction group in the sealed-bid first-price auction.

Table L12.3: Outcome of Sealed-bid, First-Price Auction

	Group A	Group B	Group C	Group D
Highest Bid				
High Bidder's Buyer Value				
High Bidder's Profits				
Highest Buyer Value				
Second-Highest Buyer Value				

■ In the sealed-bid first-price auction, was the antique bedstead sold to the person in each group with the highest Buyer Value?_____

■ In a sealed-bid first-price auction, if everyone bids intelligently, will the object necessarily be sold to the person with the highest Buyer Value? ___

_____

■ With the sealed-bid first-price auction, record the difference between the
highest bid and the second-highest Buyer Value for each group: Group A __
_____; Group B _____; Group C _____; Group D
_____.

■ In which groups, if any, would the seller have gotten a higher price if the
family portrait had been sold in an English auction rather than a sealed-
bid first-price auction (assuming that in the English auction, everyone bids
intelligently)?

_____

■ In Table L12.4, record the requested information for each auction group
in the sealed-bid second-price auction.

Table L12.4: Outcome of Sealed-bid, Second-price Auction

	Group A	Group B	Group C	Group D
Highest Bid				
Second-Highest Bid				
High Bidder's Buyer Value				
High Bidder's Profits				
Highest Buyer Value				
Second-Highest Buyer Value				

■ In the sealed-bid second-price auction, was the chamber pot sold to the
person in each group with the highest Buyer Value?_____

■ In a sealed-bid second-price auction, if everyone bids intelligently, will
the object necessarily be sold to the person with the highest Buyer Value?

_____

■ With the sealed-bid second-price auction, record the difference between
the highest bid and the second-highest Buyer Value for each group: Group
A _____; Group B _____; Group C _____; Group D ___
_____.

■ For each group, compare the price collected by the seller in the sealed-bid second-price auction with the price that the seller would have received if the chamber pot had been sold in an English auction rather than a sealed-bid second-price auction.

_____

■ Can you think of any practical reasons for using sealed-bid auctions rather than English or Dutch auctions?

_____

_____

_____

Discussion D12

Auctions

Auctions in the Real World

Although most of us are more accustomed to buying goods either from merchants who post prices on a take-it-or-leave-it basis or in bilateral negotiations with the seller, there are many interesting examples of goods that are sold by auction. The four types of auctions that we conducted during this experiment are only a few of the many auction types found round the world. A fascinating description of the variety of types of auctions used in traditional and modern societies is found in *Auctions and Auctioneering* by Ralph Cassady, Jr.[1]

A very readable account of the economic theory of auctions is found in *Games, Strategies, and Managers* by John McMillan.[7] McMillan describes many important applications of auctions in the modern economy. Some examples are the sale of oil leases, the sale of insolvent banks and savings-and-loan institutions by the Federal Deposit Insurance Corporation (FDIC) after the savings-and-loan crisis in 1988, bidding for major construction projects, wine auctions, auctions to allocate airport gate space and takeoff and landing slots, auctions to allocate tasks among computers, auctions for defense procurement, and auctions for the television broadcasting rights for the summer Olympics.

Auctions are conducted throughout the world, with many interesting variations in the rules and conduct of the auction. Among the auction types that are recorded by Cassady are the following:

- The Japanese (simultaneous bidding) auction. Bidders use hand-signals to indicate their bids. All bids are made at approximately the same time, though it takes several seconds for all bidders to get their signals up and for the auctioneer to read them. The auctioneer finds the highest signalled bid and sells to the highest bidder at his bid price. These auctions have the advantage of taking place very quickly. Of course bidders have to be good at signalling and the auctioneer must be able to read the signals quickly.

- Handshake auction. According to Cassady, "Buyers are seated in a semi-circle, each in turn having an opportunity to clasp the hand of the auctioneer and register his bid. Under cover of a piece of cloth, the bidder indicates the amount he is offering by pressing a certain number of the auctioneer's fingers at the moment that he announces a monetary unit, first 'tens', then 'rupees', then 'anas'." The auctioneer remembers the largest bid and announces the winner, but does not publicly announce the price bid by the winner. This method was used in fish markets in Karachi, Pakistan, and is reputed to have been used in China in ancient times. Cassady reports that in Karachi, in 1959, the handshake auction was replaced by the English auction.

- Whispered bid auction. According to Cassady, "The auctioneer announces that the goods are up for sale, and would-be buyers approach him and whisper offers in his ear." Whispered-bid auctions are found in fish markets in Singapore, Manila, Venice and Chioggia.

- Audible-bid rotation auction. The bid passes in rotation according to a pre-specified order. When it comes to his turn, a bidder may either make a bid that exceeds the previous high bid or say "I pass." The bidding continues around in rotation until all bidders but one have said "I pass."

- Silent auction. The seller displays the object, along with a slip of paper that states the minimum acceptable bid and the minimum increment by which bidders can increase the bid over the previous highest bid. Would-be buyers can enter their name, address, and a bid. New bids as entered must exceed the highest previous bid by at least the minimum increment. When a specified time deadline is reached, the object is sold to the highest bidder at the high bidder's bid price.

- Candle auction. There are several variants of this kind of auction, which is essentially an English auction with a time limit. A particularly colorful version is known as a "Cornish Auction." The auctioneer lights a candle and pushes a pin into the candle about an inch below the flame. As long as the pin remained in place, the bidding would proceed as in an English auction, but when the pin fell out, the object would go to the last (and highest, so far) bidder. This method of auction was common in England in the 17th century and is occasionally still used there. Samuel Pepys brags in his diary of his success in a candle auction.

Real-world Background of Experimental Auctions

The English auction is the most commonly used method for conducting oral auctions in English-speaking countries. Commodities that are frequently sold by English auction include antiques, artworks, cattle, horses, wholesale fruits and vegetables, old books, real estate, and used farm and industrial equipment.

The Dutch auction takes its name from the fact that it is used in the wholesale produce and cut-flower markets in the Netherlands. In some Dutch flower markets, the procedure is automated by a clock mechanism visible to all bidders. An indicator hand moves counterclockwise through a series of descending prices. Any buyer can stop the hand by pressing a button near his seat. Pressing the button indicates that the buyer accepts the lot being sold at the price on which the indicator hand stopped. The Dutch auction is also used in fish markets in England and in Israel, and in tobacco markets in Canada. You may be familiar with a variant of this procedure that is sometimes used to mark down clothing in retail stores.

Sealed-bid first-price auctions are commonly used in the awarding of construction contracts, which go to the *lowest* bidder. The bidders, in this case are of course suppliers, not demanders. First-price sealed-bid auctions are also sometimes used for selling real estate and art treasures.

Sealed-bid, second-price auctions do not seem to be widely used. This method of auction is used in stamp collectors' auctions and a multiple unit version of this method has been used by the U.S. Treasury to sell long-term bonds.[1]

Private Value and Common Value Auctions

The objects sold in our experimental antique auction are worth different amounts to different people. Each potential buyer is perfectly aware of the value of the object to himself or herself, but they do not know what the

---

[1]This information comes from Vernon Smith's discussion of auctions in *The New Palgrave: A Dictionary of Economics.*

object is worth to others. When this is the case, we say that the object is being sold in an informational environment of **private values**. In some auctions, however, the object that is being sold actually has the same value to anyone who buys it, but at the time it is sold, potential buyers are not sure about its value, and different people have different estimates of this value. When this is the case, we say that the good being sold is one in an informational environment of **common values**.[2]

Private Values

English Auctions With Private Values

In an English auction with a private-values informational environment, it is never profitable to bid more for an object than your willingness to pay for it. If you bid more than your Buyer Value, and if nobody else outbids you, you will lose money. It would also be a mistake to drop out of the bidding at prices lower than your willingness to pay. In fact, it is quite easy to see that in a private-values informational environment, the optimal strategy is to participate in the bidding until the price reaches your Buyer Value and then to drop out of the bidding. That is, whenever the price is below your Buyer Value and you do not currently have the high bid, you should raise the bid by the minimal increment allowed.

This simple bit of reasoning allows us to predict the outcome of an English auction with private values. If everyone bids rationally, the winning bidder will be the person with the highest Buyer Value. In order to win the object she must bid the price up high enough to make the bidder with the second-highest Buyer-Value drop out of the bidding. The final bid will therefore be close to the second-highest Buyer Value of the auction participants.[3]

In a sealed-bid, second-price auction, the object is sold to the highest

---

[2]Sometimes people speak of "private-values auctions" or "common-values auctions." These terms refer to the informational environment in which the auction is conducted and not to the institutional rules of the auction. In either informational environment, the institutional rules could specify an English auction, a Dutch auction, or a sealed-bid auction.

[3]Depending on the sequence of bidding, the final bid may be equal to the second-highest Buyer Value, or it may be $1 higher or lower. If, in the course of bidding, the person with the second-highest Buyer Value bids exactly his Buyer Value, then the person with the highest Buyer Value would have to bid $1 more than this to get the object. If the sequence of bidding is such that the person with the highest Buyer Value submits a bid that is $1 less than the second-highest Buyer Value, then the person with the second-highest Buyer Value may choose to drop out at that point, since to advance the bid by $1 would not give him a positive profit.

bidder at a price equal to the second-highest bid. In this type of auction, it is optimal for each participant to bid his or her actual Buyer Value. (To see why, take a look at your answers to the warm-up exercise.) The highest bidder will therefore be the person with the highest Buyer Value and the price that she will pay is the second-highest bid, which is equal to the second-highest Buyer Value.

We have shown that in a private-value informational environment, with either an English auction or a sealed-bid, second-price auction, the object is sold to the person with the highest Buyer Value at a price that is close to the second-highest Buyer Value. Those who have watched actual English auctions may suspect that outcomes are not always the same as in the more sedate sealed-bid second-price auction process. Auctioneers work hard to create an atmosphere of excitement and competition among bidders. Sometimes bidders seem to be "swept away" by the enthusiasm of the moment and bid more than they had initially planned to. Sometimes bidders think that they can "scare off" the competition by increasing the bid suddenly by a large amount. A bidder may make a dramatically larger bid than previous bids in the hopes that other bidders do not have time to reconsider their valuations before the object is sold. We suspect that these things happen in real auctions because the informational environment is not a private-values environment, but is more like a common-values environment. People are not entirely confident of their own judgment of the value of the object that is for sale. Seeing that someone else is eager to buy may make a bidder raise his own estimate of the object's value.

In English auctions where the buyers know each other, there are also interesting possibilities for collusion. A bidder may decide to help a rival bidder by not continuing to bid up the price against her on one object, in the expectation that she will reciprocate by not bidding up the price on some other object to be sold later. Collusive activity of this kind is sometimes done in a systematic, organized way by groups known as "bidding rings." Bidding rings are illegal, but sometimes manage to survive without being detected. An interesting account of the activities of bidding rings is found in McMillan's book, *Games, Strategies, and Managers*. It is interesting to notice that bidding rings are likely to have more difficulty in carrying out their schemes if bidding is conducted by private, sealed bids. In this case, a member of a bidding ring may be able to cheat on his supposed co-conspirators by secretly undercutting their bids.

Equivalence of Auctions

In a private-value informational environment, if all players behave optimally, an English auction leads to essentially the same outcome as a sealed-bid, second-price auction. In each case, the object being sold goes to the person with the highest Buyer Value at a price that is equal to (or nearly equal to) the second-highest Buyer Value.

In a private-value informational environment, it also turns out that a Dutch auction is equivalent to a sealed-bid, first-price auction. In each case, the object goes to the highest bidder at the highest bidder's bid price. In both types of auction, the bidder must choose a bid without knowing the bids of any other bidders. The price at which a bidder would choose to say "Mine!" in a Dutch auction is the same as the bid price that he or she would submit in a sealed-bid, first-price auction.

Optimal Strategies (Optional)

Each bidder in a sealed-bid, first-price auction will want to bid some amount that is smaller than his Buyer Value. A bidder who bids more than his Buyer Value would lose money if he gets the object. A bidder who bids exactly his Buyer Value would make zero profit whether or not he gets the object. A bidder who bids less than his Buyer Value will make a profit if his bid happens to be the high bid, and will make zero profit if his bid is not the high bid. Any bidder must decide how much below his Buyer Value his bid should be. The lower his bid, the less likely he is to win the object, but the more profit he would make if he did win the object.

The remainder of this section is more advanced than much of the material in this book. If you are really terrified by probability and simple algebra you will want to skip this section. But if you like to see striking results emerging from simple mathematics, you will find it interesting.

In general, working out an optimal strategy for a bidder in a sealed-bid auction is very difficult. But for the case of our in-class experiment, this calculation can be worked out with a bit of elementary mathematics. Recall that your Buyer Value was determined by two digits from your social security number. Knowing the Buyer Value of one class member gives no information about the probability distribution of Buyer Values of other class members. When this is the case, we say that Buyer Values are **statistically independent**. The Buyer Value of a randomly chosen individual is equally likely to be any integer from 0 to 99. Therefore the Buyer Values are said to be **uniformly distributed** on the integers from 0 to 99.

We can now prove the following theoretical result.

Proposition. *(Optimal bidding strategies) In a sealed-bid, first-price auction in an informational environment of private values with n bidders, if private values are uniformly distributed over the integers from 0 to 99, then there is an equilibrium in which each individual bids the fraction $\frac{n-1}{n}$ of his or her Buyer Value. The object is sold to the person with the highest Buyer Value at a price equal to the fraction $\frac{n-1}{n}$ of the highest Buyer Value.*

The proof of this proposition is outlined below.

For starters, consider the case where there are only two bidders. Suppose that your Buyer Value is V and you make a bid of B. If you win the bidding, then your profits will be your Buyer Value minus your bid, or $V - B$. If you want to maximize your expected profits, then you will try to maximize the probability that you have the high bid times your winnings, $V - B$.

The probability that you win the object with a bid of B depends on the strategy of the other bidder. Suppose that the other bidder has Buyer Value X and bids the amount αX, where α is some fraction between 0 and 1. Then the probability that you will win the object is the probability that $\alpha X < B$, or equivalently, the probability that $X < \frac{B}{\alpha}$, where X is the other bidder's Buyer Value. Since Buyer Values are uniformly distributed over the integers from 0 to 99, the probability that $X < \frac{B}{\alpha}$ is just $\frac{1}{100}\frac{B}{\alpha}$.[4] The expected profits that you will make from bidding B are therefore

$$\frac{1}{100}\frac{B}{\alpha}(V - B) = \frac{1}{100\alpha}B(V - B).$$

Since $1/100\alpha$ is a positive constant independent of your bid, B, it must be that to maximize your expected profit you should choose B to maximize $B(V - B) = BV - B^2$. If you don't know any calculus at all, you might at this point have to solve the problem by trial and error. But just the tiniest bit of calculus will tell you that you can maximize this expression by setting the derivative of $BV - B^2$ with respect to B equal to zero. When you do this, you find that $V - 2B = 0$, or equivalently $B = V/2$. This shows that when there are two bidders, your optimal strategy is to bid one-half of your Buyer Value.

If there are 3 bidders, then in order to win the auction, you have to outbid *both* of the other bidders. If each of the others bids the fraction α of his

---

[4]This is not exactly right, since $\frac{B}{\alpha}$ may not be an integer. For simplicity we work the rest of this example as if Buyer Values were randomly chosen real numbers between 0 and 100. With a little more work, one can show that the answers are also correct when Buyer Values are required to be integers.

Buyer Value, then the probability that you outbid one specific competitor is $\frac{1}{100}\frac{B}{\alpha}$ and the probability that you outbid both of them is $\left(\frac{1}{100}\frac{B}{\alpha}\right)^2$. More generally, if there are n bidders, each of whom bids the fraction α of his Buyer Value, the probability that you win the auction with a bid of B is $\left(\frac{1}{100}\frac{B}{\alpha}\right)^{n-1}$. With a bit of algebra and a bit of calculus, you can then show that when there are n bidders, you will maximize your profits by setting $B = \frac{n-1}{n}V$, that is, by bidding $\frac{n-1}{n}$ of your Buyer Value.

Common Values and the "Winner's Curse"

When oil companies bid for oil leases, each company asks its geologists to estimate the value of the oil deposit that lies beneath the tract that is being offered. The companies may do some preliminary drilling on or near this tract to learn more about the amount of oil that is available. Each company realizes that it is working with partial information, and each realizes that its information may be wrong. Moreover, each company realizes that the other companies have gathered useful information which they are unlikely to share with their competitors.

On the basis of its own information, each company can estimate the expected value of the oil deposit. If in a sealed-bid auction, each company were to bid its expected value, then the company that had the highest estimate of the value of the oil deposit would win the contract and would pay its expected value. If several companies each make an estimate and a bid, it is very likely that at least one of them *overestimated* the value of the oil. The company that most badly overestimated the value would "win" the bidding. But this victory would be a hollow one, since winning the bidding with a higher bid than the object is worth means that you will lose money. This effect has acquired the colorful name, the **winner's curse**, since with naive bidding, those who win the auction are likely to be "cursed" by paying more than the object is worth.

Two Common Values Experiments

Counting Pennies

The following simple experiment illustrates the notion of a common-values informational environment. (Your instructor may do this in class with you. It only takes a few minutes.) The instructor brings a jar of pennies to class and passes it around for everyone to inspect. The instructor knows the number of pennies in the jar, but he will not tell you. You are not allowed to open the jar and count the pennies, but you can look at the jar and feel its weight. After you have had a look, you can submit a bid for the object on a piece of paper. After everyone has submitted a bid, the instructor will "sell the jar" to the highest bidder. The highest bidder will receive a payment equal to the total value of the pennies in the jar. In this experiment, the jar of pennies will be worth the same amount to every buyer, but at the time of bidding none of the bidders know just how many pennies are in the jar. Everyone is aware that the other bidders are also making guesses about the number of pennies in the jar.

The Unreliable Accountants

We are going to run another quick experiment in class to illustrate the winners' curse. A carload of merchandise is being auctioned off. It has been evaluated by several different accountants. Each accountant has written his evaluation on a slip of paper and dropped it into an envelope. The average of the accountants' estimates is the true market value of the merchandise. Some of the accountants have overestimated the true market value and some have underestimated it. The highest of the overestimates is $50 higher than the true value. The lowest of the underestimates is $50 below the true value. Each of you will be able to draw one slip of paper from the envelope, giving the evaluation of one accountant. You must not show your slip of paper to anyone or look at anyone else's slip of paper. We will have a sealed-bid, first-price auction for the merchandise. Put your identification number and your bid on a slip of paper. We will collect the bids and announce the high bidder and the gains or losses made by this bidder.

An Escalation Auction

(Your instructor may have conducted this experiment in an earlier class meeting.)

The instructor offers to auction off an ordinary dollar bill, using a rather unusual method of auctioning. In this auction, the dollar bill will go to the highest bidder, but *both* of the two highest bidders have to pay their bids. In this auction, the bidding probably got well above $1, in which case both bidders lost money (and the "house" made money). Yet there was no time during the auction where one person was doing an obviously stupid thing. For example, suppose you are the second-highest bidder with a bid of $1.10 and the highest bidder has a bid of $1.20. If you quit bidding, you will lose

$1.10 and get nothing in return. If you bid $1.30, the other bidder may quit, and if so, you will have to pay $1.30, but since you are the high bidder, you will get the dollar bill. Thus you will lose only $.30 instead of $1.10.

You might think this is a bizarre form of auction, but in the real world there are a number of phenomena that are similar to this auction which is known as the **escalation auction** or sometimes as an **all-pay auction**.

- Two opposing lobbyists try to win a congressman's favor by bribing him. The congressman will vote on the side of the lobbyist who pays him the most money, but collects bribes from both.

- Two firms are in a race to invent and patent the same product. Each hires a research staff to work on the invention. The firm that finds the invention first gets the patent and all the profits from the invention. But both firms in the patent race have to pay the costs of their research staffs.

- One person sues another over ownership of a piece of property. Each party hires a lawyer. The more one spends on legal fees, the more likely one is to win the lawsuit. Both sides have to pay their legal fees, but only one side gets the piece of property. (An interesting twist on this story is the case where the losing party has to pay the winning side's legal fees as well as its own.)

- Two countries dispute ownership of an area of land that lies between them. Each raises an army to buttress its claim to the land. The country that raises the largest army gets to invade the disputed area, but both countries have to pay the cost of raising the army. (As in the case of the lawsuit, the winning side may sometimes also be able to force the losing side to pay "reparations.")

NAME _____

Home Work–Experiment 12

We claim that in the sealed-bid, second-price auction, the most profitable thing to do is to always bid exactly your Buyer Value. This exercise should help you to see why this is true. Let V be your Buyer Value, let B be your bid, and let X be the highest bid made by anybody else in the auction. Suppose that you bid more than your Buyer Value, so that $B > V$.

If $B > V$, then ignoring ties[5] there are three possibilities, depending on X. These possibilities are:

- (a) The highest bid made by anybody else is greater than your bid $(X > B > V)$.

- (b) The highest bid made by anybody else is greater than your Buyer Value, but smaller than your bid $(B > X > V)$.

- (c) The highest bid made by anyone else is smaller than your Buyer Value and smaller than your bid $(B > V > X)$.

■ In Case (a), your profits from bidding B would be (greater than, smaller than, equal to) _____ your profits from bidding your Buyer Value V. In Case (b), your profits from bidding B would be (greater than, smaller than, equal to) _____ your profits from bidding your Buyer Value V. In Case (c), your profits from bidding B would be (greater than, smaller than, equal to) _____ your profits from bidding your Buyer Value V.

---

[5]For the time being we will ignore the possibilities that $X = B$ or $X = V$. With a little more work, this result extends to these cases.

■ Explain why it follows from these answers that it never pays to bid *more than* your Buyer Value.

_____

_____

_____

Suppose that you bid less than your Buyer Value, so that $B < V$. When $B < V$, there are three possibilities, depending on X. These possibilities are:

- (d) the highest bid made by anybody else is smaller than your bid $(X < B < V)$.

- (e) the highest bid made by anybody else is greater than your bid but smaller than your Buyer Value $(B < X < V)$.

- (f) the highest bid made by anyone else is greater than your Buyer Value $(B < V < X)$.

■ In Case (d), your profits from bidding B would be (greater than, smaller than, equal to) _____ your profits from bidding your Buyer Value V. In Case (e), your profits from bidding B would be (greater than, smaller than, equal to) _____ your profits from bidding your Buyer Value V. In Case (f), your profits from bidding B would be (greater than, smaller than, equal to) _____ your profits from bidding your Buyer Value V.

■ Explain why it follows from these answers that it never pays to bid *less than* your Buyer Value.

_____

_____

_____

■ If in a sealed-bid, second-price auction it never pays to bid more than your Buyer Value and it never pays to bid less than your Buyer Value, how should you bid in this type of auction?

_____

■ If you know the Buyer Values of all participants in a sealed-bid, second-price auction, and if everybody is bidding rationally, can you predict the high bid? Can you predict the price paid by the high bidder? Explain.

_____

_____

_____

Experiment 13

Bargaining

Deals for Wheels

The term is over and the dormitory is almost empty. You, however, plan to stay on campus to take summer courses. Now that the weather is warm, you would like to have a bicycle. You have checked the prices of used bicycles at the local shops and know that a bicycle of the kind you want costs $150. You also know that the local bicycle shop buys used bicycles from students for $100, and that this shop does no repairs on bicycles before it resells them. You have discovered that a departing senior is about to take her bicycle down to the shop to sell it. (You are not personally acquainted with this person and will not see her again after she leaves campus.) The senior knows that you would be willing to pay $150 for her bicycle and that she can get only $100 from the shop if she doesn't sell it to you.

Today's experiments deal with bargaining in situations like this.

Instructions

A Single Ultimatum

In this experiment, each buyer sends a message to a seller, making an offer for the seller's bicycle. The seller can either accept or reject a buyer's offer, but does not have an opportunity to make a counteroffer. If the buyer offers X, and the seller accepts the offer, the buyer gets profits of $(150 - X)$ and the seller gets profits of $(X - 100)$. If the seller rejects the offer, buyer and seller both get profits of 0.

In the first round of this session, half of the people in class will be designated as buyers and half will be designated as sellers. (At the instructors' discretion, a second round may be run, in which those who were sellers in the first round play the role of buyers in the second round, and those who were buyers in the first round play the role of sellers in the second round.)

In each round, activity proceeds as follows:

- Each buyer writes his identification number and a bid for the bicycle on a sheet of paper.

- The market manager collects all of the bid sheets and mixes them so that buyers and sellers are not aware of their trading partners' identities.

- The manager distributes one of the bid sheets to each of the sellers. The sellers then decide whether to accept or reject the bid. Each seller writes her identification number and marks "accept" or "reject" on the bid sheet that she received.

- The market manager collects the sheets and announces the outcomes and the resulting profits for each player (without revealing the identities of trading partners).

A Two-Stage Bargaining Process

In this experiment, each buyer again sends an offer to a seller, but this time the seller can either accept the offer, or reject it and make a counteroffer to the buyer. If the seller rejects the buyer's offer and makes a counteroffer, the buyer then must decide whether to accept or reject the counteroffer. If the buyer rejects the counteroffer, then there is no sale and buyer and seller both make zero profits.

Making offers and counteroffers takes time and reduces the value of the bicycle to the buyer. The value of the bicycle to the buyer is $150 if his first offer is accepted, but only $130 if the first offer is rejected and he buys it at the price proposed by the seller.

If the seller accepts the buyer's bid, then profits of buyer and seller are as in the previous session. If, however, the seller rejects the buyer's bid and makes a counteroffer of a price Y which the buyer accepts, then the buyer's profits will be $(130 - Y)$ and the seller's profits will be $(Y - 100)$. Finally, if the seller rejects the initial bid and makes a counteroffer which the buyer rejects, then buyer and seller both get zero profits.

Bargaining will proceed as follows:

- Each buyer writes his identification number and a bid for the bicycle on a sheet of paper.

- The market manager collects all of the bid sheets and shuffles them.

- The manager distributes one of the bid sheets to each of the sellers. Each seller writes her identification number on this bid sheet and either writes "accept" or writes a counteroffer on the sheet.

- The market manager collects the sheets, records the profits of buyers and sellers for those bids that are accepted, and returns those with counteroffers to the original bidders.

- The original bidders who receive counteroffers mark either "accept" or "reject" and return their sheets to the market manager, who records sales, prices, and total profits.

A Three-Stage Bargaining Process

In this session, if the seller rejects the buyer's first offer and makes a counteroffer, the buyer will get a chance reject the counteroffer and make one more offer before the bargaining is over. As in Session 2, making offers and counteroffers takes time and reduces the value of the bicycle to the buyer. If the buyer's first offer is accepted, the bicycle is worth $150 to him. If his first offer is rejected and the buyer accepts the seller's counteroffer, the bicycle is worth $130 to him. If, after the seller rejects the first offer and the buyer rejects the seller's counteroffer and makes a second offer, the seller accepts the second offer, then the bicycle is worth $118 to the buyer.

Bargaining will proceed as follows:

- Each buyer writes his identification number and a bid for the bicycle on a sheet of paper.

- The market manager collects all of the bids and shuffles them.

- The manager distributes one of the bid sheets to each of the sellers. On her bid sheet, each seller writes her identification number and either writes "accept" or writes her counteroffer.

- The market manager collects the sheets, records the profits of buyers and sellers for the accepted bids and returns those bids that are sent back with a counteroffer to the original bidders.

- The original bidders either write "accept" or they write a second offer on the paper.

- The market manager collects the sheets, records profits of buyers and sellers for the accepted bids, and returns those on which buyers have made a second offer to the sellers.

- Sellers who have received second offers now write either "accept" or "reject" on the bidding sheets.

- The market manager collects the remaining sheets and calculates profits.

Warm-up Exercise

A Single Ultimatum

■ In Session 1, what is the Buyer Value of the bicycle if his offer is accepted

by the seller? _____

■ In Session 1, suppose that the buyer knows that the seller would take any deal that gave her at least \$1 profit, but would refuse a deal that gave her less than \$1 profit. How much should the buyer bid to maximize his

profit? _____

■ In Session 1, if you were a seller and a buyer offered you a price of

\$101, what would your profits be if you accepted the offer? _____

What would your profits be if you rejected the offer? _____ If you are trying to maximize your profits, should you accept or reject this offer?

_____ If you are a seller and an anonymous buyer offers you \$101 for your bicycle, do you expect that you will accept the offer or reject the offer? Explain.

_____

_____

_____

■   In Session 1, what is the smallest offer that you would accept for your

bicycle? _____ (This answer is for your own benefit only. You will
not have to show it to any buyers.)

■   In Session 1, if you are a buyer and you anonymously offer the seller
a price of $101 for her bicycle, how likely do you think it is that she will

accept your offer? _____ (Remember that she will get no
other offers, and she knows that if she turns you down, she gets zero profits.)

What will your profits be if she accepts your offer? _____ What will

your profits be if she rejects your offer? _____

■   If you are a buyer in Session 1, what do you think would be the advantage
and what would be the disadvantage to you of offering more than $101 for
the bicycle?

_____

_____

_____

■   If you are a buyer in Session 1, how much do you expect to offer for the

bicycle? _____

Two-Stage Bargaining

■   In Session 2, what is the Buyer Value of the bicycle to the buyer if the

seller accepts his initial offer? _____

■   In Session 2, what is the Buyer Value of the bicycle to the buyer if the
seller rejects his first offer and the buyer accepts the seller's counteroffer?

_____

■ In Session 2, suppose that you are a seller and the buyer offers you $110 for your bicycle. If you refuse the offer and make a counteroffer of $125,

what will the buyer's profit be if he accepts the counteroffer? _____

What will the buyer's profit be if he rejects the counteroffer? _____ If the buyer is a profit-maximizer, should he accept the counteroffer or reject

the counteroffer? _____

■ In Session 2, suppose that you are a seller and you refuse the buyer's first offer. What is the highest counteroffer price that you could propose

and expect him to accept if he is a profit-maximizer? _____

■ In Session 2, suppose that you are a buyer. The seller refused your first offer and made a counteroffer of $129. Would your profits be higher if you

accepted the counteroffer or rejected the counteroffer? _____ If you find yourself in this position, do you think you would accept or reject the

seller's counteroffer? _____

■ In Session 2, if you are a buyer and the seller has refused your first offer and made a counteroffer. What is the highest counteroffer that you would accept? Explain.

_____

_____

_____

■ In Session 2, if you are a seller and you decide to reject the buyer's first offer, what price will you ask for in your counteroffer? Explain.

_____

_____

_____

■ In Session 2, if you are a seller, what is the lowest offer that you would accept from the buyer? _____

■ In Session 2, if you are a buyer, how much do you plan to offer for the bicycle as your initial offer? _____ How likely do you think it is that your offer will be accepted?

_____

Three-Stage Bargaining

■ In Session 3, what is the Buyer Value of the bicycle to the buyer if the seller accepts his initial offer? _____

■ In Session 3, what is the Buyer Value of the bicycle to the buyer if the seller rejects his first offer and the buyer accepts the seller's counteroffer?

_____

■ In Session 3, what is the Buyer Value of the bicycle to the buyer if the seller rejects his first offer, the buyer rejects the seller's counteroffer, and the buyer makes a second offer which the seller accepts? _____

■ Suppose that in Session 3 you are a buyer. You made a bid for the bicycle and the seller rejected your bid and made a counteroffer of $125. If you accept the counteroffer, you will make a profit of _____. If you reject the counteroffer and make a second offer, how much will the bicycle be worth to you if you get it? _____ If you reject the counteroffer and offer the seller $101 for the bicycle, will she accept this offer if she is a profit-maximizer? _____ If she does accept a second offer of $101, how much will your profits be? _____

■ Suppose that in Session 3 you are a buyer and that the seller has rejected your first offer and made a counteroffer. What is the highest counteroffer price that you would accept? Explain.

_____

_____

_____

■   Suppose that in Session 3, you are a seller. You decided to reject the
buyer's first offer. What price do you expect to demand as a counteroffer?
Explain.

_____

_____

_____

■   Suppose that in Session 3, you are a seller. What is the lowest first offer
price from the buyer that you would accept? Explain.

_____

_____

_____

NAME _____

Lab Report–Experiment 13

A Single Ultimatum

Round 1 of Session 1

■ In Table L13.1, record the offers made by each buyer in the first round of Session 1. In the column "Accept Reject", write the letter "A" if the offer is accepted and "R" if it is rejected by the buyer. In the next two columns record the buyer's profit and the seller's profit.

Table L13.1: Offers and Outcomes–Session 1, Round 1

Price Offered	Accept Reject	Buyer 's Profit	Seller's Profit	Price Offered	Accept-Reject	Buyer 's Profit	Seller's Profit

■ Use the information in Table L13.1 to complete Table L13.2 For each range of offers, find the number of offers that were in this range, the percent of these offers that were rejected, and the average profit made by all demanders who made offers in this range (including those whose offers were refused).

Table L13.2: Offer Range and Outcomes–Session1, Round 1

Offer Range	Number of Offers	Percent Rejected	Average Profit of Buyers
100-110			
111-124			
125			
> 125			

■ On the basis of the results of this round, what would you recommend that a selfish profit-maximizer should offer for the bicycle? Explain.

_____

_____

_____

■ How much were the total profits of buyers and sellers in this round?

_____

■ In this round, what would total profits of all buyers and sellers have been if no offer had been rejected? _____

■ Where we define the efficiency of an experimental market to be the ratio of the total profits made by buyers and sellers to the maximum possible total profits, what was the efficiency of the market in the first round of Session 1? _____.

Round 2 of Session 1

(To be completed only if two rounds were conducted in class.)

■ In Table L13.3, record the offer made by each buyer in Round 2 of Session 1. In the column Accept-Reject, write the letter "A" if the offer is accepted and "R" if it is rejected by the buyer. In the next two columns record the buyer's profit and the seller's profit.

Table L13.3: Offers and Outcomes-Session 1, Round 2

Price Offered	Accept-Reject	Buyer's Profit	Seller's Profit	Price Offered	Accept-Reject	Buyer's Profit	Seller's Profit

■ Use the information in Table L13.3 to complete Table L13.4 For each range of offers, find the number of offers that were in this range, the percent of these offers that were rejected, and the average profit made by buyers who made offers in this range.

Table L13.4: Offer Range and Outcomes-Session 1, Round 2

Offer Range	Number of Offers	Percent Rejected	Average Profit of Buyers
100-110			
111-124			
125			
> 125			

■ On the basis of the results of this round, what would you recommend that a selfish profit-maximizer should offer for the bicycle? Explain.

_____

_____

_____

■ How much were the total profits of buyers and sellers in this round?

_____

■ In this round, what would total profits of all buyers and sellers have been if no offer had been rejected? _____

■ Where we define the efficiency of an experimental market to be the ratio of the total profits made by buyers and sellers to the maximum possible total profits, what was the efficiency of the market in the second round of Session 1? _____.

Two-Stage Bargaining Process

■ Record the results of Session 2 in Table L13.5. In the first column, record the buyer's offer. In the second column, if the offer was rejected, write the seller's counteroffer and if the offer was accepted, write "A." In the third column, write "A" if the counteroffer was accepted and "R" if the counteroffer was rejected. In the last two columns, write the buyers' and sellers' profits. Remember that if the first offer is rejected, the bicycle is worth only $130 to the buyer.

■ What fraction of all buyers' offers were rejected? _____Of those sellers who rejected the buyers' initial offer, what fraction ultimately got a _lower_ price for their bicycles than the initial offers made to them by sellers?

_____

Table L13.5: Offers and Counteroffers–Session 2

Buyer's Offer	Accept or Counteroffer	Counteroffer Accepted?	Buyer's Profit	Seller's Profit

■ Use the information from Table L13.5 to complete Table L13.6.

Table L13.6: Offer Range and Outcomes–Session 2

Initial Offer	Number of Offers	Percent Rejected	Average Profit of Buyers
100-110			
111-124			
125			
126-129			
130			
> 130			

■ On the basis of the results of this round, what would you recommend that a selfish profit-maximizer should offer for the bicycle? Explain.

_____

_____

_____

■ How much were the total profits of buyers and sellers in this experiment?

_____

■ In this experiment, what would total profits of all buyers and sellers have been if no offer had been rejected? _____

■ Where we define the efficiency of an experimental market to be the ratio of the total profits made by buyers and sellers to the maximum possible total profits, what was the efficiency of the market in the last round of Session 2?

_____.

■ Use the information from Table L13.5 about the cases where offers were rejected and counteroffers made to complete Table L13.7. In the second column, record the number of counteroffers made in each price range. In the third column, record the percentage of the counteroffers in each range that were rejected. In the fourth column, record the average price received by sellers who made counteroffers in each range.

Table L13.7: Counteroffer Range and Outcomes-Session 2, Last Round

Offer Range	Number of Counteroffers	Percent Rejected	Average Price
129-130			
116-128			
115			
< 115			

Three-Stage Bargaining Process

■ Record the results of Session 3 in Table L13.8. In the first column, record the buyer's first offer. In the second column, write "A" if the seller accepts the buyer's first offer, or write her counteroffer if she rejects the buyer's offer. If the seller accepted the buyer's first offer, then leave the third column blank. If the seller rejected the buyer's first offer and made a counteroffer, then either write "A" in the third column if the buyer accepted the seller's counteroffer, or write the buyer's second offer if the buyer rejected the sellers' counteroffer. If the buyer made a second offer to the seller, then write an "A" in the fourth column if the seller accepted the second offer or an "R" in the fourth column if the seller rejected the second offer. In the last two columns, record the buyers' and sellers' profits.

■ What fraction of all buyers' initial offers were rejected? _____

_____What fraction of those sellers who rejected the buyers' initial offer ultimately got a lower price for their bicycle than the amount first offered

by the buyer? _____

Table L13.8: Offers and Counteroffers–Session 3

Buyer's Offer	Seller Accepts or Counteroffer	Buyer Accepts or Second Offer	Second Offer Accepted?	Buyer's Profit	Seller's Profit

■ Use the information from Table L13.8 to complete Table L13.9.

Table L13.9: Initial Offer Range and Outcomes-Session 3

Offer Range	Number of Offers	Percent Rejected	Average Profit of Buyers
100-112			
113-115			
116-124			
125			
126-130			
> 130			

■ On the basis of the results of this round, what would you recommend that a selfish profit-maximizer should offer for the bicycle on the first round? Explain.

_____

_____

_____

■ How much were the total profits of buyers and sellers in this experiment?

_____

■ In this experiment, what would total profits of all buyers and sellers if every seller had accepted the initial offer made by every buyer? _____

■ Where we define the efficiency of an experimental market to be the ratio of the total profits made by buyers and sellers to the maximum possible total profits, what was the efficiency of the market in Session 3? _____.

Discussion D13

Bargaining

Have you heard this fine old joke?

> Two economists have just completed a leisurely restaurant dinner. For dessert, the waiter brings a plate with two pieces of chocolate cake, one of which is much larger than the other. He offers the plate to the first economist, who takes the large piece.
>
> The second economist says, irately: "If the waiter had offered me the plate first, I would have taken the smaller piece."
>
> The first replies: "What are you complaining about? You *got* the smaller piece."

Session 1–The Ultimatum Game

The experiment that we ran in Session 1 is known as the "ultimatum game." The buyer in this experiment gets to make a single offer, an "ultimatum," which the seller must either accept or reject. If the seller rejects the ultimatum, buyer and seller both get zero profits from the transaction. If the seller is a profit-maximizer, then the buyer knows that the seller will accept any offer of a price that is higher than the seller can get from her outside option, which is selling the bicycle to the second-hand dealer for $100. Therefore the buyer would maximize his own profits by offering the seller a price of $101. In this case, the buyer makes a profit of $49 from the deal and the seller gets a profit of $1.

Suppose that you are a seller, and a buyer offers you $101 for your bicycle. You know that the bicycle is worth $150 to him, but the most you can get elsewhere is $100. Would thoughts like this cross your mind? "That rat! He is trying to cheat me. If he were playing fair, he would split the difference between $150 and $100 and offer me $125. I'll teach him a lesson. I'll reject his lousy offer!" This strategy would probably be a good idea if you think that you will deal with this buyer again, and that he would remember that you were tough the last time he tried to exploit you. But we have arranged this experiment so that buyers and sellers will never discover each others' identities. "Teaching the buyer a lesson" does not directly increase your future profits, since you will not encounter him again, and since he does not know who refused his offer. In fact, if there is a second round of this session, you will be a buyer rather than a seller, so you have nothing to gain from making buyers behave more generously.

Suppose that you are a buyer in Session 1. When you think about what offer to make, do you wonder whether an offer of $101 will offend the seller? There are two things that you should notice about offering her only $101: 1) the seller may be annoyed by your small offer and want to punish you, and 2) it doesn't cost the seller very much to inflict a big punishment on you. It costs her just $1 in lost profits to reject your offer, and her rejection will inflict a $49 punishment on you. If you offer her, say, $115, she still may be annoyed that you did not offer an equal split, but now it will cost her $15 to punish you and the punishment only inflicts $35 harm on you. If you offer her $125, she will probably think that you are fair and generous, and will most likely accept your offer. The downside of offering $125 is that your profits are smaller than they would be if you could get a smaller offer accepted.

Many people who participate in this experiment feel a tension between a desire to maximize profits and an impulse to "play fair" and to punish "wrongdoing" by others. In recent years, economists and other social scientists have been engaged in an intense debate about this matter. When people meet each other in anonymous one-time bargaining encounters, do they eventually learn to behave is such a way as to maximize their own profits, or is their behavior determined by their notion of fairness? And where do notions of fairness come from? How can we predict what people will regard as "fair" in various environments.

Participants in this debate have devised and run a large number of clever experiments in attempts to distinguish between alternative theories. These experiments have typically been conducted under carefully controlled conditions, using paid volunteer subjects. The experiments have revealed some interesting and perhaps surprising regularities. If you want to read more about the controversy and the resulting experiments, we recommend that you look at the survey article on bargaining experiments by Alvin Roth in the *Handbook of Experimental Economics* [6] and the discussion of bargaining games in *Experimental Economics* by Davis and Holt. [3]

In the published results of controlled ultimatum game experiments, the most common proposal made by the buyer is to split the total payoff equally. (In our ultimatum game experiment, this means that the buyer would offer $125 for the bicycle.) In the reported experiments, some of the buyers proposed lower prices, which would give themselves more than half of the profit. When this happened, sellers receiving the offers frequently rejected them, even though they would make more money by accepting.

Researchers have debated whether the buyers in ultimatum games offered equal divisions of profit because they were concerned about fairness, or because they were afraid that an "ungenerous" offer would be rejected by spiteful sellers. In an attempt to answer this question, researchers devised a game called the "dictator game." In the dictator game, one player is allowed to propose a division of a fixed sum of money between himself and another player, and this division will be the outcome whether the second player likes it our not. If we were to run the bicycle market as a dictator game, the buyer could offer the seller any price greater than $100, and the seller would have to accept it. When the dictator game experiment was run, the most common outcome was for dictators to take about 3/4 of the profits, but about 1/5 of the dictators took the entire profits and about 1/5 of them divided the profits equally. Later, this experiment was conducted as a "double-blind experiment," in which even the experimenter could not determine how individual dictators behaved. In the double-blind experiment, dictators chose to take the entire profits in 2/3 of the cases, and only a very small percentage of the dictators made offers as generous as an equal split. These results suggest that a large portion of those who propose equal division in the ultimatum game do so not out of a desire for a fair outcome, but because they fear that a small offer will be rejected.

We are left with the question of why, in so many cases, the player receiving the offer is willing to give up profits to punish an ungenerous offer. One explanation is that most subjects do not logically solve for the action that gives them the highest payoff, but base their actions on previous experience. Although it is true that in the experiment, a seller would make greater profits by accepting a low offer, many market participants do not realize this, but simply take the kind of action that they have found to be most successful in similar situations that they have experienced in the past. Everyone has had to deal with bullies and exploiters and most people have learned that it is worthwhile to stand up for their own interests. In normal life, people who accept insulting offers are likely to become known as easy marks and to be exploited in the future. Therefore it is valuable to earn a reputation for firmness in bargaining situations. The ultimatum game experiment is very different from our usual experience in bargaining with others, because it has been designed to make dealings between buyers and sellers anonymous and to ensure that there is no chance for further bargaining after a first offer is rejected. But experimental subjects may not take these differences into account in choosing the action that "feels right."

A second explanation is that people are willing to pay at least something to punish "injustice" even if they realize that punishing the wrong-doer will not influence their future profits. We suspect that many of us harbor feelings of this kind, and that we are likely to impose such punishment if it is relatively cheap to do so. For example, in the experiment in Session 1, if a buyer offers you a price of $101 for your bicycle, it only costs you $1 to reject the offer and this rejection will cost the greedy seller $49.

Session 2–Two-Stage Bargaining

The experiment that we conducted in Session 2 is known as a two-stage, sequential bargaining game. This experiment, like the ultimatum game has been run many times by experimental economists. As in the ultimatum game, experimental behavior does not fully correspond to the predicted behavior of two selfish, profit-maximizing players each of whom knows that the other is a selfish, profit-maximizer.

In the two stage bargaining experiment, there is a fixed sum of money to be divided between Players 1 and 2. Player 1 proposes a division to Player 2. Player 2 can either accept or reject the proposed division. If she accepts the division, the money is divided as proposed by Player 1. If she rejects the division, she can make a counteroffer, but less money is left to be divided than if the first offer had been accepted. If Player 1's offer has been rejected and Player 2 has made a counteroffer, then Player 1 can either accept the counteroffer, in which case the division is as proposed by Player 2, or reject the counteroffer, in which case both players get zero.

In the ultimatum game, in order to determine his own action, Player 1 must first figure out which offers Player 2 would accept and which she would reject, and then choose to make the offer that is best for him, given Player 2's response. The procedure of solving for best strategies by working backwards through the course of play from the end of the game to the beginning is known as **backwards induction** and can be extended to games where each player has several turns in which to take action. The solution that is found by solving in this way is known as the **subgame perfect** outcome.

Let us apply the method of backward induction to the two-stage bargaining experiment in Session 2. We first think about the last possible move in the game. This occurs when the seller rejects the buyer's initial offer and makes a counteroffer. In this case, the last move occurs when the buyer decides to accept or reject the counteroffer. At this stage of the game, the value of the bicycle to the buyer is $130. So the buyer will accept the counteroffer if it is $129 or smaller, and will otherwise reject it. This means that if the seller rejects the buyer's initial offer, she can expect to get $129 by making a counteroffer. The buyer therefore knows that his initial offer will be rejected if it is smaller than $129, and will be accepted if it is $130 or greater. Knowing this, the buyer will make the lowest offer that the seller will not refuse, which is $130. So the subgame perfect outcome is for the buyer to make an initial offer of $130 and for the seller to accept this initial offer.

It is interesting to see that although the subgame perfect outcome is that the buyer's first offer is accepted, the *possibility* of rejection and a counteroffer influences the outcome, because the buyer realizes that if his initial offer is too low, the seller will exercise this option. In fact, in our two-stage sequential bargaining game, the buyer must offer the seller *more* than half of the total profit from the transaction. This is true because if the seller rejects the buyer's offer, she will be able to play an ultimatum game with the buyer, in which she would offer the buyer a profit of only $1 and take the remaining profits of $29 for herself.

In two-stage sequential bargaining experiments that have been conducted under laboratory conditions, researchers have found that most initial offers lie between equal division and the subgame perfect solution. For Session 2 of the bicycle experiment, this would mean that most offers would be greater than $125, but less than $130. Researchers have found that in the two stage sequential bargaining experiments, about 15% of the first offers are rejected, and in more than 2/3 of the cases where the player corresponding to our seller rejected the first offer, her counteroffer gave her a lower payoff than she would have received if she had accepted the offer.

Session 3–Three-Stage Bargaining

The experiment in Session 3 is known as a three-stage sequential bargaining game. This experiment is similar to that of Session 2, except that if the buyer's first offer is rejected and the seller makes a counteroffer, the buyer can reject the counteroffer and make a second offer. If bargaining reaches the stage where the buyer makes a second offer, the value of the bicycle to the buyer will have fallen to \$118.[1] The seller must then either accept the second offer or there will be no sale.

In order to find the subgame perfect outcome, we again work backwards from the end of the game. If the game goes as far as the last round, in which the buyer makes a second offer, then in the last round, the seller would accept any offer of \$101 or more. At this stage the bicycle would only be worth \$118 to the buyer, so if the buyer's second offer is \$101, the buyer would make a profit of \$17 and the seller would make a profit of only \$1. Therefore in the previous stage of bargaining, the seller knows that the buyer would accept any counteroffer that leaves him with a profit of more than \$17. If the buyer accepts the seller's counteroffer, the bicycle will be worth \$130 to the buyer. If the seller offers it to him for \$112, then the buyer would make a profit of \$18 by accepting the seller's counteroffer, which is better than the \$17 profit he could get by rejecting the counteroffer and making a second offer. Therefore the highest price that the seller can guarantee herself by refusing the buyer's first offer and making a counteroffer is \$112. Working back one more stage, when he makes his initial offer, the buyer knows that the seller will accept any offer greater than \$112 and would refuse an offer smaller than \$112. So the subgame perfect outcome for our three-stage sequential bargaining game is that the buyer offers \$113 for the bicycle and the seller accepts this offer.

In three-stage sequential bargaining experiments conducted under laboratory conditions, researchers have found that most first offers are between equal division and the subgame perfect outcome, but closer to equal division.

Conclusion

There are at least two interesting lessons to be learned from this experiment. It is instructive to see how you should behave if you are trying to maximize your profits *and* if you are bargaining with a clever and selfish profit-maximizer. It is also important to think about how to behave if you or some of the individuals you deal with are not motivated only by profit-maximization, but also by some notion of fairness.

In the ultimatum game and sequential bargaining games (as in many interpersonal relationships), the best way to figure out your own most-

---

[1] In each successive round of bargaining, the total profit of buyer and seller is 60% of that in the previous round. Thus total profit falls from \$50 to \$30 to \$18.

profitable action is to "put yourself in the other person's shoes" in order to determine how that person will react to what you do. For example, in the ultimatum game in Session 1, the buyer needs to ask himself, "If I were the seller, which offers would I accept and which would I reject?' In the sequential bargaining games, the same kind of reasoning has to be carried out, but with more steps. In two-stage bargaining, before making an offer, a buyer needs to know which offers will be accepted by the seller, and which will lead to counteroffers. But the seller's willingness to accept a first offer, rather than reject and make a counteroffer, depends in turn on which counteroffers the seller thinks the buyer will accept. Thus in choosing a first offer, the buyer must think about what the seller thinks the buyer will do in response to various counteroffers. The way to solve these things is to work backwards. That is, to think about what will happen in the last turn of bargaining and then, having decided this, to think about what will happen on the next-to-last turn, third-to-last turn, and so on.

In the subgame perfect outcome for the ultimatum game, the buyer got almost all of the profit, but in the two-stage sequential bargaining game, where the seller gets to make the last offer, he seller gets more than half of the profit. In the three-stage sequential bargaining game, the buyer again gets to make the final offer, but the subgame perfect outcome is less extreme than in the ultimatum game. If you solve for the subgame perfect outcome in the four-stage and five-stage sequential bargaining games, you will find that as more stages are added, in the subgame perfect outcome the buyer's initial offer is always accepted, but as the number of stages gets larger, this offer gets ever closer to an equal division of profits. This is a special case of a remarkable general result, that was discovered by Ariel Rubinstein. A very informal statement of Rubinstein's theorem as applied to examples like this, is the following:

Rubinstein's theorem (informal version). *If the exchange of offers and counteroffers is fast enough so that the value of the object being sold decreases only slightly between each offer and counteroffer, and if the buyer and seller are approximately equally impatient to finish the bargaining, then the outcome of multistage bargaining where many rounds of offers and counteroffers are permitted, is that the buyer makes an initial offer that divides buyer's and seller's profits approximately equally, and this initial offer is accepted.*

It is likely that most of the bargaining situations that people experience in everyday life are not of the single take-it-or-leave-it type, but are part of a process in which there is time for several offers and counteroffers. It is plausible that in experimental bargaining games, people call upon their experiences in more open-ended situations where the best strategy is to offer approximately an even split of profits and to reject offers that do not give you about half of the total gains. This policy, which is usually sensible, is carried over to experimental situations, even though this happens not to be the best way to play in the ultimatum game or the two-stage bargaining game.

Even if ultimatum games and two-stage bargaining games are simpler than the bargaining situations encountered in ordinary life, they are worth studying, because their simplicity makes it possible for us to work out exact answers to how rational, selfish profit-maximizers would play. The lesson that one learns about the need for putting yourself into the other player's shoes in order to imagine their responses to your own actions is an important principle that extends to much more complicated and realistic bargaining environments.

Please be warned that the games in this experiment are artificially concocted in such a way that the pursuit of self-interest leads to actions quite contrary to ordinary notions of politeness and fairness. It would be a great mistake to conclude from these examples that treating other people with kindness, respect, and generosity is not worthwhile, or that the correct response to bullies and tyrants is to knuckle under whenever resistance is costly. The world in which we live is one of repeated encounters, usually not anonymous, in which people develop reputations and affections, and in which rational people often return generosity with generosity. But, you may ask, "doesn't the theory suggest that it is in our interest to take what we can get when we are sure that nobody is looking?" The answer, we think, is "no." It is extremely difficult, if not impossible, to deceive others consistently. Arguably, the best way to convince others that you will play cooperatively in long-term relationships is to develop in yourself a genuine concern for their welfare which will prevent you (at least most of the time) from deceiving them, even when it is possible.

NAME _____

Home Work–Experiment 13

Sequential Bargaining Against a Robot

Suppose that you are bargaining against a robot that is programmed to choose a strategy that maximizes its own profit. Assume that you are a profit-maximizer who understands that the robot is programmed to maximize its own profit. If two alternative options are equally profitable for the robot, it will toss a fair coin to decide what to do. You don't care at all how much money the robot makes, but you do want to maximize your own profit.

You are trying to buy an object from the robot that is worth $0 to the robot. It is worth $100 to you if you get it on your first offer. Each offer or counteroffer that is made uses up one period of time. Each period of time that passes before the object is sold causes the value of the object to you to fall to 80% of its value in the previous period. For example, if your first offer is rejected and the robot makes a counteroffer which you accept, the object will be worth $80 to you when you get it. If your first offer is rejected and you reject the robot's counteroffer, and it accepts your second offer, the object will be worth $64, and so on. Neither you nor the robot can make change for a dollar, so you and the robot have to make offers and counteroffers in dollar units. If at the end of the time allotted for offers and counteroffers, no agreement is reached, then you and the robot both get $0.

■ If you can make only one offer, and the robot must either accept your

offer or reject, it how much should you offer the robot for the object? ____

_____

■ Suppose that the robot is allowed to make a counteroffer to your first offer, and you must either accept or reject the robot's counteroffer. If the robot rejects your first offer, what price will the robot ask for the object in

its counteroffer? _____ What price should you offer the robot when you make your initial offer? _____

■ Suppose that the robot is allowed to make a counteroffer to your first offer, and that if you reject the robot's counteroffer, you can make a second offer which the robot must accept or reject. If the bargaining process gets to your second offer, at the time of sale the object will be worth only $64 to you. What price would you offer on your second offer? _____ and what would your profits be? _____ If the robot rejects your first offer and you accept the counteroffer, the object will be worth $80 to you. What price will the robot propose in its counteroffer in order to prevent you from rejecting the counteroffer? _____ What would the robot's profits be if it made that offer? _____ What price should you offer in order to ensure that the robot will take your first offer? _____

■ ■ Suppose that bargaining can go on to a fourth stage, in which the robot can make a counteroffer to your second offer, but you have to either accept or reject this counteroffer. If the bargaining goes this far before a deal is struck, the object will be worth $51 to the buyer at the time he gets it. Work backwards to calculate your best initial offer. _____

■ ■ Assuming that at each extra stage of bargaining, the value of the object falls to 80% of the value at the previous stage (or the nearest integer to this value), what do you think would happen if there is a fifth stage? _____ Do the first offered prices seem to be converging to a limit as the number of stages get large? _____ If so, what can you say about this limit?

Food for Thought

■ Labor negotiations between unions and firms are in many ways similar to the bargaining problem in this experiment. Explain how it is that the value to the workers and to the firms of a labor contract decreases as time passes without an agreement.

_____

_____

_____

_____

_____

■ Sometimes the bargaining problem posed here is said to be a problem of "how to divide a shrinking cake." Can you think of other real world examples of bargaining over the division of a shrinking cake?

_____

_____

_____

Index